MW01613816

Roadmap to Success

Through High School to College:
A Step-By-Step Student Guide

published 2016

PUBLISHED AND DISTRIBUTED BY
Education Opens Doors

Education Opens Doors is a nonprofit organization whose mission is to empower students to purposefully navigate through high school to college. To learn more, provide feedback, or inquire about potential partnerships please contact us directly at:

P.O. Box 601971

Dallas, TX 75360

Website: www.educationopensdoors.org

Email: info@educationopensdoors.org

This manual is dedicated to each and every student who is able to use it as a guide on your journey to college and your career. You have a bright future ahead of you!

We also dedicate this manual to the students in Dallas, Texas whom the authors have had the pleasure of teaching. Each of you has inspired the creation of Roadmap to Success.

Education Opens Doors would like to acknowledge our dedicated team, both past and present, who have significantly contributed to the continued improvement of the Roadmap to Success student manual.

A special thank you to Courtney Fadley for leading the revisions of the 7th Edition.

Paris Ball	Emily Cook	Amy Tran
Brianna Ballard	Megan Grable	Abigail Wilson
Jayda Batchelder	Andrew Lovley	Asil Yassine
Courtnee Benford	Sean Planchard	Rebecca Zivin

In addition, Education Opens Doors would like to thank the following educators and community members, without whom this project would not have initially been possible!

Ashley Bryan, Matthew Busch, Brad Earl, Chelsea Johnson,
John Maher, Allyson Stromer, Paula Tyler,
Jack Wallace, and Kristen Watkins

Table of Contents

MAP YOUR JOURNEY

DIRECTIONS: Read the topics of this unit on the roadmap. Draw an "emoji" of your emotions about this content as you start the unit.

What steps do I need to take in order to achieve my educational goals?

How is this manual going to be helpful to me?

Message to Students	MY Roadmap to Success	How to Read This Manual	Unit 1 Vocabulary
page 8	page 9	page 11	page 12

My 7 Year Checklist
page 13

What information do I already know about college?

Education Pays
page 20

Is college worth the expense?

Unit 1 Summary
page 22

DIRECTIONS: In reflection of the information you learned in this unit, draw an emoji of how you feel now.

Dear Student,

Congratulations on taking the next step toward your personal success! This manual is meant to be your guide as you work hard and continue to move forward in your education.

Have you ever thought about the person you want to become in the future? Perhaps you have thought about where you want to live, the kind of job you aspire to have, or the kind of life you would like to live. YOU have the potential to turn all of those dreams into a reality by committing to your education. Your future career, college, and perhaps the end of high school, may seem like they are in the distant future. However, it is important to start preparing now; time will move quickly and you want to be ready.

There might be questions that arise or challenges that you are faced with on the road stretching ahead. Don't be discouraged, but instead be prepared and empowered by the resources within your reach. Your teachers, parents, mentors, school counselors, peers, and this *Roadmap to Success* will all help you on your journey as you turn your college aspiration into a reality.

During each step of the way, use this manual as a resource and a guide. It will provide you with the information you need to be successful beginning as early as middle school, through high school, and on to your graduation four years later. It is meant to be interactive, so feel free to write in it and take notes along the way.

Inside you will find a checklist of important reminders, dates and advice that you don't want to miss. There are also tips to help you stand out when you apply to school or your first job, steps to apply to college and secure scholarships as well as financial aid, and so much more.

Don't forget to look for over 75 roadside tips found throughout the units. These are critical pieces of advice that you should not miss out on! Plus, there are interactive pages and templates for you to complete. You can build your own résumé, practice interview questions, learn more about your favorite college, and calculate potential income based on your level of education.

This is your chance to learn how to pave the way for your own road to success! Good luck on the journey ahead! You are college bound, and your dreams are within your reach!

We look forward to supporting you on your personal path to success.

All Our Best,

The Education Opens Doors Team

MY Roadmap to Success

This manual belongs to: _____

Name of school I currently attend: _____

Current grade level: _____   Graduating Class of: _____

Professional email address: _____

My personal goal(s) for this school year: _____

_____

I _____(Print name) **will commit myself fully to my academic and personal goals this year and use my new knowledge and skills to become a bright, motivated, college-ready scholar.**

_____ (Signature)

About ME (Fill in the following information as you use your manual and learn more about the steps that will get you to college)**:**

> **Key Point**
> *Personal ownership of one's education should start as early as middle school, and includes class selection, extracurricular involvement, goal setting, and utilizing resources including the RTS manual and your guidance counselor.*

Goals during High School:

1. **My goal GPA:** _____
2. **My goal SAT/ACT Score:** _____

Clubs, sports, or organizations that I would like to be a member of:

1. _____
2. _____
3. _____

Top 3 Colleges, Universities, or other options after High School that I would like to pursue:

1. _____
2. _____
3. _____

Careers I am interested in:

1. _____
2. _____
3. _____

My Turn! Create My Personal Shield

1. Write your name in the banner running across the shield.

2. Choose 4 of the 7 questions below that you would like to answer.

   - What are three of your positive qualities or skills?
   - What do you like most about your family?
   - What do your friends like about you?
   - What do you think you can do better than almost anyone else your age?
   - What do you dream about doing one day?
   - What is something you have already done that makes you feel really proud?
   - What is one thing you are planning to change about yourself so you will be even better in the future?

3. Draw or write each of your answers in one of the 4 sections of the shield. Be sure to write the question in that section as well. Repeat this for the remaining 3 sections until you have answered all 4 of your questions on your shield.

4. Decorate your shield however you would like!

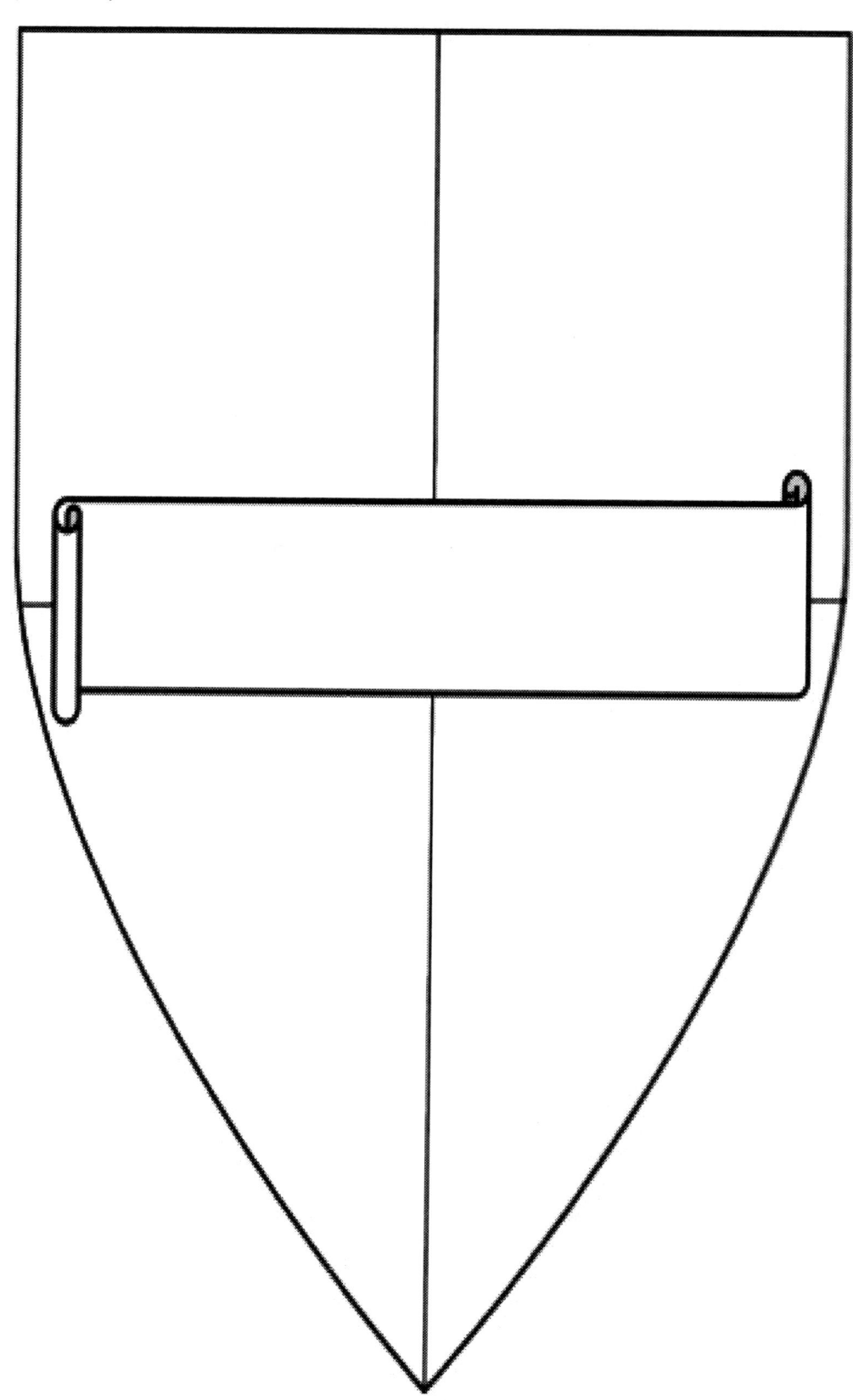

How to Read This Manual

The *Roadmap to Success* manual is designed for YOU, the student! Read the notes on this page to understand the layout of the manual and how to interact with the information most effectively.

How to Use The Margins

On most pages, the margins (the blank space on the side of each page) have been left blank for you to write in. We encourage you to make this *Roadmap to Success* manual your personal roadmap to success. Take notes, add comments, highlight important information that you want to remember later - do whatever works for you!

Formatting Used Throughout This Manual

- **Boldface** is used throughout this manual to emphasize important information and vocabulary.
- *Italics* are used throughout this manual for special notes or disclaimers.
- The font `Courier New` is used for web addresses in order to help you easily find and refer to them later.

How *Roadmap to Success* is Organized

This manual is organized into six units. Each unit covers a broad, but essential, topic on the pathway to college and your career as well as answers specific questions that you may have. The six units are:

1. **Map Your Journey** – What steps do I need to take in order to achieve my educational goals? What information do I already know about college? How is this manual going to be helpful to me? Is college worth the expense?

2. **Navigate High School and Life Outside of the Classroom** - What are the different types of high schools? Which one would be the "right" fit for me? Which classes should I take? What can I do outside of school in order to improve my chances of success? What is an internship?

3. **Practice Professionalism** - What is a résumé? Why are they important? How do I ace an interview?

4. **Explore Career Paths** - What are my options after high school? What makes each type of school different? What is a major? How should I choose the major and career for me?

5. **Pursue Financial Aid** - How expensive is college? What is financial aid and how do I apply for it? What are the differences among grants, loans, and scholarships? How do know if a financial aid package is right for me?

6. **Apply to College** - What are the steps for applying to college? What are the SAT and ACT? Are there any tips for scoring well on them? Whose help do I need in the application process?

Icons Used in This Manual

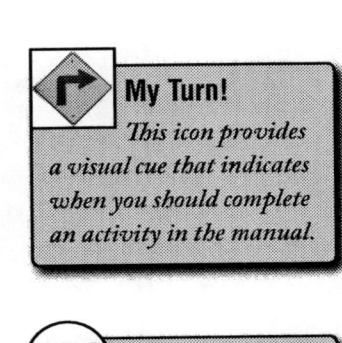

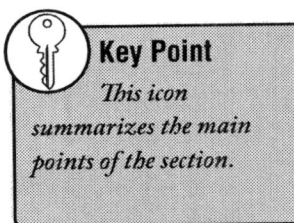

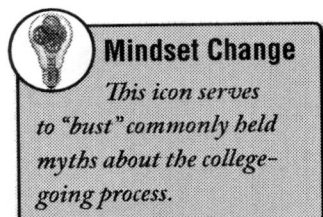

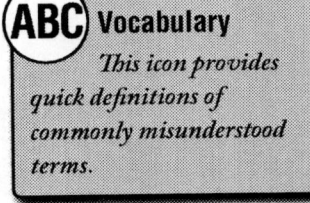

Unit 1 Vocabulary

Freshman	Sophomore	Junior	Senior

DIRECTIONS: In the space below, select several unfamiliar words from the vocabulary word bank. Then, define each word using the glossary or a dictionary. Last, create an original sentence for each of the selected words.

Vocabulary Word	Definition	Your Original Sentence

My 7 Year Checklist

A Checklist for Middle School and High School

Follow these steps to help you reach your goals! This checklist will ensure that you are on the right path to both a high school diploma and acceptance to a college of your choice. Your checklist contains important reminders, dates, and helpful advice to guide you each step of the way. Remember, being on track to reach your dreams starts in middle school!

6th Grade

- ☐ Believe in yourself and start setting goals for your future now!
- ☐ Familiarize yourself with the contents of your *Roadmap to Success* student manual in preparation for your journey ahead.
- ☐ Calculate your own GPA at the end of each grading period (such as Six Weeks, Quarter, or Semester). This will be something you should do from now until the end of your education.
- ☐ Figure out your personal learning style. As a middle school student, you will start to have more homework, projects, tests, etc. Ask yourself if you learn better by seeing, doing, or listening. You can also take a learning styles inventory test to find out the answer. Based on the type of learner that you are, develop study habits throughout the year.
- ☐ Take a career/interest inventory. These are surveys that help to match your interests to possible career choices. This will help you begin to think about your future and brainstorm career possibilities.
- ☐ Ensure that your ITBS scores are at or above grade level
- ☐ Work hard to pass all of your standardized test exams (from now until the end of high school!)
- ☐ Strengthen your skills in reading and writing as you move through middle school and high school. Both are invaluable skills for your future! Strong writing skills are important for your résumé and application for high school and college admission.
- ☐ Participate in school activities, clubs, and sports to learn more about your interests, but make sure you stay focused on homework and grades.

7th Grade

- ☐ Meet with your school counselor and decide which courses you need to take to be on track as you prepare for high school and for college.
- ☐ Stay involved in extracurricular activities and pursue leadership roles.
- ☐ Take advanced or Pre-AP math, which in most cases will be Pre-Algebra, to prepare for 8th grade.
- ☐ Take tough classes and challenge yourself. Colleges will look to see that you take challenging classes in high school, so get ready now!
- ☐ Seek help from teachers if you are scoring low on standardized test or ITBS tests.

TIPS **Not A 6th Grader?**
Even if you are in a higher grade, look through all of the lists to make sure that you have completed everything.

 Key Point
Utilizing the grade level checklists in the manual will keep you on the path to achieve success in your educational journey.

TIPS **Writers Are Readers Too**
The strongest writers often read more than they write! Picking up a book can improve your writing skills.

8th Grade

☐ Take advanced or Pre-AP math, which in most cases will be Algebra I.

☐ Take a language other than English (Spanish, French, etc).

☐ Be aware that you will be taking a number of statewide or national standardized tests, such as the ITBS (Iowa Tests of Basic Skills). These tests are very important in determining your odds of acceptance to some of the high schools you can apply to and which classes you will be placed in.

☐ Begin reaching out to teachers and counselors about applying to magnet schools or charter schools.

☐ Take the ACT Explore Tests (These can be taken in 8th or 9th grade, but don't take them until you finish algebra!)

☐ Apply for a Social Security Number (if you do not already have one). Do this by visiting a social security administration office in your city.

☐ Sign up for high school classes. Be sure that the classes you sign up for are the most advanced you can take and succeed in (usually a B- average or above).

☐ Remain involved in your extracurricular activities and pursue leadership roles.

☐ Start researching colleges and college majors that you are interested in.

☐ Attend Magnet, Charter, Private, and other high school fairs.

TIPS **Remember!**

See if your school offers a summer orientation program that you can attend!

Freshman Year

August – September

☐ Find a school counselor, teacher or mentor whom you trust for guidance, help and support. Talk with them about your goals for college as well as for after graduation.

☐ Find out now what classes you'll need to graduate and try to take challenging courses. This includes college prep and advanced classes such as AP or IB classes.

☐ Focus on academics and get your grade point average as high as possible. Maintaining at least a 3.0 grade point average (an overall B GPA) is crucial for getting into good colleges.

☐ Join clubs, sports and activities at your school and/or outside of it, especially those that will allow you to eventually take on leadership positions. Start now, since colleges will be impressed if you have a high level of involvement with a group for 3 or 4 years.

☐ Most large cities have numerous colleges and universities. If your family visits a city, see if you can go check out some of the campuses.

October - June

☐ Visit **www.college.gov** for info on financial resources. Through this website, you can also access **www.studentaid.ed.gov** to create your Student Planner and **www.fafsa4caster.gov** to estimate how much financial aid you might be eligible to receive.

☐ Start making a high school résumé and save all awards, honors, certificates, etc. that you receive.

☐ Manage your time. Make sure you are able to stay involved in activities while keeping a high GPA.

Mindset Change

Many students and families believe that they should only start worrying about financial aid once they know where they're going to college. Don't fall into this trap! You should be trying to earn as much financial aid as possible as early as possible.

Summer after Freshman Year

☐ If you anticipate having a hard time paying for college, get a summer job and start saving now.

☐ Take summer school classes. If you failed any classes, take summer school to get credit for those classes. If you don't need to make up classes, take summer school to get ahead!

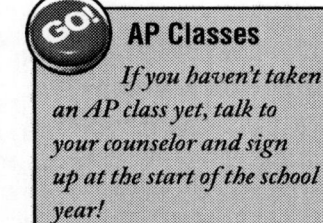

Mindset Change
Many students who drop out do so between their freshman and sophomore year. Don't fall into this statistic. Use your Roadmap to Success to guide you!

Sophomore Year

August – June

☐ Visit your counselor to make sure that you are taking the right classes to graduate on time.

☐ Keep your grades up. Maintain at least a 3.0 GPA. Take as many college prep or AP classes as possible.

☐ Stay involved in, or join, additional clubs, sports, and activities outside of school. Also, enroll in courses that could allow you to receive college credit, such as AP or Dual Credit.

☐ Take the PSAT in October, whether or not you've taken it before, and take it seriously. It's good practice for when you take the SAT or ACT your Junior and Senior year. Doing well will also make you eligible for several scholarships.

☐ Begin considering potential majors, college options and what you would look for in a school.

☐ Visit a college fair in your area. They can be found by searching online.

GO! AP Classes
If you haven't taken an AP class yet, talk to your counselor and sign up at the start of the school year!

Summer after Sophomore Year

☐ Continue working in order to save money for personal expenses and to maintain a personal savings account.

☐ Continue working in jobs, internships, and/or community service positions. As you do, don't forget to add these items to your résumé.

☐ If you want to play a sport in college, start contacting college coaches so they can scout you during the coming year. Contact them by writing letters, sending e-mails and calling their offices. You can get their information through their college website.

☐ Check into SAT or ACT test prep courses at your school. Go to **www.sat.collegeboard.org** for free test prep for the SAT. Ask your counselor about or research free or low-cost community programs that offer free study support and materials.

Junior Year

August – October

☐ Focus on academics! Maintain at least a 3.0 GPA. Colleges take junior year grades very seriously, and you only have two more years to make your overall grade point average look good for your college application.

☐ Visit your counselor to make sure you are going to graduate on time.

☐ Make a top 10 list of the colleges you would like to attend and make sure they offer the major or majors you're interested in. Look at admission requirements for those colleges, and make sure you meet their requirements.

☐ Take the PSAT again. Only students who take the PSAT by their Junior Year qualify for the prestigious National Merit Scholarship Qualifying Test (NMSQT), which can lead to scholarship money or recognition!

☐ Remain involved in your extracurricular activities and pursue leadership roles.

☐ Go to a bookstore, buy an ACT or SAT prep book, and start reviewing on your own. This is important – there will be material in those books that may have never been taught to you! A good ACT or SAT prep book will make sure you review all the material you need to know, which will raise your score on the test.

☐ Sign up to take the December ACT or sign up to take the December/January SAT. You can do this online, just search for ACT or SAT, or ask your school counselor to help sign you up.

November – January

☐ Find out whether the colleges you would like to attend require you to take the SAT or ACT. Many will accept either, so see which test format suits you.

☐ Visit another college fair. Also, visit college campuses that you are interested in applying to. Information on how to set up a college visit will be found on the college's website.

☐ Take the ACT, SAT, or both.

February – June

☐ If you don't think you did well on the ACT or SAT, register to take it again in June. You may need to register BEFORE you get your original scores back.

☐ Register for AP exams through the Counseling Center.

☐ Complete all AP exams in May (Remember, a score of 3 or higher can earn you college credit at some colleges!)

☐ Finalize your senior schedule. Make sure it meets all the requirements for high school graduation.

☐ Gather more information about college scholarships and financial aid at `www.fafsa.gov`.

☐ If you plan to play sports in college, complete the NCAA Clearinghouse application. (Simply type "NCAA clearinghouse" into your favorite search engine to find the application). If you don't apply, you will not be eligible to play your sport in college!

Summer after Junior Year

☐ Keep working and saving money for personal expenses in college. If possible, try to get a job in a professional environment (with a business or an office). This will look good on your college application.

- ☐ Visit colleges. Call ahead for appointments with admissions, the financial aid office and academic advisors at the schools you are interested in attending.
- ☐ Go online to view college application essay prompts. Practice writing essays based on the prompts.
- ☐ Check your college deadlines and develop a calendar of when you should submit your materials (application, essay, deposits, etc). Pay particular attention to early decision or early action deadlines (these are extra-early application deadlines).
- ☐ Think of whom you would like to write letters of recommendation for you when you start applying to schools. Core teachers are usually the preferred choice.

Senior Year

August - September

- ☐ Visit with your counselor to make sure you are on track to graduate on time. Do you have enough credits? Have you taken and passed all of the classes you need to get into the colleges to which you are applying?
- ☐ Attend college fairs to get more information on schools and their exciting opportunities.
- ☐ Research the colleges that you plan to apply to online. Print a copy or PDF of each college application and create a physical or virtual folder for each school. Write all of the deadlines for those colleges on the front of each folder or in the file name so you won't miss any of them.
- ☐ Double check application deadlines for your colleges and begin filling out applications online. Pick 6-8 colleges you are interested in, and apply to at least 3 or 4 of them. If you need a counselor letter of recommendation, be sure you obtain the necessary materials from the counseling center.
- ☐ Ask a teacher or teachers from a recent core subject to write your letters of recommendation and supply them with a form from the application packet to go with each application. Remember to allow at least 3 weeks for them to write your letter. If you need a teacher recommendation letter, provide the teacher with a résumé and stamped, addressed envelope (so the teacher may mail the recommendation directly to the college).
- ☐ Begin working on your college essays. If possible, seek help from an adult who is a good writer or editor.
- ☐ Register to take the September ACT or October SAT if you haven't done so yet or want to retake the test. If you also need to take SAT Subject tests, be sure you have registered to take them. Remember that it's best to take these tests more than once if it increases your chances of getting into your dream school or receiving better scholarships.

GO! Register to Vote!
When you turn 18, one of the most important things that you can ever do in your life is register to vote. Not only will this allow you to share your political voice, it will help you make a difference in your community.

October – December

- ☐ Continue to search and apply for scholarships. Don't forget to read the financial aid websites of each school you are applying to.
- ☐ Fill out the FAFSA. You can either do this online or by submitting the form to your counselor as soon as possible after October 1st.
- ☐ Begin gathering forms needed (tax documents) to prepare for financial aid application.

- ☐ Beginning October 1st, you can fill out your CSS/Finanical Aid PROFILE from the College Board. This is an application for nonfederal financial aid from colleges and scholarships.
- ☐ Go online and set up a communication account with each campus you are applying to. This will give you access to the details of the application for that individual campus.
- ☐ Submit college applications and send a transcript to each college you are applying to. No later than one month after submitting your applications, call the admissions offices at those schools and confirm they have received your application. Aim for completing all applications by December 1st.

January

- ☐ Once you receive your Student Aid Report (SAR) after completing the FAFSA, send it to other colleges you may not have listed previously on your FAFSA. Do this as soon as possible after receiving it in the mail.
- ☐ If you fail a class necessary for graduation in the fall, be sure to add it to your spring semester schedule and inform your counselor how you will complete the class.

April - May

- ☐ Make a decision on which college you want to attend. If you're wait-listed at the school you want to attend, accept another school's admission offer while remaining on the wait-list.
- ☐ Send all of the necessary forms you need to attend the college you've decided upon.
- ☐ Meet all deposit deadlines for your college.
- ☐ Sign up and take AP Exams.
- ☐ Keep your grades up and make sure you graduate on time!

My Turn! Status Update

> What's on your mind...

> Do you wish you could check more tasks off of your checklist?

> Are unchecked items mostly because you were unaware of needing to complete them, or because you do not want to complete them?

> What prevents you from checking ALL of the boxes? i.e.: resources, a person, group of people, personal motivation, etc.

> What can you start doing today in order to ensure you are able to achieve your goals?

Students and alumni (graduates of a school) have several reasons they attended college. Some of those reasons include personal development, gaining independence, social and networking opportunities, and many more. Ask a teacher or other college graduate about their experience in college and why they went. One huge advantage of getting a college degree is the financial security it can provide.

My Turn! Time to Crunch Some Numbers

DIRECTIONS: Below you will find the average amount of money people make based on their level of education and the amount of an average person's living expenses. Use this information to calculate the total for each education level and see whether it pays as much as you thought.

Monthly Income

Without a High School Diploma:

Earn an average of $12/hr x 40hrs per week = $_____ a week

$_____ a week x 4 weeks =   **$_____ a month**

With a High School Diploma:

Earn an average of $17/hr x 40hrs per week = $_____ a week

$_____ week x 4 weeks =   **$_____ a month**

With a College Degree (Bachelor's):

Earn average $28/hr x 40hrs a week = $_____ a week

$_____ a week x 4 weeks =   **$_____ a month**

Monthly Expenses

Apartment or house mortgage?	$ 1,000
Utilities (gas, electric, phone, cable)?	$ 250
Car?	$ 350
Gas?	$ 150
Insurance?	$ 150
Cell Phone (Without a data plan)?	$ 40
Groceries and fast food?	$ 300
Entertainment (sports, movies, shopping, going out)?	$ 100
Donations to charitable, religious, or non-profit organizations?	$ ____
Other	$ ____
TOTAL per month	$_____

1. If you DON'T have a high school diploma, how much will you still owe or have left over? _____

2. If you only have a high school diploma, how much will you still owe or have left over?
_____

3. If you have a college degree, how much will you still owe or have left over?
_____

Key Point

Attendance records, age of becoming a parent, level of education, and time commitment to a job have statistical connections to future economic success.

TIPS Don't Forget Taxes...

Taxes are money that the government (Federal, State, and Local) collects from every citizen each year to pay for public services (e.g. police and firefighters). The amount you owe is based on how much money you make each year, but everyone is required to pay them. Taxes should always be included in your budget.

Notes

A famous author, Fyodor Dostoyevsky wrote in one of his books, "To go wrong in one's own way is better then to go right in someone else's." What he is telling his readers is that independent thinking is better than conforming to the thinking of others. You have the opportunity to shape your own future by focusing on the decisions and actions you take now. You can set goals of what success looks like in your life. Every person is unique, with special and significant thoughts, strengths, qualities, and skills, all of which are important contributions to the community where you live, work, learn, and have fun.

Setting goals is a crucial (and often overlooked) step in the process of mapping your journey. Use the information in your *Roadmap to Success* student manual to help guide you on the path you create.

My Turn! 3-2-1... Map Your Journey!

List THREE different steps you can take to help you reach your goals this school year:

-
-
-

List TWO expenses adults must pay every month other than rent:

-
-

Write ONE reason you want to finish high school and go on to college, trade school, or other post-secondary education option:

-

DIRECTIONS: Read the topics of this unit on the roadmap. Draw an "emoji" of your emotions about this content as you start the unit.

What are the different types of high schools? Which one would be the "right" fit for me?

DIRECTIONS: In reflection of the information you learned in this unit, draw an emoji of how you feel now.

What classes should I take?

What can I do outside of school in order to improve my chances of success?

What is an internship?

Unit 2 Vocabulary

Academic Advisor / Guidance Counselor	Cumulative GPA	International Baccalaureate (IB)	Semester
Advanced Placement (AP)	Dual Credit	Internship	Semester GPA
	Early College		Study Group
Class Rank	Grade Point Average (GPA)	Percentile	Syllabus
Community Service		Recommendation Letter	

DIRECTIONS: In the space below, select several unfamiliar words from the vocabulary word bank. Then, define each word using the glossary or a dictionary. Last, create an original sentence for each of the selected words.

Vocabulary Word	Definition	Your Original Sentence

Grade Point Average (GPA) and Class Rank

What is a "Grade Point Average?"

Your **grade point average (regularly called GPA)** is exactly what it sounds like – an average of all of your grades. When you get into high school and college, each letter grade you receive will be represented by a different number. Your grade point average is calculated by taking the sum of all of your grades and dividing that sum by the total number of credits or courses taken. Grade point averages are typically calculated on what is called a 4.0 scale, yet some schools may use a 5.0 weighted GPA or even an 11.0 scale. If your school uses a 4.0 scale, then your GPA will be between a 0.0 and a 4.0, with a 4.0 being the best. The number representations that are most generally used for letter grades are listed to the right. It is important to note that some schools give plus/minus grades while others do not, and some high schools may not use this exact number scale for grades.

Letter Grade	Percent Grade	4.0 Scale
A+	97-100	4.0
A	93-96	4.0
A-	90-92	3.7
B+	87-89	3.3
B	83-86	3.0
B-	80-82	2.7
C+	77-79	2.3
C	73-76	2.0
C-	70-72	1.7
D+	67-69	1.3
D	65-66	1.0
E/F	Below 65	0.0

(ABC) Grade Point Average (GPA)
Grade point average (GPA) is an average of all of your grades from your freshman year through your senior year.

Key Point
Cumulative GPA is a number that is used by colleges and scholarship providers to determine your acceptance and eligibility.

Whichever scale is used at your school, just know that the higher your GPA, the better (remember from your 7-year checklist that you want to maintain at least a B, or 85, average).

Semester GPA vs. Cumulative GPA

On your report card, you will typically see two types of GPAs – semester and cumulative. A **semester GPA** calculates your grade point average from that semester only. Your **cumulative GPA** calculates your grade point average from the very beginning of your freshman year. You will have a separate high school cumulative GPA and college cumulative GPA (so your high school GPA will not rollover into your college GPA). While it's great to have a high semester GPA, you want to work on keeping your cumulative GPA as high as possible since that is what colleges and potential employers will be looking at when you apply.

(ABC) Semester
A semester is a half-year term in a school or college, typically lasting fifteen to eighteen weeks.

Weighted GPA and Unweighted GPA

Key Point

Unweighted GPA typically assigns an A – 4 points, B – 3 points, C – 2 points, D – 1 point, and an F – 0 points.

Key Point

Weighted GPA goes beyond a 4-point scale as a result of taking accelerated or advanced courses.

The previously mentioned GPA examples based on a 4.0 scale are considered "unweighted." However, many schools offer accelerated and Advanced Placement (AP) classes, IB classes, Dual Credit classes, and honors classes. Since these classes are more advanced than regular courses, schools often assign a different point system to the harder classes. To weight the GPA, the semester grade in each course is added to the course weight. All weighted courses are totaled and divided by the total number of courses to get the weighted GPA.

For example, a student earns a grade of 4.0 in Mrs. Blackwell's AP Chemistry class for the spring semester. This student's points will be calculated using a weighted GPA since it is an advanced course. Think of it as earning an additional point because you are in an advanced course. So instead of earning a 4.0 for an "A," this student would receive a 5.0 (4.0 for the A + 1.0 for the advanced course) for the semester class.

Check with your school to learn more about their weighted GPA scale and which classes it applies to. Taking advanced classes and doing well in them can help to raise your GPA. Your transcript will most likely show both your weighted GPA on a 5.0 scale and your unweighted GPA on a 4.0 scale. These numbers will be decimals and are used to calculate your class rank.

What is "Class Rank?"

Key Point

Class rank compares your weighted GPA to other students at your high school.

TIPS Class Rank

Competition can be good. Graduating with a high class rank will increase your chances of getting into the college of your choice.

Your **class rank** measures where you stand academically compared to others in your graduating class. For example, if you have a GPA of a 3.7 and your friend has a GPA of 3.8, your friend will rank higher than you do. Class rank may be used as a number (such as 6th in a class) or as a **percentile** (top 25% of a class). Admission officers for colleges and scholarships usually look at both your GPA and class rank together, so it is just as important to have a high class rank as well as a high GPA. A "really good" class rank is typically considered to be in the top 25% of your class and to be in the top 10% is considered "highly competitive" or "excellent." Think of it as a friendly competition between you and all of your classmates.

How to Calculate GPA

To calculate your GPA, remember to ADD all of your grades together and DIVIDE by the total number of classes. Round to the nearest hundredth. For example:

$$A+A+B+B+C+A+B = \frac{4.0 + 4.0 + 3.0 + 3.0 + 2.0 + 4.0 + 3.0}{7} = \frac{23}{7} = \mathbf{3.28}$$

My Turn! Practice Calculating GPA

DIRECTIONS: Sandra's report card is missing some information! Follow the 4 steps to help her calculate her GPA. Use the GPA Scale Table below to help!

Letter Grade	Percent Grade	4.0 Scale
A+	97-100	4.0
A	93-96	4.0
A-	90-92	3.7
B+	87-89	3.3
B	83-86	3.0
B-	80-82	2.7

Letter Grade	Percent Grade	4.0 Scale
C+	77-79	2.3
C	73-76	2.0
C-	70-72	1.7
D+	67-69	1.3
D	65-66	1.0
E/F	Below 65	0.0

Step 1: Change your letter grades to grade points.

Subject	Letter Grade	Grade Points
English	A	4.0
History	A-	3.7
Math	B+	3.3
Science	B	3.0

Step 2: Add up all of your grade points.

4.0 + 3.7 + 3.3 + 3.0 = **14 Grade Points**

Step 3: Count the number of classes you have.

English + History + Math + Science = **4 Classes**

Step 4: Divide your Total Grade Points (TGP) by your Number of Classes (NC).

```
TGP              14
------ = GPA    --- = 3.5
NC                4
```

Step 1: Change Sandra's letter grades to grade points.

Skyrise High School Sandra Medina Semester 1		
Subject	Letter Grade	Grade Points
Algebra II	A	4.0
English II	A	4.0
World History	B-	2.7
Art I	B	
Biology I	A	
Team Sports	B+	
Newspaper	A	

Step 2: Add up all of Sandra's grade points.

Step 3: Count the number of classes Sandra has.

Step 4: Divide Sandra's grade points by # of classes.

What is Sandra's GPA? _____

Now, look at Darrion's report card. Follow the steps to calculate his GPA.

Cityview High School Darrion Maher Semester 2		
Subject	Letter Grade	Grade Points
Yearbook	A-	3.7
Choir	A	4.0
Geography	B	3.0
Algebra II	B+	
Chemistry	A	
English II	C+	

Step 1: Change letter grades to grade points!

Step 2: Add total grade points:

Step 3: Count total # of classes:

Step 4: Divide grade points by # of classes:

What is Darrion's GPA? _____

Calculating My GPA

My Turn! What's My GPA?

After speaking with your guidance counselor, fill in the chart below:

What numerical value does your school assign for each of the following grades (just in case it's different from the previous page)?

A+ =	B+ =	C+ =	D+ =
A =	B =	C =	D =
A- =	B- =	C- =	D- =

TIPS **GPA**
You should be calculating your GPA frequently over the school year based on your current grades. You want to always know where you stand!

Use this specific scale and your report cards to calculate your own GPA and make sure you are staying on track! To practice, fill in the chart below with each of your classes and the grade you earned from last semester.

Class	Letter Grade Earned	Numerical Value
Example: Math	B	3.0

Step 1: Change letter grades to grade points!

Step 2: Add total grade points:

Step 3: Count total # of classes:

Step 4: Divide grade points by # of classes:

My Calculated GPA = _____

Unit 2: Navigate High School

Types of High Schools

Key Point

There are different types of high schools, all with benefits and limitations. Each vary in size, entrance requirements, selectivity, and difficulty of coursework.

As early as the 7th grade you want to start thinking about where you want to go to high school, because by the 8th grade you will be able to apply to the high school of your choice. This section will help you understand the differences between the various types of high schools that your town or city may have to offer.

Public High Schools

Public schools get their financing from local, state and federal government funds. Therefore, public schools are free and do not charge tuition. Public high schools are part of a larger school district, and teachers must abide by state and district guidelines regarding curriculum and testing. Most public high schools (unless they are magnet or charter schools) have an open admission, meaning any student living within the school's limits may attend.

Private High Schools

Private schools receive funding from student tuition and are allowed to be more selective on whom they allow to go to their schools. Some private schools may require family interviews, essays, and testing before granting admission. Many private schools typically have smaller class sizes, and their students often produce higher test scores. Since they are not a government institution, many private schools require religious classes along with the normal curriculum or have their own set of guidelines about life and class on campus.

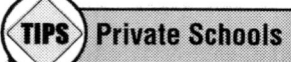

Private Schools

It's worth looking into scholarship opportunities at private high schools in your area.

Magnet High Schools

Magnet schools are public schools with specialized courses (such as health, business, engineering or performing arts). They are referred to as "magnet" schools because they attract students from many areas outside of normal school boundaries. Students must apply to magnet schools and many are highly competitive. Students may need to complete application forms, write essays, take admissions tests months in advance, go for interviews and even participate in auditions to gain admission into magnet schools. Magnet schools look at a student's 7th and 8th grade academic history as well, so it is important for students who are interested to have good grades and try hard on state tests throughout all of middle school.

Home School

The idea of home schooling typically comes with many misconceptions. Students in a traditional education setting often equate their own time at home with what home schooling would be like. This could not be farther from the truth! Students who are home schooled must be highly motivated as well as their teacher.

Home School is sometimes called interest-motivated education or self-motivated education. You get interested in something for whatever reason, that interest motivates you to learn about it, and you do learn about it by doing your own research. The reality is, in this country, that regardless of where you attend school, you are accountable to learning the information. Home school environments can range from being project based where families take a child's curiosity and interest in a topic and help the child explore the topic. Other families buy all of the textbooks and follow the state curriculum just like a normal school would. The material is simply taught at home in a smaller setting.

Charter High Schools

Charter schools were created to give students and families other options besides their designated public schools within their districts. Charter schools receive state funding (and some private donations) and do not charge tuition, yet they do not have to follow all of the rules and regulations that district public schools must follow. Since they do not have to follow the guidelines of a specific district, they are held more accountable for student achievement.

Any student may enroll in a charter school. If too many students try to enroll in a charter school, a "lottery" or some other form of random selection must take place to randomly select who is enrolled. If a student is not picked in the lottery, he or she may be placed on a waiting list.

Early College

Early College is a school that gives students the opportunity to obtain both a high school diploma and an Associate's degree within four years by enrolling in dual credit classes. Early College requires students to take a mixture of both high school and college classes, receiving credit for both. To enroll in Early College, one must typically go through an application process, write an essay, submit his or her academic history and provide letters of recommendation. Important point of clarification: most high schools offer dual credit courses, but the high schools are not early college. If you're interested in pursuing a great number of dual credit courses or an Associate's degree during high school, you have the option of applying to an Early College High School.

My Turn! Status Check

DIRECTIONS: Complete the following sentence stem. Then write a brief paragraph explaining your choice.

I feel I will fit in best at a _____ **type of high school because...**

TAG highSchool / career high School

_____

_____

_____

_____

_____

_____

_____

Types of High School Scavenger Hunt!

DIRECTIONS: Below is a table that summarizes the differences between the various types of high schools that students can attend. Using the information in the surrounding boxes as clues, search for the correct answers to complete each box. Hint: hunt for the correct information in the previous pages and/or by using your outside knowledge.

	Public	Private	Charter	Magnet	Early College
Expenses	Public schools get money from the state so they are free for students to attend.	Private schools receive no money from the state so students are required to pay to attend.	Charter schools receive money from the state, so it is free for students to attend.	_____	_____
Application Policies	No application is required.	_____	_____	_____	Applications are required. These require an essay, academic history, and letters of recommendation.
Attendance Policies	As long as you live in the boundaries of that particular school zone, you have a right to attend public school.	_____	_____	_____	If you apply and are accepted you are, of course, allowed to attend!
High School Examples	Research local examples	Research local examples	Research local examples	Research local examples	Research local examples

My Turn! Does the Perfect School Exist?

DIRECTIONS:

Step 1: In the center box, draw a picture of THE perfect school. It can be a view from the outside or the inside.

Step 2: Answer the following questions in text or pictures around your center image.

- How many students will be in each grade level?
- How would the class schedule work? (i.e. how many classes per day, lunch schedule, etc.)
- What would be the mission statement of the school?
- What would a typical teacher be like?
- What would the demographics (characteristics of students) of the school be?
- What will the application requirements be?
- How much homework should be given?
- Any other questions you can think of!

My Turn! Research Local High Schools

DIRECTIONS: Using the information you have learned in the previous sections, please use this space to research high school options in your community by answering the questions below.

Think of the names of some high schools you have heard of. Please write down the names of a few local high schools you want to know more information about as well as what type of school you think it is.

	Name of School	Type of School (ie: magnet, charter, public, etc.)
A		
B		
C		

Use this list of questions to help guide your research. Include any additional questions you want to look up in the space provided.

Where is the school located?
- School A: _____
- School B: _____
- School C: _____

If it's far away from your home, what are the transportation options available?
- School A: _____
- School B: _____
- School C: _____

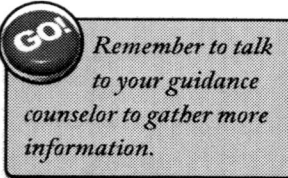

Remember to talk to your guidance counselor to gather more information.

What types of programs are available to students? (IB, AP, dual credit, etc.)
- School A: _____
- School B: _____
- School C: _____

What are the steps to take in order to apply?
- School A: _____
- School B: _____
- School C: _____

What is the school website and phone number?
- School A: _____
- School B: _____
- School C: _____

Researching Local High Schools Continued

What are the application deadlines?
- School A: _____
- School B: _____
- School C: _____

What are the fees/tuition/costs to students?
- School A: _____
- School B: _____
- School C: _____

Are there scholarships available for students unable to pay fees/tuition/costs?
- School A: _____
- School B: _____
- School C: _____

What is the graduation rate?
- School A: _____
- School B: _____
- School C: _____

What are the average SAT and ACT scores of seniors?
- School A: _____
- School B: _____
- School C: _____

What is the college acceptance rate?
- School A: _____
- School B: _____
- School C: _____

Are sports available?
- School A: _____
- School B: _____
- School C: _____

Are trade, vocational, and technical courses available?
- School A: _____
- School B: _____
- School C: _____

Additional information:
- School A: _____
- School B: _____
- School C: _____

High School Fit

Every student in the U.S. is guaranteed a public education through high school — meaning that if you choose to go this route, you will not be required to apply.

While the application process to apply to other high school options can be much more difficult, students that put forth the effort and earn admission to these schools generally enjoy a smoother path to success than their peers. The application process is rigorous and varies uniquely depending on which school(s) you choose to apply to. To help organize most of the application requirements that you will be asked to meet, the most important information has been organized in the table below:

Key Point

All students have options for high school outside of their neighborhood public school. Applying to other schools can offer unique learning opportunities.

ABC Percentile

Percentiles are a way of comparing scores or GPAs across a population of students. For example, a percentile rank of 50% means that the student scored or had a GPA the same or better than 50% of the students in his or her population of students. It does not mean the student scored a 50 on the test.

School Type	Application* Due + Fee	Entrance Exam	Approximate GPA Required	Essay	Interview	Special Notes
Private	✔ Applications are generally due in early January. *Fee ~ approx. $175, ask about fee waivers*	✔ **Independent School Entrance Exam (ISEE)** *Score ~ 50th/60th Percentile*	✔ Solid "A/A+" Student	✔ Applicants are typically asked to write at least one (1) 500 word essay	✔ Applicants are typically required to interview before being accepted	*Financial aid is available and usually awarded for students that earn admission*
Magnet	✔ Applications are accepted throughout January. *Fee ~ FREE for your home district*	✔ Iowa Test of Basic Skills (ITBS) *Score ~ 65th–85th Percentile*	✔ Solid "B" Student	✔ Applicants are typically asked to write at least one (1) 500 word essay	✔ Applicants are typically required to interview before being accepted	*You may be asked to submit a portfolio, an original project, or even audition to be accepted.*
Charter	✔ Check their websites for application due dates. *Fee ~ FREE*	✘ No Entrance Exam Requirement	✘ No GPA Requirement	✘ No Essay Requirement	✘ No Interview Requirement	*Charter school admission is based entirely on a lottery system. Every applicant has an equal chance of being accepted. Preference may be given to residents of the area nearby the school.*
Early College	✔ Check their websites for application due dates. *Fee ~ FREE*	✔ Satisfactory scores on state tests may be required	✔ GPA may be a consideration in application. Check with your local Early College high school.	✘ No Essay Requirement	✔ If students advance, they and their parents are invited to a family interview	*Early Colleges prioritize "effort-driven" students who are prepared for college work.*

NOTE: The applications to each of these school types usually require letters of recommendation from your teachers and/or administrators.

Which Option is Right for Me?

TIPS Essays are Important!

High schools often look at essays first when determining applications. Practice your writing skills!

There is no "right" or "wrong" option when it comes to high school. It's about finding the best fit for you. Some students may thrive the best in a highly rigorous academic environment at a private high school. Others may find more success at a traditional public high school where they can make the transition to college-level work on a more gradual basis.

Here are some questions worth considering when it comes to researching which high school will fit you the best:

My Turn! Questions to Answer When Thinking About High School Options

DIRECTIONS: Answer the following questions. Be honest in your responses.

1. How close to home do you want to be for high school? Some schools may require you to travel very far each morning and evening.

   _____

   _____

2. What do you think about uniforms? Some schools have dress codes, some schools do not. Would you be comfortable wearing a shirt and tie to school every day?

   _____

   _____

3. What subjects are most interesting to you? Are the classes that you are most interested in offered at the high school you're enrolling in?

   _____

   _____

   _____

4. Extra-Curricular Participation? Some of these options require participation in afterschool programs such as sports. Some schools do not offer sports programs. How involved do you want to be in programs such as these? Keep in mind, that the more involved you are, the more attractive your applications to college may be!

   _____

   _____

   _____

   _____

   _____

GO! Need an Application Essay?

Skip to "Unit 6: Apply to College" and read the tips on writing essays and personal statements. They relate to High School applications as well as college!

Unit 2: Navigate High School

Questions To Think About For Yourself:

1. Are you ready for college-level work? In general, the academic expectations will be higher than traditional high schools at schools of choice. Are you prepared to produce college-level work?

2. To reach your goals, what do you need to improve? Not even Einstein was a perfect student! What steps do you need to take to ensure that you submit a strong application that will result in acceptance at one of these competitive schools?

3. What do you want for your future? How will your high school choice affect your long-term goals? Do you want to be a doctor? A musician? An artist?

4. Are you mature enough to handle more work? No matter where you go to high school, you will be expected to handle an increased workload. This pattern will only strengthen as you advance through school – how does your maturity match up with you in this area?

The Final Word on Applying to High School

In the end, it's not only where you go to high school, but more importantly how you handle the challenges that arise once you are in school. No matter where you end up going, high school will present its own unique set of challenges, and opportunities for you to pursue and thrive within! Take advantage of the opportunity to apply for various high school options in order to find the choice that will lead to the future you envision for yourself!

Notes

Which Path Will You Choose?

Have you ever thought to yourself...?

> *"I believe sophomore year is when I need to start thinking more about which classes to take."*... This is not the case. From the moment you start high school, your course schedule should be well thought out.

> *"I am already too far behind in my grades or classes"*... There is always an opportunity to learn and do more! Summer camps, tutorials, private tutors, or even just scheduling extra with your teachers can help improve your college choices.

> *"I want to have a lot of college opportunities and make the choice that is best for me."*... You absolutely can! You just need to stay resilient and remember that hard work pays off.

"Two roads diverged in a wood and I - I took the one less traveled by, and that has made all the difference."
~Robert Frost

Whether you are currently in middle school, or already in high school there are multiple paths that you can choose for your future.

My Turn! Which Path Will I Choose?

1. What did Robert Frost mean when he said that the road less traveled made all of the difference? How do you think that same idea relates to your future path? _____
_____
_____

2. How do the choices that you make today, both in and out of school, impact your future? _____
_____

3. Why is it important to be purposeful in selecting your high school classes?
_____
_____

4. How many times have you spoken with your guidance counselor? _____

5. How many advanced courses have you taken/are you planning to take in high school?
_____

6. What do you want to do after high school? How will your time in high school affect whether or not you are able to reach that goal? _____
_____

Which Path Will You Choose? Continued

Middle School

High School

Roadmap to Success

?

Unit 2: Navigate High School

Which student do you want to be?

Which student are you currently most similar to? -- Student A, Student B, or Student C?

Student A
Never speaks with guidance counselor, takes whatever s/he is placed in, has a 2.6 GPA, graduates on time.

Student B
Takes 1 or 2 advanced courses, speaks with guidance counselors, has a 3.5 GPA, and graduates on time.

Student C
Meets with guidance counselor each quarter to make sure s/he is on track, takes as many advanced courses as possible, has a 3.8 GPA, graduates on time.

Student A
4 Total College Choices
0 Scholarship Options

Accepted to:
- 2 Public Schools
- 2 Community College Options in the Local Area

Although Student A had decent grades, he/she had not taken any advanced or unique courses. No scholarships are available.

Student B
10 Total College Choices
3 Partial-Scholarship Options

Accepted to:
- 2 Private Schools
- 5 Public Schools
- 3 Community Colleges Options in the Local Area

Accepted into their first choice school

Student C
17 Total College Choices
10 Scholarship Options

Accepted to:
- 6 Private Schools
- 6 Public Schools
- 5 Community College Options in the Local Area

Received multiple Academic Scholarship Awards, covering all finances for attendance to 4 highly selective schools across the country, now they just have to choose which one suits them best!

Planning for College Admission Requirements

You may have already chosen your high school, or currently be in high school, so the next step is to carefully select the classes that you are enrolled in!

Universities and colleges often have specific high school coursework required for acceptance. These can be different than the classes that your high school requires you to take, so make sure that you check with your colleges of choice early in your high school career.

Not only do you have to take certain classes, but also it is important to make sure you have taken the correct number of courses (and credit hours) in each subject area. Below is a generic chart of admission requirements based on the type of college or university that you may be interested in. On the following pages you will learn more about high school course credits and types of advanced courses you can take in high school. You will also build your own plan for high school.

Type of College/University				
Ivy League or Highly Selective Private School	**Highly Selective Public School**	**Selective Private School**	**Selective Public School**	**Community College**
Example: Princeton	*Example: University of California, Berkeley*	*Example: SMU*	*Example: Louisiana State University*	*Example: LaGuardia Community College*
Course Work Requirements *These requirements are subject to change for each college and based on your major, but give a general guideline for specific types of schools. Be sure to check with your school of interest for exact requirements.*				
• 4 years of English (including continued practice in writing) • 4 years of mathematics (including calculus) • 4 years of the same foreign language • At least 3 years of laboratory science (including physics, chemistry, and biology) • At least 3 years of history/social science • 1 year of visual or performing arts	• 4 years of English • 4 years of math • 2 years of same foreign language • 3 years of laboratory science • 2 years of history/social science • 1 year of visual or performing arts	• 4 years of English • 4 years of math (algebra I, II, geometry) • 2 years of social science • 3 years of science (of which 2 must be lab science) • 2 years of same foreign language • 1 year of visual or performing arts	• 4 years of English • 4 years of math • 2 years of foreign language • 4 years of natural science • 4 years of social science • 1 year of visual or performing arts	• A high school diploma or General Equivalency Diploma (G.E.D.)
Testing Requirements				
Require SAT, SAT Subject Tests, or ACT	Require SAT, SAT Subject Tests, or ACT	Require SAT or ACT scores	Require SAT, SAT Subject Tests, or ACT	SATs and ACTs are not required.
Approximate GPA Requirements				
Roughly 3.9+	Roughly 3.7+	Roughly 3.5+	Roughly 3.2+	no minimum GPA

Understanding Course Credits

My Turn! My High School Course Credits

DIRECTIONS: Using the course names listed on this page, draft a copy of your ideal course schedule by writing each course name in the blocks.

Common Electives

- Visual Arts
- Drawing
- Sculpture
- Painting
- Photography
- Film Studies
- Art History
- Performing Arts
- Choir
- Drama
- Band
- Orchestra
- Dance
- Guitar
- Vocational Education
- Woodworking
- Metalworking
- Computer-aided Drafting
- Automobile Repair
- Agriculture
- Cosmetology
- FFA
- Sewing

- Computer Science
- Word Processing
- Programming
- Graphic Design
- Web Design
- Web Programming
- Video Game Design
- Music Production
- Journalism/Publishing
- School Newspaper
- Yearbook
- TV Production
- Foreign Languages
- American Sign Language
- Business Education
- Accounting
- Data Processing
- Management
- Culinary Arts
- Childhood Development
- Nutrition
- Weight Training

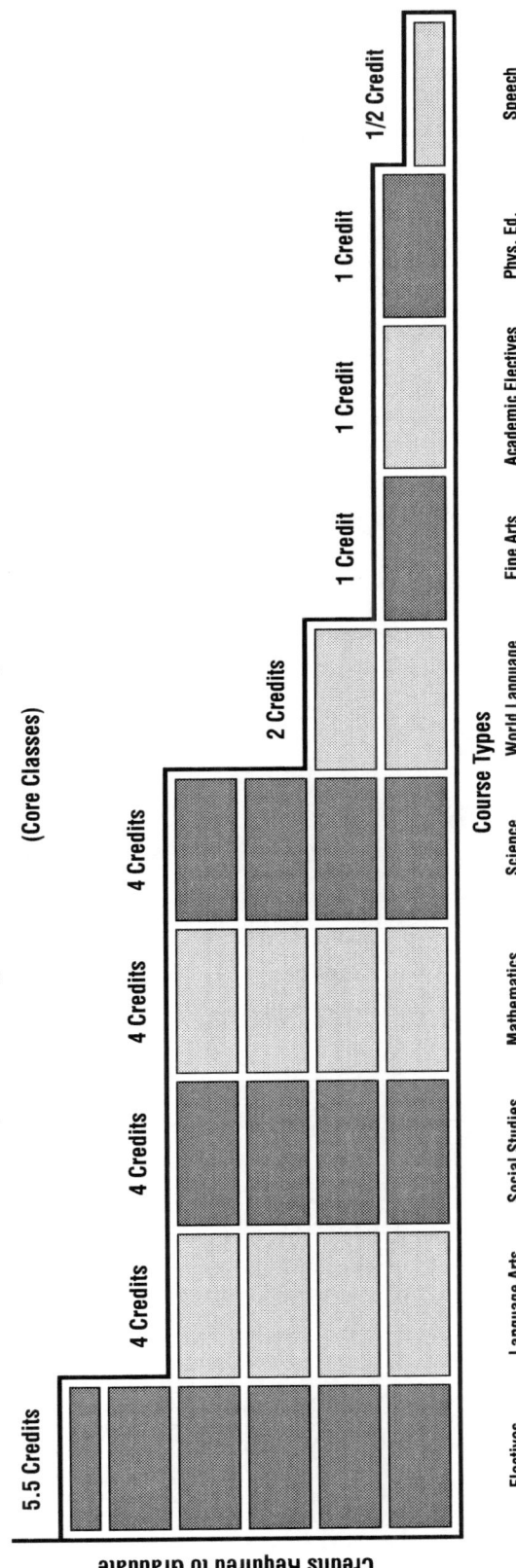

High School Graduation Requirements (Core Classes)

Credits Required to Graduate

	5.5 Credits	4 Credits	4 Credits	4 Credits	4 Credits	2 Credits	1 Credit	1 Credit	1 Credit	1/2 Credit

Course Types

Electives	Language Arts	Social Studies	Mathematics	Science	World Language	Fine Arts	Academic Electives	Phys. Ed.	Speech
Course options will vary by school.	Composition I	Geography	Algebra I	Earth Science	*Such As...* Spanish	*Such As...* Drama	*Such As...* World History Studies	*Such As...* P.E. or Equivalent	*Such As...* Communication Applications
	English Lit.	U.S. History	Geometry	Biology	French	Drawing/Painting	World Geography Studies		Professional Communications
	World Lit.	World History	Algebra II	Chemistry	German	Media Arts	Other Science Courses		
	Composition II	Economics	Trigonometry	Physics	Chinese	Music			
		Government	Calculus		Japanese				

Notes:
* 1 credit = 1 year of class in certain subject
* Ask your guidance counselor for the actual graduation requirements at your local high school. These are a representative of what is most common.

Dual Credit Enrollment

TIPS College Credit

There are ways to receive college credit while you are in high school. Ask your counselor for more information.

Dual credit programs allow high school juniors and seniors to take college-level classes and receive high school and college credit for them. These classes are normally taught on a high school campus, yet some students can take them on a college campus, usually at a community college. Dual credit courses may be academic (such as AP Biology or Government) or technical (Drafting or Automotive Repair). Some districts pay for students' tuition fees while others may require students to pay for the dual credit themselves.

Schools usually require many of the following: an application, a copy of the applicant's most recent grades, ITBS and state standardized test scores, an essay, parent statement/support, teacher recommendation(s), and a family interview. Once students are admitted, they must pass a college readiness exam. This test is used to determine if students can read, write, and do math on a college level.

Mindset Change

Not all dual credit classes will directly transfer to a 4-year bachelor degree program.

Dual credit enrollment has many benefits:

- Studies show that students who take dual credit are more likely to graduate from high school and continue on to college.
- Taking these courses in high school decreases future tuition fees one may have to pay.
- If students enter college with a lot of credits, they can graduate from college and enter the workforce sooner.
- Students who take college-level courses in high school are much more prepared for college once they graduate as opposed to students who do not take college-level courses.
- Any Dual Credit course taken and passed is typically guaranteed to transfer to any PUBLIC four-year university in the same state.
- Diverse courses. Often, dual credit courses are taken at a community college with college students of all ages and backgrounds.

Regardless of the high school you attend, remember that the more college-level courses you take the better prepared you will be!

Advanced Placement (AP)

AP (Advanced Placement) Courses are college-level courses you can take in high school. AP exams take place in May and are the final exam after you complete an AP course. These standardized exams measure how well you mastered the content and skills of the course. The AP Exam is scored on a 1-5 scale, with a 1 as the worst and a 5 as the best. A passing score is a 3, 4, or 5, and, depending on the college, you will receive college credit if you receive a score of 3, 4, or 5.

Advantages of AP Courses:

- Help prepare you for college
  - The pace, workload, and expectations are higher (like they will be in college) than in non-AP classes.

- You will be challenged to strengthen and improve your learning and studying skills.
- Receive college credit
  - If you receive passing scores on your AP exams, many colleges will give you college credit. This can lead to several possibilities!
  - You will have more time for classes you are interested in outside of the required general education.
  - You will be ahead of the game for college and may be able to graduate early.
  - You will save money on college courses because you've already completed some college level courses!
- Preference in the college application process.
  - Students who take AP courses stand out to colleges and universities. The most prestigious universities will be more likely to admit a student who challenged themselves in high school as opposed to one who took regular courses.

Mindset Change

"Wait. Isn't it better to take easier classes in high school and get better grades?" This is another misperception about college applications. One of the best things you can do is to take rigorous classes and do your best to succeed.

There are up to 34 AP courses that your school can choose to offer. Ask your guidance counselor which AP courses are available at your high school. Teachers and counselors can help you decide which courses you should consider, how you can prepare for them, and how to enroll. Some schools offer more AP courses than others. If the courses you are interested in are not offered at your school, talk to your counselor about possible opportunities to take the class online.

To get more information search online for "College Board-AP."

International Baccalaureate (IB) Diploma Program (DP)

The **International Baccalaureate** Program is a multi-level curriculum developed for students K-12. It's mission statement "aims to develop inquiring, knowledgeable, and caring young people who help to create a better and more peaceful world through intercultural understanding and respect."

Diploma Program

The Diploma Program (DP) is a challenging, two year curriculum (offered only to juniors and seniors) that requires students to study courses across all disciplines. The diploma program is recognized by colleges and universities around the world as a superior education. Success with IB can even result in course credit or advanced standing. A common precursor to the Diploma Program is the Middle Years Program (MYP), completed through the ages of 11-16. Talk to your counselor to see if your campus offers IB coursework and learn more about what the DP can do for you!

Advantages of the Diploma Program

- Preparation for college-level courses
  - The DP is based upon rigorous academics within a broad curriculum, focusing on developing intellectual knowledge and social awareness. This will serve students well as they prepare for the rigor of higher education.
  - DP courses will include a great deal of independent research and large-scale projects to be presented to an audience multiple times in your 2-year experience.
- Through the mission of IB, students will develop empathy to opinions different from their own and be able to formulate intelligent arguments encompassing multiple viewpoints.
- Students are required to participate in community service, in the form of large-scale student projects within the curriculum that are largely based around community development.

Talk to Your Guidance Counselor

(ABC) Academic Advisor/Guidance Counselor

This person will help you pick the right courses, review the course requirements for the major you want and help you with any academic problems you run into.

High school can be a new, exciting, and challenging place to navigate. Generally speaking, school **guidance counselors** are at every high school to help students successfully navigate the high school journey and beyond. Often times there are far more students than counselors at one school, so take the initiative and be proactive about building a relationship with your guidance counselor (and/or a trusted, knowledgeable teacher, or school staff).

Here are some tips for making the best out of your relationship with your counselor:

1. **Be proactive and start early!** Meet with your guidance counselor early in your freshman year and continue to build a relationship with your counselor throughout your four years.

2. **Make appointments with your counselor!** Often times, counselors are working with a large number of students and may not have a lot of time for unscheduled visits. If you make an appointment, your counselor will have time to prepare for your meeting and you are more likely to have his/her full attention for that period of time.

3. **Seek academic advising!** Talk to your counselor about your favorite subjects and your plans after high school. Your counselor can be more intentional about planning your high school class schedule based on your interests and goals. They can also keep you on track for high school graduation and college admission. You and your counselor should have frequent conversations to make sure you are:

   • Taking all the classes you need to graduate on time
   • Taking the types of classes that most colleges look for
   • Getting the help you need if you're having trouble in class
   • Taking classes and participating in activities that will challenge you

(GO!) *Who is your guidance counselor?*

_____

What are the top 2 questions you have for them today?

1) _____
   _____
   _____

2) _____
   _____
   _____
   _____

4. **Be curious and ask questions!** Exemplar questions to ask your guidance counselor:

   • What are the graduation plans at this school?
   • What are the course requirements and credit hours needed for each graduation plan?
   • What pieces am I currently missing (if any) in order to be on track for the best possible graduation plan?
   • What advanced courses (AP, IB, and dual credit) are offered at this school?
   • Can we schedule a meeting to discuss my courses each semester?
   • If I choose to participate in athletics or fine arts that take a significant number of credit hours, how will my credits be affected?
   • Does this school have any trade programs or opportunities to earn course credit while working off campus?

My Plan for High School

TIPS *Please keep in mind that high school graduation requirements vary from state to state, district to district, and often are continually changing. Talk to your guidance counselors for your school's graduation requirements.*

DIRECTIONS: After meeting with your guidance counselor(s), and obtaining graduation requirements for your school, complete the chart below. List the classes you will take each year by listing the course name (i.e.: English Composition 1) as well as credit hours for that course. Remember, a yearlong course (if each semester is passed) will give you a total of 1 credit hour. That means each semester is .5 credit hours. Be sure to include any advanced courses you may be considering.

Freshman Year (9th Grade)				
Fall Semester		**Spring Semester**		
Course Name	# of Credit Hours	Course Name	# of Credit Hours	**Total number of Credits at the end of Freshman year *You MUST pass the course to receive a credit hour** **Total:** _____
Total		**Total**		

Sophomore Year (10th Grade)				
Fall Semester		**Spring Semester**		
Course Name	# of Credit Hours	Course Name	# of Credit Hours	**Total number of Credits at the end of Sophomore year *You MUST pass the course to receive a credit hour** **Total:** _____
Total		**Total**		

Note: Keep in mind that you can participate in any extracurricular sport or fine art for more than 1 year, and likely will not receive course credit for them beyond the first year. (Example: Playing soccer all 4 years: 2 semesters of P.E. credit per year, however you are only given 1 year's worth of credit. The remaining 3 years you will receive some elective credit and eventually receive no credit at all for your time in soccer.)

Junior Year (11th Grade)

Fall Semester		Spring Semester		Total number of Credits at the end of Junior year *You MUST pass the course to receive a credit hour Total: _____
Course Name	**# of Credit Hours**	**Course Name**	**# of Credit Hours**	
Total		**Total**		

Senior Year (12th Grade)

Fall Semester		Spring Semester		Total number of Credits at the end of Senior year *You MUST pass the course to receive a credit hour Total: _____
Course Name	**# of Credit Hours**	**Course Name**	**# of Credit Hours**	
Total		**Total**		

Notes

_____

_____

_____

_____

_____

_____

_____

Time Management

Staying organized is an essential part of ensuring your success in high school and in college. There are three general ways to make certain that you stay on track from a monthly basis to a daily basis.

You can organize your responsibilities and commitments in 4 steps:

STEP 1 Create a monthly calendar

STEP 2 Build weekly calendar using the monthly calendar

STEP 3 Create a to-do list of tasks from the weekly calendar

STEP 4 Log your calendars and to-do lists in a planning tool

Key Point
The three most commonly used organizational tools are monthly calendars, weekly calendars, and daily to-do lists.

ABC Syllabus
an outline of the important information about a course that typically includes important dates, assignments, expectations and policies specific to that course.

Monthly Calendar

At the beginning of the school year, purchase a school calendar (if one is not supplied for you) and update it regularly. For each month, fill in the general overview with specific dates and activities.

- Write down your tests and school assignments with their due dates. These can sometimes be found on your course **syllabus** for each class.
- List your planned school extracurricular activities and out-of-school extracurricular activities. Some examples:
  - "Football Games" on Fridays
  - "Math Tutoring" on Tuesdays and Wednesdays

Example Monthly Calendar

The picture to the right is an example of a typical monthly calendar you might use to help plan your time. Keep in mind that this is just an example.

Weekly Calendar

Use your weekly calendar to keep track of activities and assignments. Organization is key.

- List your daily classes.
- Transfer things to be done for the coming week from your monthly calendar and from the past week.
  - Example: "Science project due Wednesday."
- Add all extracurricular activities for the week.
  - Example: "Soccer practice Monday through Friday from 4 to 6."
- Include times for completing assignments, working on projects, and studying for tests.
  - Example: "Work on Science project from 3 to 5 on Sunday."
- Include tutoring times from your teachers for each of your core classes.
  - Example: "Science tutoring on Tuesdays from 4 to 5:30."

Daily Organizer (To-Do List)

Each night, you should prepare a daily organizer for the next day. Check off each task as you complete it.

- Transfer activities and assignments to do for the coming day from your weekly calendar.
- Transfer everything that you may have not completed from yesterday's daily organizer.
- Include any additional out-of-school activities you will be involved in that day.

My Turn! Create a To Do List

DIRECTIONS: Brainstorm a list of tasks you need to complete this week.

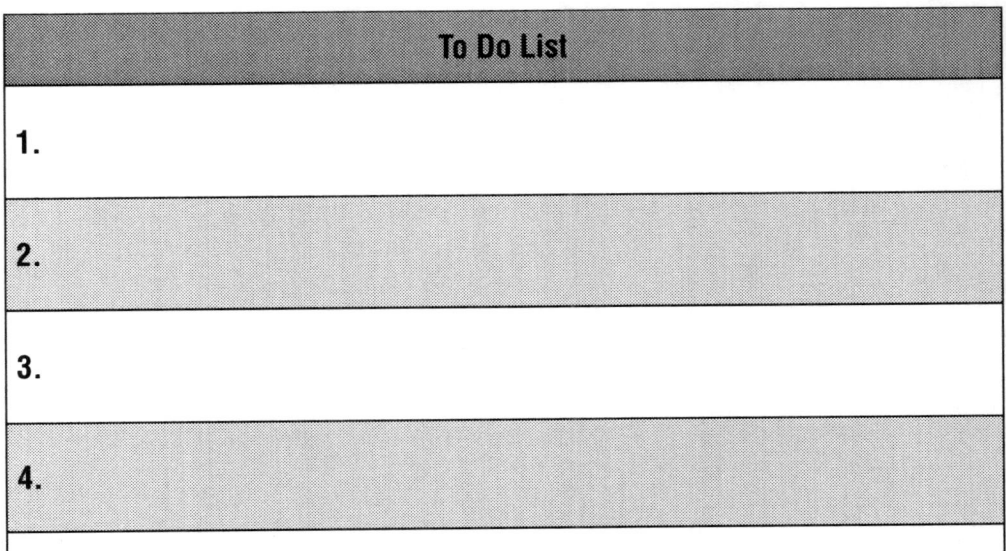

To Do List
1.
2.
3.
4.
5.

My Turn! Student Planner

DIRECTIONS: Staying organized is not easy. Using a student planner like this one can help a lot! Complete the weekly planner template below.

Monday, __/__/__

Before School To Do's	☐ _____
	☐ _____
	☐ _____

Class Name/ Period	Task/Assignment	Due Date

After School To Do's	☐ _____
	☐ _____
	☐ _____

Thursday, __/__/__

Before School To Do's	☐ _____
	☐ _____
	☐ _____

Class Name/ Period	Task/Assignment	Due Date

After School To Do's	☐ _____
	☐ _____
	☐ _____

Tuesday, __/__/__

Before School To Do's	☐ _____
	☐ _____
	☐ _____

Class Name/ Period	Task/Assignment	Due Date

After School To Do's	☐ _____
	☐ _____
	☐ _____

Friday, __/__/__

Before School To Do's	☐ _____
	☐ _____
	☐ _____

Class Name/ Period	Task/Assignment	Due Date

After School To Do's	☐ _____
	☐ _____
	☐ _____

Wednesday, __/__/__

Before School To Do's	☐ _____
	☐ _____
	☐ _____

Class Name/ Period	Task/Assignment	Due Date

After School To Do's	☐ _____
	☐ _____
	☐ _____

Events this week...

Upcoming Assessments

Planning for Success

Many people use different types of planning tools to help organize their time. Some of these are described in the paragraphs below!

There's an App for That!

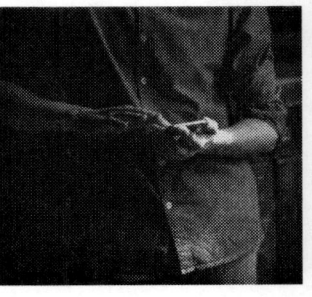

Some people love having a physical calendar, such as the examples you have seen so far in this section, to use in order to help organize their time. However, for other individuals keeping track of a calendar or "To Do List" can be a burden and can cause more stress than help. This is obviously not the goal of being an organized person and using these tools to help plan your time.

Calendaring Electronically

If you prefer an electronic calendar on your phone or computer, practice these same skills using your preferred technology. Just make sure you stick to it!

If this is you and you are not the handwritten calendar type of student, do not fear! Many electronic options exist to help you stay on top of your responsibilities, events, and activities.

As cell phone technology, and most smart phones continue to improve, most electronic devices come standard with powerful software to help calendar your time. Some of the latest models and devices even have voice-activated technology, making setting reminders as easy as holding a button and having a virtual assistant set an alarm right there from your phone! Find what works best for you, but stick to it and use it to stay organized.

The Last Word on Planning

No matter who you are or what you decide to do with your life, one thing is for certain: as you get older, you will continue to earn more privileges as well as more responsibilities. No two people live exactly the same lives and, therefore, it follows that no two people will organize their responsibilities precisely the same way.

This is perfectly ok! There is no single "right" way to plan. Some people write down their to do list, some use electronic applications, and some people use both! The most important part of planning is finding a system that works for you and allows you to take care of your business and enjoy your life at the same time!

My Turn! Plan to Plan

DIRECTIONS: Brainstorm a list of tasks you need to complete this week.

> Prior to this lesson, what organization or planning methods did you use?

> After this lesson, what tools do you think will work well for you?

Study Tips for Success!

Staying on track includes being a successful student and developing good study habits that you can apply to all of your classes. Here are some tips on studying effectively:

1. **Set specific goals for your study times.**

   Do not simply sit down to study, you must set goals on what you want to accomplish during your study time. For example, "review chemistry notes from last week's lab" is going to be more productive than "study science."

2. **Try not to study too much at one time.**

   Don't cram or you will eventually lose focus. Make sure you take short breaks once in a while. Let yourself rest for a short period of time when you reach a certain point in your studying. Set an alarm on your kitchen timer or phone for 25 minutes of work then take a 5-minute break. Just make sure you are focused and working during all your 25-minute blocks!

3. **Plan routine times for studying and reward yourself.**

   Schedule specific times throughout the week for your study time. Make it a routine so that it becomes a regular part of your day. This is important – a student who plans to work on their Science Fair Project on "Tuesday from 5 to 7" is much more likely to get it done than a student who plans to get it done "whenever". Don't put it off. After a successful study session, reward yourself with a treat like spending time on your favorite hobbies.

Key Point
Good study habits aren't innate, they must be learned and are critical for success in high school and college.

4. **Avoid distractions.**

   Your work is interrupted when your phone rings, and this will distract you from studying. Your friends and social activities can wait. Things like TVs, video games, your phone etc. will make it harder to get your work done.

5. **Work on difficult assignments first.**

   You will have the most energy and focus when you start studying, so do the assignments that require the most effort at the beginning of your study time.

6. **Review your notes before beginning an assignment, focusing on studying the main concepts first.**

   You want to make sure you are doing your assignment correctly and are able to explain the big picture before you begin memorizing the details.

7. **Study in a comfortable environment.**

   Find a place you like, such as a library, your room, a teacher's classroom, etc. to study. Different people prefer different environments. Choose the one that works best for you! Don't be afraid to switch it up sometimes if you lose focus in one place, move to another to help your brain refresh!

8. **Review your schoolwork over the weekend.**

Yes, you should relax on weekends, but you also need to prepare yourself for the week ahead. You do not want to start out the week behind.

9. **Join afterschool programs.**

There are many free or low-cost tutoring programs run by community centers and community-based organizations that offer both individual and group support. Ask your counselor or research online for these opportunities.

10. **Change up your study materials.**

Rewrite your notes or change the order of notes that you are studying. Use different numbers in your math problems.

My Turn! Weekly Study Flow Chart

DIRECTIONS: First, study the flow chart below, then explain it to a partner. Underline all of the tasks you already complete. Lastly, answer the reflection question under the chart.

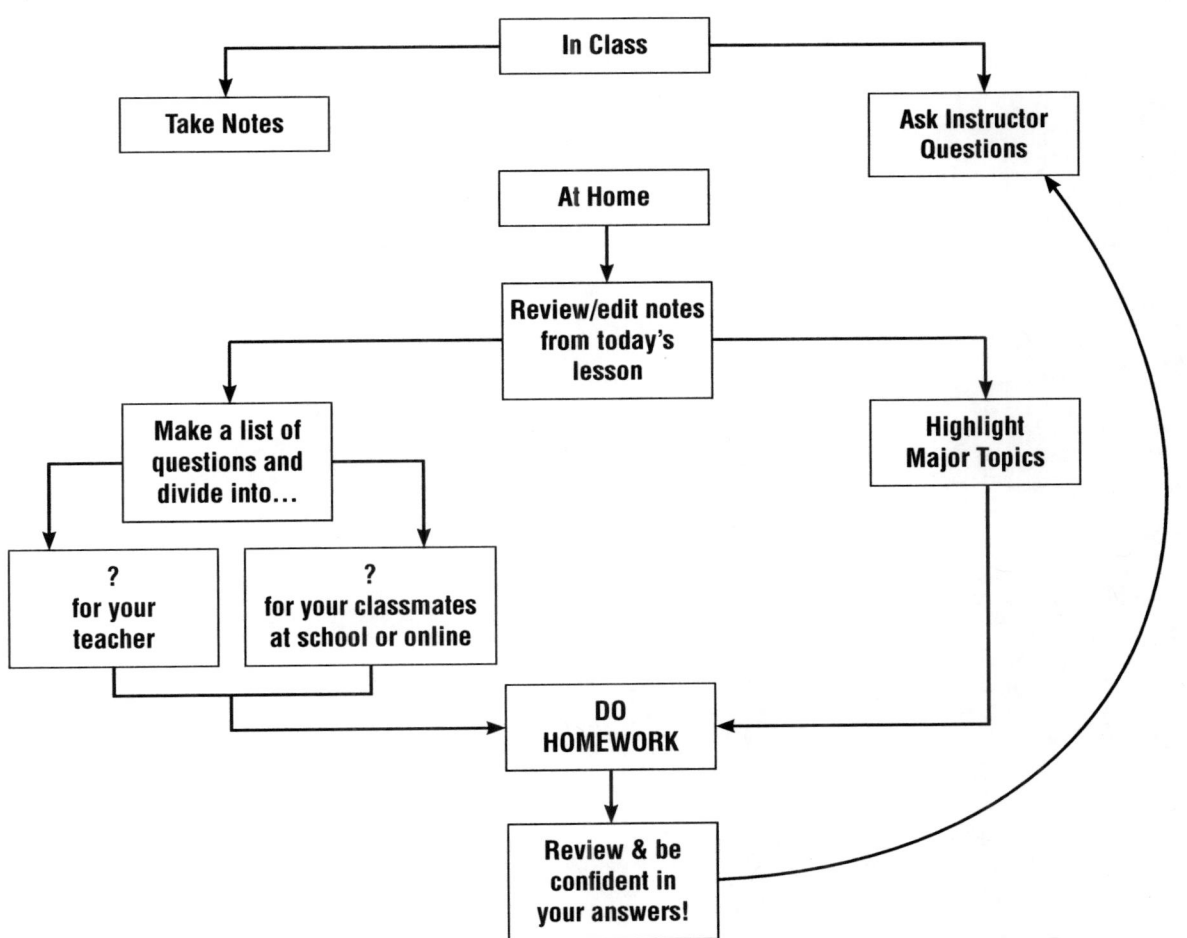

Which task in the flow chart will be the most difficult for you? Why?

Joining or Starting a Successful Study Group

Many high school and college students are part of study groups. A **study group** is a group of people (usually 4-6 students) who meet often (usually weekly depending upon need) to help each other with schoolwork, prepare for tests, share information, and discuss knowledge gained in class. This is NOT a group to share answers and copy work.

TIPS **Study Groups**

Discussions during a study group can help ensure that you didn't overlook or misinterpret any information from class.

A study group environment offers an opportunity to have in-depth discussions about class material. When students work in groups, they have the opportunity to explain concepts, discuss ideas, disagree with one another and reason through why one person's answer is different than another. Often when a student is struggling with a concept, it can immediately make sense when explained by another student rather than a teacher. Study groups can be especially helpful for students whose native language is different than the language of instruction.

1. Group members come prepared to work on time.
2. The group stays on task with respect to its agenda and to each other.
3. Every group member participates in the group discussions.
4. Group members listen to one another without interruption, with only one person speaking at a time.
5. Group members feel comfortable to ask one another questions.
6. Group members may constructively criticize one another. This can encourage group members to reveal and strengthen their weaknesses.
7. Most importantly, group members should keep a positive attitude throughout each study session.

Tips for the Classroom

Tips on Becoming a Better Listener in Class

- Sit up straight. Slouching makes you much more likely to lose focus or fall asleep.

- Focus on what the teacher is saying, not on the students around you.

- Try to find the important details and try to connect those details to other information. Ask yourself: *"How does this relate to what we talked about yesterday, to what I read in the text, or to my life outside of school?"*

- Picture scenes being described, or draw diagrams in your notes to help you understand the material.

- Ask questions and participate in class discussions.

TIPS **Class Tip**

If you are struggling in a class, ask your teacher for help! They are there to help answer your questions!

Note Taking Tips in the Classroom

- Don't try to write every word. Instead, use abbreviations, symbols, diagrams and drawings.

- Try to find similarities between your own experiences, knowledge and the class material.

- Look for a structure in your teacher's lecture. If he or she says Newton has three laws, look for those three laws to be clearly defined, and listen for details about each one.

- Try to review your notes as soon as you can after class. Mark or highlight the most important points, and do a little reorganization if you need to.

- Put the most important information on flash cards – these are incredibly useful when it's time to study for a test.

Caution: The Senior Slump (A.K.A. "Senioritis")

Senioritis is a noticeable decrease in motivation towards schoolwork and studies is detected in students as they are nearing the end of high school. Side effects can include a drop in academic performance, the desire to drop out of school, poor behavior in class, truancy, excessive absences and frequent tardiness to name a few. The senior slump is a danger zone that you want to avoid by staying organized and keeping up with your schoolwork. A decrease in your academic performance, as a consequence of senioritis, may result in a difficult transition to the next step of your education. Be aware that many colleges do not look favorably upon students who slack off during their senior year! Be careful – a similar effect can happen towards the end of middle school on your way to high school.

Mindset Change

Many students believe senior year doesn't matter; this could not be further from the truth. Your education builds on itself, and the classes you take during your senior year in high school will often determine which classes you will take your first year in college.

Unit 2: Navigate High School

High schools offer various types of graduation plans, endorsements, and diplomas depending on where you go to school. Choose the plan that challenges you and gives you the best chance for acceptance into the college and career of your choice. Think of your high school plan like a budget; follow it closely in order to avoid trouble in the future. Participate in extra-curricular activities, learn a foreign language, take advanced courses to boost your GPA, and above all else, align your classes with the type of college you want to enroll in. High school is a launching point for your future. Choose wisely!

And since high school is so important, if you are in middle school, you have many things to consider when choosing a high school! Do I have to wear a uniform? Does the school have a good athletic program? Does it offer advanced classes and/or the opportunity to take dual credit? You should choose a high school that will best prepare you for the field of study you wish to pursue in the future!

My Turn! 3-2-1... Navigate High School!

List THREE different types of high schools:

-
-
-

List TWO ways you can earn college credit during high school:

-
-

Based on your current GPA, list ONE study or organizational tip you can add into your life to improve your GPA, and explain how you plan to do so:

-

Life Outside of the Classroom

Enrichment Opportunities

The word enrichment means to make something more meaningful, substantial, or rewarding. Enrichment improves something that already exists. In this case, enrichment opportunities like community service, jobs, internships, and extracurriculars all add meaning and substance to both you as a person as well as your résumé.

Colleges want to know what makes you different. Having good grades is crucial, but you need more to really set yourself apart from other students applying to college. Professional experience gained through jobs, internships, extracurricular activities, and being involved in the community will help you stand out and get into the college of your dreams!

There are lots of opportunities out there for you to take advantage of, but the sooner you start looking, the better. Look to set yourself up with a job, camp, internship or community service experience by the summer before your freshman year of high school! You are going to want to take advantage of activities every summer until you enter college, and continue into your college years.

While you're looking for activities that will improve your résumé and set you apart, make sure it's also something that you enjoy. Whether it's a club at school, a charity, or a community organization, you want to be involved in something that will not only improve your college application, but enrich your life as well. Remember that summer jobs, extracurricular activities and community service activities ultimately help develop you as a person and give you life skills that you will need in college and beyond.

In the following pages you will find categories that contain examples and websites you can explore to find the perfect fit.

Key Point

Professional and volunteer activities provide opportunities to use your skills to help others, work in teams, gain leadership experience, and effectively manage your time outside of the classroom.

Unit 2: Navigate High School

Summer Job Benefits

There are many advantages to having a job over the summer. Consider the following:

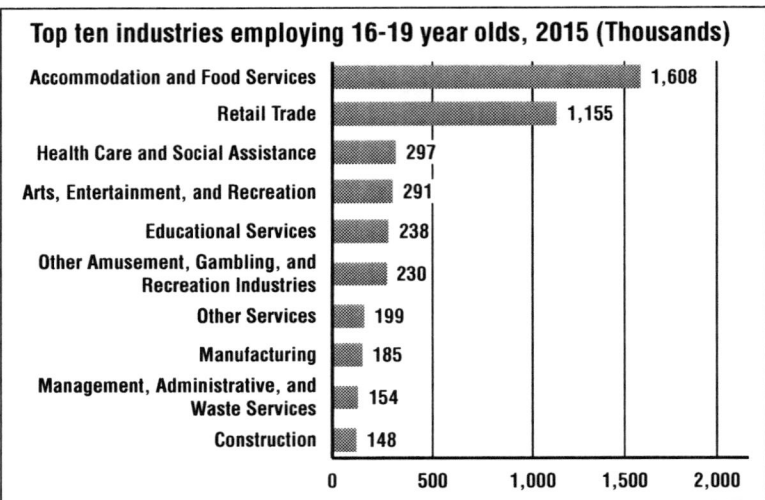

Top ten industries employing 16-19 year olds, 2015 (Thousands)

Accommodation and Food Services	1,608
Retail Trade	1,155
Health Care and Social Assistance	297
Arts, Entertainment, and Recreation	291
Educational Services	238
Other Amusement, Gambling, and Recreation Industries	230
Other Services	199
Manufacturing	185
Management, Administrative, and Waste Services	154
Construction	148

source: Bureau of Labor Statistics

1. **Jobs help you improve your résumé.** Applying for future jobs (and colleges) will be easier if you have work experience.

2. **Summer jobs keep you busy.**
   When you're busy, you won't get bored as easily and often will keep yourself from getting into trouble.

3. **Jobs come with lots of benefits!**
   In addition to being paid for the work you do, you may get discounts, free tickets, specialized training and other exciting perks!

4. **Jobs prove to colleges that you're responsible.**
   Showing that you held a job proves you are dependable and motivated. It is important that your college application is well rounded. Having worked a summer job in addition to having good grades and being involved in extracurricular activities can help you get into the school that you really want.

5. **Jobs pay.**
   Who couldn't use some extra cash? By having a job you can make as much as a few thousand dollars over the summer, even just working part-time. Who couldn't use some extra cash? By having a job you can make as much as a few thousand dollars over the summer, even just working part-time. Money saved can be used for things you need, or if you are lucky enough to be able to save, you can use that money for college!

How to Get a Summer Job

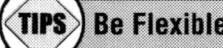

TIPS **Be Flexible**
Being flexible and having availability in your schedule will help you secure a job.

1. **Decide what type of summer job you want. Consider these questions:**
   - How much money do you want/need to earn?
   - What type of job do you want?
   - When are you available to work?
   - How will you get to work?
   - Do you need to work close to home?

   You may not be able to find a job that meets all your needs, but you should strive to find one that meets as many as possible.

2. **Think about your qualifications. Consider these questions:**
   - What do you have to offer an employer?
   - What kind of skills do you have?
   - What other kind of work have you done? Was it paid work or were you a volunteer?
   - What have you learned at school that might be useful in your summer job?

3. **Develop your résumé.**
   You will make a great first impression if you present a professional-looking résumé to potential employers. A good starting point would be reading over the résumé section of this book. From there, follow up with an online search to find additional résumé resources. Make sure you do the same for cover letters; employers will expect you to include them in applications.

4. **Research job opportunities.**
   In order to land your ideal summer job, you need to take advantage of every resource. Ask every adult you know about summer job opportunities. This list should include your family, your friends' parents, teachers and any others. Give them copies of your résumé to pass along to potential employers. Don't stop here though – you can also read newspaper "help wanted" ads, hunt for jobs online or just walk into a store.

TIPS **Be Prepared**
Be prepared in case you are interviewed on the spot when you drop off your application.

5. **Apply to jobs.**
   This is where your résumé comes in, as you will need to submit it as part of your application. Before sitting down to complete the application, make sure you have all the information you'll need to fill it out (your address, phone number, social security number, names and phone numbers of people who might recommend you, etc..). Before going in for your interview, make sure you research the company and think of a few questions you could ask during the interview.

TIPS **Reach Out**
Tell recommenders to expect calls before you submit your application.

What do Employers Look for in Teens?

Employers want motivated teens that work hard, have a good attitude, show up on time, and demonstrate leadership qualities. You need to prove to your employer that you will be a valuable employee if they hire you! They are sizing you up starting with the first time that they meet you, so dress appropriately and do your research.

Final Words of Advice

The important thing is to remember why you are working – to earn money, to build up your résumé for future job and college applications, and to develop your skills.

- **National Chains:** Stores like Best Buy and Target are frequently hiring – year round.

- **Local Businesses:** Every community has locally owned businesses, ranging from beauty salons to auto repair shops, and they often hire during the summer. Talk to your friends and family – they may know an owner who would hire you.

- **Restaurants:** Fast food chains and restaurants are usually hiring, and many provide employees with free or discounted food (Taco Bell, McDonald's, Sonic, Chili's, CiCi's Pizza, etc).

TIPS **Bonus Cash**

Jobs at restaurants will usually allow you to earn an hourly wage and tips.

- **Summer Camps:** Being a camp counselor is a great way to have fun and experience camp life while getting paid at the same time. Do some research online to find the ones in your area.

- **Major Corporations:** Lots of big companies have summer jobs and internships that will look great on your college application, but be aware that these jobs can be hard to get. (Ernst & Young, Teach For America, Chase Bank, etc).

- **Mall Stores:** There are a variety of stores located in malls, and if you work at one of them you will typically get an employee discount. So, why not apply to a store you like to shop at? (Hollister, Hot Topic, Apple Store, etc).

- **Hotels & Resorts:** Most hotels and resorts are busy during the summer months, so they usually hire extra people to help out (The Hyatt Regency, Doubletree Hotel, Sheraton, etc).

- **Grocery Stores:** Getting a job at a local grocery store will be convenient and you can probably keep the job during the school year (Fiesta, Minyard Food Store, Albertsons, Kroger).

- **Tourist Attractions:** Regardless of where you live, your city or town likely has some tourist attractions. Tourist attractions usually need extra help during the summer tourist season and will likely be hiring (aquariums, theme parks, museums, etc.).

- **Parks & Recreation Departments:** Parks and recreation departments often have special summer programs, and thus have job opportunities (YMCA, Parks and Recreation, etc).

- **Working for Yourself:** Don't want to work for a boss? Can't find a summer job? Set up your own business in your neighborhood and be your own boss (lawn service, babysitting, dog walking, etc).

Don't just stop with this list! Use the Internet to research additional job opportunities. You might be surprised at what you find!

Internships

An **internship** is a temporary job (almost always over the summer) that allows you to see what it is like to work in a certain area. In turn, this can help you decide what career you want to pursue when you graduate from college. Interested in science? You could be an intern at a laboratory. Want to learn more about jobs in finance? You could intern at a bank. In general, summer internships are fantastic learning experiences during high school – and almost a necessity for students in college. Colleges want high school students who have "real world" experience, and internships are one of the best ways to get it. Internships also help you explore possible career paths before you have to pick a major in college.

So what are the steps for finding the perfect summer internship?

1. **Decide What You Want From Your Internship**
2. **Polish Your Application Skills**
3. **Find Internship Sources**

Key Point
Internships are short-term jobs that help you explore career paths and gain "hands-on" experience, and can be paid or unpaid.

My Turn! Read and Reflect

DIRECTIONS: Fill out the Venn Diagram below as you read to pull out the similarities and differences between jobs and internships. Additionally, as you are considering the questions that successful students ask about the types of internships they want to pursue, use the lines provided on the following page to write your answers.

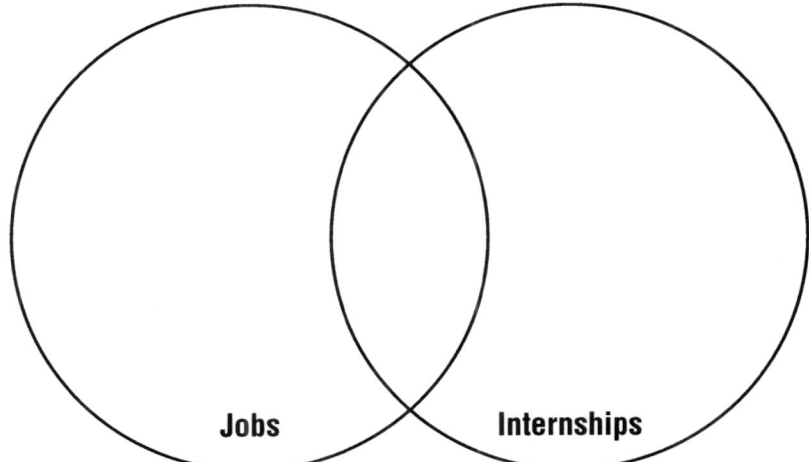

Jobs   Internships

Decide What You Want From Your Internship

Before you start hunting for internships, you should figure out what you want to get out of it. Here are some general questions to help you get started:

What are Your Specific Career Interests?

Whenever possible, make sure your internship aligns with your career goals. If you want to be a scientist, you probably want to explore an internship in the field of science. That said, if you're not entirely sure about what you want to do after college, an internship is a great way to help you define your career goals. For example, if you're interested in government but aren't sure you want to make it your career; you might consider an

Why Get an Internship?
Ask yourself, "**Why would someone want to get an internship?**" *When you have an answer, share your thoughts with a friend, teacher, or classmate.*

internship with a local or state politician. In other cases, an internship can help refine your career goals. For example, if you want to help sick people but you're not sure how, volunteering as an intern in a hospital may help you find a career that's right for you. If you like getting people excited about products, but are not sure whether you want to go into advertising or public relations, you should consider getting internships in both areas to help you decide which is best for you.

_____

_____

What do you want to gain from your summer internship?

There are many reasons to apply for an internship, including deciding what type of job you would like to have after graduation. Other reasons include meeting new people, improving your résumé (especially for college applications), developing your skills and helping you get a full time job with the same organization or company after graduating college.

_____

_____

What kind of organization do you want to work for?

There are many different types of organizations, from small charities to huge corporations. You need to think about where you want to work. Issues to consider include size (big vs. small), location (close/far from home?), atmosphere (What would it be like to work there? Do you like the people?) and whether the organization is a not-for-profit (charity), government agency, or for-profit company.

_____

_____

Is it paid or unpaid?

While there are some internships that pay, most (especially the popular ones) do not. If the internship you want is unpaid, you need to decide whether you can afford to work for free.

Why "unpaid?"

Ask yourself, **"What would motivate you to take a job that wasn't paid?"** _When you have an answer, share your thoughts with a friend, teacher, or classmate._

Polish Your Application Skills

Internships are highly competitive, so you need to make a good impression in your application and interview. The interview information in Unit 3 will help you polish these skills:

- **Cover letter writing.** After reviewing cover letter examples, it is recommended that you do some more research online until you feel comfortable creating your own cover letter. Make sure you have someone read over and edit your cover letter before you submit it.

- **Résumé preparation.** Just like the cover letter, make sure you have someone read and edit it before you submit it.

- **Interviewing strategies.** Read Unit 3 of this book for a detailed guide on interviewing best practices. Make sure you review it before your interview.

Finding a Summer Internship

Once you've determined your internship goals and polished your applications skills, it's time to find the internship that's right for you. Here are some resources to use:

Internship Websites

There are a few internship websites that list information on thousands of different internship opportunities. These are definitely worth investigating, but don't rely on them too much because many internships for high school students won't be listed there.

Your Community

Tell everyone you know about the kind of internship you're looking for, as you never know who might be able to help. These people should include your family, friends, teachers and past employers (among others).

Organization Websites

Once you have a rough list of which organizations you'd like to intern for, visit their websites. In particular, check out the careers/internships section and see if they have an online application or people to contact about internships.

Call Them

If none of the approaches above are working, it might be worth calling or emailing the organization directly. It's a long shot, but it sometimes pays off. You can find the contact information you need on the organization's website.

Final Words of Advice

After you've applied to several internships, you need to make sure you follow up with each organization. Don't call the companies every day, but be persistent. Follow up your initial contact with a phone call, your interview with a thank you letter or email, and your thank you letter or email with a phone call.

My Turn! So, What are My Next Steps?

DIRECTIONS: Pretend you are a senior in high school and want to get an internship for the summer. What would be the first step you would take? Think about the people who you know or people within your network that would be able to connect you to individuals in the industry that you're interested in. Networking is almost always the best way to get a job!

_____

_____

_____

_____

Community Service

TIPS **Where to Volunteer?**

Churches and community centers often have lists of volunteer opportunities.

ABC **Community Service**

Community service may include any experiences you have giving back to your classmates, school, or community. Activities such as tutoring a classmate, walking your neighbor's dog, or reading to the kids at your sibling's daycare may all be considered community service!

Why is it important to give your time? Though there are many reasons, most of them boil down to three key points. First, and most importantly, it's the right thing to do. Community service is a way to help others and to make sure that the causes and initiatives that you care about are not overlooked. Second, it looks really good on your college applications. Volunteering shows that you care about the world around you and that you are willing to take action for your beliefs. Third, it benefits you as an individual. Just like jobs and internships, community service develops skills and interests that will stay with you for the rest of your life. Volunteering at an animal shelter might, for example, lead you to a career as a veterinarian. Similarly, time spent working as a tutor could lead you to become a teacher. The opportunities are nearly limitless. Here's the bottom line: If you can, get involved in community service!

Examples of Volunteer Opportunities

- Boys and Girls Club
- Salvation Army
- Ronald McDonald House
- Hispanic Youth Foundation
- Soup kitchens/food banks
- Church volunteer opportunities

Don't just stop with the list above – there are many more volunteer opportunities available. Do some research online to find community service areas that interest you.

Final Words of Advice

While volunteer opportunities do not benefit you by paying money, they do show friends, family, community and colleges that you care about issues larger than yourself. Volunteering not only allows you to help others, but by getting involved, you will also develop your own personal skills as well as make new friends. Not to mention, you will be making the world a better place.

My Turn! When Have I Helped Someone?

DIRECTIONS: Write a brief paragraph about a time when you helped someone else. Describe how you felt while you were helping them, how you felt after you finished helping, and how it benefited them.

_____

_____

_____

_____

_____

_____

_____

Extracurricular Activities

Colleges are looking for well-rounded students. A well-rounded student is someone who works hard in the classroom AND is involved in several additional activities outside of the classroom. Having great grades is not enough; you also need to be actively involved in extracurricular activities such as athletics and clubs. This proves to colleges that you have the ability to succeed at the next level and that you can manage your time wisely. When you are considering which extracurricular activities fit you, follow these guidelines:

(ABC) Extracurricular Activities

Non-classroom activities that students can get involved in at school. examples are: athletics, clubs, student government, recreational and social organizations and events.

1. **Go with your gut!** If you want to join a team or a club then do it. Don't worry about what other people may think about your choice. Make a choice that is right for you.

2. **Explore different options.** Colleges look for people who take advantage of many different activities on campus, so it is important to be well-rounded. If you think you are only an athlete, think again! Get out of your comfort zone and try something new.

3. **Be a leader.** Find an activity where you can develop your leadership skills. Being a member of a club is a great start, but it's even better if you have a leadership position (such as president, secretary, treasurer, etc.). This shows that you are dedicated to the club and that you are a leader on your campus.

GO! Be a Leader!
When you join a club, listen for when leadership positions open up or elections are being held.

4. **Don't overextend yourself.** Being well-rounded does not mean taking on every extracurricular activity that interests you, especially if you won't have enough time to maintain a good GPA. Participate in the activities that are most important to you. Choose activities that you can commit to for all four years and where you have the potential to hold leadership roles.

5. **There is something for everyone.** If you are a student who isn't into school, then make school work for you. Start a skateboarding club, a film club, or an art club. Below you will find a list of many potential clubs, sports and volunteer opportunities outside of the classroom.

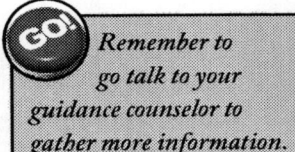

GO! *Remember to go talk to your guidance counselor to gather more information.*

Sports

Football	Soccer	Baseball	Drill/Dance Team
Basketball	Track & Field	Softball	Cheerleading
Volleyball	Cross Country	Golf	
Tennis	Wrestling	Swimming	

Clubs

Student Council	Newspaper	UIL – Academic Competition	DECA – International Association of Marketing Students
National Honor Society	FCA – Fellowship of Christian Athletes	Yearbook	
Language Clubs		Choir	Men & Ladies of Distinction
Dance	Mock Trial	Band	
Jr. ROTC	Speech and Debate		Book Club

Off-Campus Extracurriculars

Big Brothers Big Sisters	Boy and Girl Scouts	Music Lessons	Young Life
Vacation Bible School	Piano	Dance Lessons	Boys and Girls Club
Church Choir	Select Sports Teams	Steppers' Groups	YMCA Youth Leadership

My Turn! Extracurricular Activities

DIRECTIONS: Think of activities and experiences you have had in your life. Write a list of all activities in the chart below, including the type of activity and the dates if you can remember.

Example:

GO! *Later, you can add these activities to your resume. You will learn about resumes in Unit 3.*

Activity	Type of Activity	Dates You Were Involved
Soccer	Extracurricular Activity	2011-Present
Help in kids class at Sunday School	Community Service	Fall 2013
ROTC	Extracurricular Activity	2014-Present
MVP in soccer game	Award	January 2016
Play guitar	Skill	2010-Present

Activity	Type of Activity	Dates You Were Involved

Healthy Choices for a Healthy Life

You may ask yourself why there is a nutrition section in a manual that is meant to prepare you for college. Well, it is important to know that recent research has shown a direct relationship between poor nutrition and poor test scores. Taking care of your body will help you feel better and improve academically.

That being said, making healthy choices can be tricky. You get information from television, movies, the Internet, and your friends that is often conflicting. You need to know where you can turn for information that is correct and straightforward. You will find information regarding nutrition below as well as some resources to help you on your path to a healthy life!

Nutrition and Teenagers

According to the Centers for Disease Control (CDC), 40% (nearly half!) of the calories most teens consume during the day comes from soda and other sugary drinks (like juice), dairy desserts (like ice cream), grain desserts (like donuts), pizza, and whole milk. As a teen, you might think, "I can worry about what I eat later," or "I eat junk food a lot, and I'm perfectly healthy." But the truth is that the nutritional choices you make today will shape your health for the rest of your life. Unhealthy habits and nutrition can lead to Diabetes Mellitus (a disorder in which your body doesn't use sugar the way it should), high cholesterol and cardiovascular disease (increasing your risk of a heart attack or stroke in the future), back and joint pain, and even cancer. All of these can be a risk even if you are not considered overweight.

The Key to a Healthy Diet: Moderation

It's very easy to say "Eat healthy and don't eat junk food," but it's much easier said than done. With all of the unhealthy choices available at restaurants and the convenience of fast-food chains, making healthy food choices can be a challenge. Not to mention, sometimes the food that is bad for our bodies tastes great! The key to any healthy diet that becomes a part of your lifestyle is to eat in moderation. One cookie is fine but a box of cookies followed by a gallon of soda is not. An orange is great for you, but an entire bag of oranges is not. If you eat too many calories, you will gain weight no matter what type of food you are eating. However, if you eat more calorie dense foods, you might be surprised to know you can eat more of them than foods that contain "empty" calories (food with little nutritional value). Let's look at the cookie – orange nutrient information to get a clearer picture of this.

TIPS Moderation is Key!

The key to any healthy diet that becomes a part of your lifestyle is to eat in moderation.

Frosting-filled sandwich cookie	Medium sized navel orange
160 calories, with 7 grams of fat (average)	64 calories, with 0 grams of fat (average)

Considering the high number of calories in a cookie, you can eat 2 medium navel oranges, feel more full, and still consume fewer calories than if you chose to eat 1 cookie. Not to mention, oranges are loaded with vitamin C (which boosts the immune system and helps to keep people from getting sick), vitamin A (good for vision and immunity), calcium (good for strong bones), and fiber (which keeps the gastrointestinal tract running smoothly).

Nutrition Myth Busters

Have you ever wondered why you often hear from one source that something is good for you and from another that it is bad for you? How do you know for sure that a "fruit" smoothie is as good for us as the store says it is? Keep reading to learn about different food myths and truths.

- **Myth #1:** "Eggs are bad for you." Mostly myth! One large egg has 71 calories, 6 grams of protein, and many other vitamins needed for the body to stay healthy, including choline (a vitamin responsible for attention, learning, and memory). Think of an egg as brain food! But also use your brain to remember that an egg yoke (the yellow part) is high in cholesterol and saturated fat, two things linked to heart disease and to be eaten in low amounts. Eggs are unhealthy if you eat too many.

- **Myth #2:** "A diet soda is better for me than a regular soda." Myth! No matter how you look at it, soda is bad for you. While diet soda has no calories and no sugar, it also has nothing else in it-- no protein, no vitamins, and no minerals making it completely the opposite of healthy. Even a few brands of regular soda can claim a tiny bit of calcium and iron in it. If you must drink a soft drink, keep it to a 12 ounce can and only a few days a week.

- **Myth #3:** "If it's got a fruit or a vegetable on the label, it's good for me." This one is definitely a myth. Take a frozen dinner, for example. On the label, it's got vegetables and meat, usually with a rice or a potato side. While the calorie content isn't too high, there is more sodium (preservative used to help keep food fresh) in one of those little plastic trays than some people on special diets are allowed to have in one day. So say no to frozen dinners and choose fresh or frozen vegetables and fruits instead.

We all eat food that is not good for us from time to time. Just remember to limit the bad stuff, read the food label, and don't be fooled just because it looks healthy. See the chart below to get a clearer picture of our myths.

Food and Serving	Calories	Sugar/Fat/Protein	How Often?
1 Large Egg	71	5 grams Fat/6 grams Protein	2-3 times a week
12 oz. Diet Soda	0	Nothing!! Remember, the opposite of healthy!	Less than 3 times a week
12 oz. Regular Soda	136	35 grams Sugar, a little Calcium, and a little Iron	Less than 3 times a week (less if you drink diet too)
Frozen dinner	626	45 grams Sugar/39 grams Fat/23 grams Protein/2200 Sodium	Never ever, or as rarely as possible!

Understanding Serving Size

You have probably seen the words "serving size" on a food label, but have you ever stopped to ask yourself what that means and why it is important for you?

Let's pretend you are munching on a bag of your favorite chips; they are cheesy and crunchy and taste delicious. Out of curiosity you decide to look at the food label and it says "Calories 150." That must be a good thing because that doesn't seem like a big number. But wait a minute; the number of calories listed on a food label only represents a small portion. A cup of chips may only have 150 calories in it, but you have to multiply that number by the size of the bag to discover how many calories are in the WHOLE bag. You may have just eaten more calories in that short period of time than you should eat all day to be considered healthy!

My Turn! Track My Calories

DIRECTIONS: Look at the following example and use the template to start managing your calorie intake. This will give you a better idea of what you are eating during the typical day.

What you will need: The food label from your favorite food, or you can go to www.nutritiondata. self.com to type in the food and you will find the food label.

What to do: Read the food label (usually found on the back) carefully in order to find the necessary information to fill out the table. Remember to multiply the calories in one serving size by the total number of servings you ate. Lastly, subtract the total number of calories you ate from 2,800 if you are a boy or from 2,200 if you are a girl. If you get a negative number, you have already eaten too many calories for one day.

Example: Megan is on her way to school and forgot to pack a lunch; she stops at the convenience store on her way and buys a bag of her favorite chips. Throughout the day, she shares a few with her friends but eats 75% of the bag by herself.

	Food: Cheese Flavored Chips	Calories	Grams of Fat	Carbs (Sugar)
Serving Size	1 ounce (21 chips)	150	10 grams	13 grams
Package Size	20.5 ounces	3075	205 grams	266.5 grams
Amount eaten	75% of the bag (total ounces 20.5 x .75)= 15.375 ounces	15.375 x 150 (calories per ounce)= 2306.25	153.75 grams	199.88 grams

Calorie Calculations:

Total Calories **(2,200 --Megan is a girl)** – *Calories Consumed* **(2,306) = -106**

This means she has already eaten more calories than she needs in an entire day!

My Turn! Now You Try!

	Food: _____	Calories	Grams of Fat	Carbs (Sugar)
Serving Size				
Package Size				
Amount eaten				

Calorie Calculations:

Total Calories recommended – Calories Consumed = _____

Did you eat more or less than your recommended calories? _____

My Turn! Nutrition Reflection

DIRECTIONS: After learning new facts about teen nutrition, the importance of moderation, the meaning of "serving size," and doing calorie calculations-- please reflect on the following questions.

Why is it important to keep track of serving size when you are eating dinner or a snack, no matter how healthy the food is? _____

_____

What does it mean to enjoy "in moderation?" _____

_____

Which myth buster surprised you the most and why? _____

_____

Why is it beneficial for you to regulate the number of calories you eat each day? How can this prevent you from being unhealthy? _____

_____

Other than eating in moderation and consuming nutritional foods, what else can you do to keep yourself healthy? _____

_____

If you are an athlete, do you think you should eat more or less calories than the recommended amount? (Hint: You will be burning more energy when you work out.)

_____

Here are some additional resources to find out what is healthy and what is not! www.nutritiondata.self.com, www.nutrition.gov, www.fda.gov

Notes

As you already know, steps taken on your path to success do not end when the school bell rings. Working a summer job, taking on an internship, and volunteering in the community are all fantastic ways to develop personally as well as improve your future opportunities. The number of experiences that you can pursue are almost limitless. There are multiple organizations out there to help you find an interesting and exciting match. The most important thing is to take the initiative in starting the search. Your life is destined for success, make sure you're taking the steps to enjoy it for as long as possible!

My Turn! 3-2-1... Life Outside of the Classroom!

List and explain THREE activities you can pursue outside of the classroom this year:

-

-

-

List TWO differences between a job and an internship:

-

-

List ONE place you can find a summer job or internship:

-

UNIT 3
PRACTICE PROFESSIONALISM

DIRECTIONS: In reflection of the information you learned in this unit, draw an emoji of how you feel now.

What is a résumé?
Why are they important?

How do I ace an interview?

DIRECTIONS: Read the topics of this unit on the roadmap. Draw an "emoji" of your emotions about this content as you start the unit.

Unit 3 Vocabulary

Business Casual	Extracurricular Activities	Informational Interview	Résumé
Business Professional			References
	Interview	Networking	
Cover Letter			Professionalism

DIRECTIONS: In the space below, select several unfamiliar words from the vocabulary word bank. Then, define each word using the glossary or a dictionary. Last, create an original sentence for each of the selected words.

Vocabulary Word	Definition	Your Original Sentence

The Job Application Process

Applications are a multi-step process. When you submit your résumé and cover letter, multiple people will often view them in order to determine if you should be a potential candidate. A hiring manager often views hundreds of résumés to fill a position, so it is vital to make sure that yours stands out. They will dismiss the applicants who do not stand out or who do not seem to be a potential match for the position. After this process, the hiring manager often selects a small number of applicants to invite to an interview. It is normal to interview with a company multiple times and with more than one person.

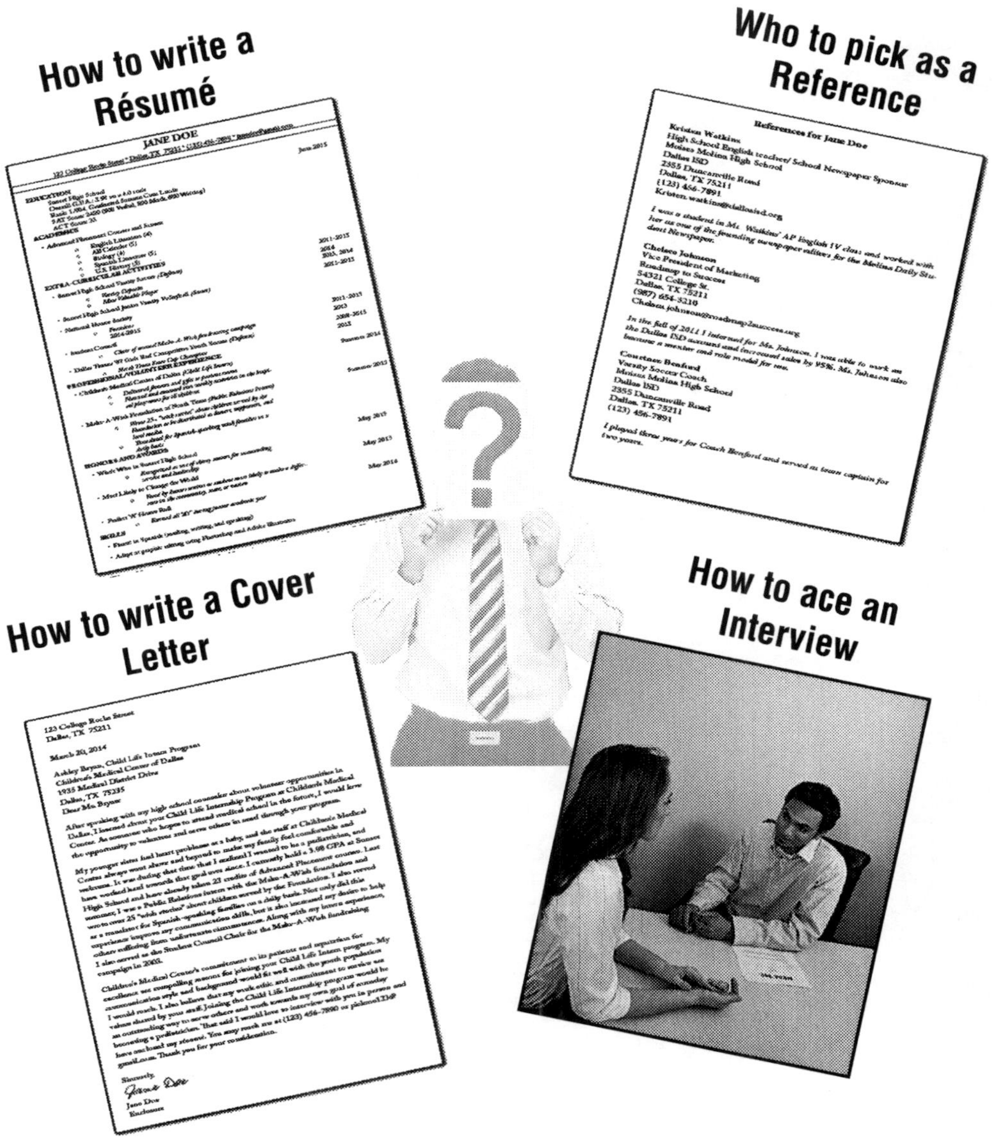

How to write a Résumé

Who to pick as a Reference

How to write a Cover Letter

How to ace an Interview

Unit 3: Practice Professionalism

Professionalism is about doing the little things and doing them the right way. It is a scientifically supported truth that people form their first impressions of you within the first three seconds of meeting you. How you carry yourself – how professional you are – and the decisions you make when interacting with others can add up to a lifetime of chances missed, or a world of opportunities that can transform your future.

The importance of professional dress is discussed later in this section. Therefore, the three aspects of professionalism we will focus on here are:

1. **Networking** – Tips to grow your real-life social network.

2. **Conducting a Follow-Up Phone Call** – Guidelines for successful phone conversations

3. **Writing a Thank You Note** – Style notes and quick formatting to communicate how much you care.

> **Key Point**
> *Creating and maintaining a positive and professional identity in-person and online is an essential part of success.*

Networking

Networking is all about people: meeting people, interacting with people, and following up with people that could use your help or who could help you. Truly any interaction with another person is a networking opportunity and you are never too young, or too old, to start spreading your networking wings!

How can networking help you? You might be surprised. These face-to-face connections can open many doors you might not expect. Frequently, business deals for the largest and smallest companies are made largely because there are people on both sides of the transaction who know and trust each other. These business friendships often develop as a result of networking events (such as art shows, dinners, and professional mixers) and can even blossom into personal friendships over time.

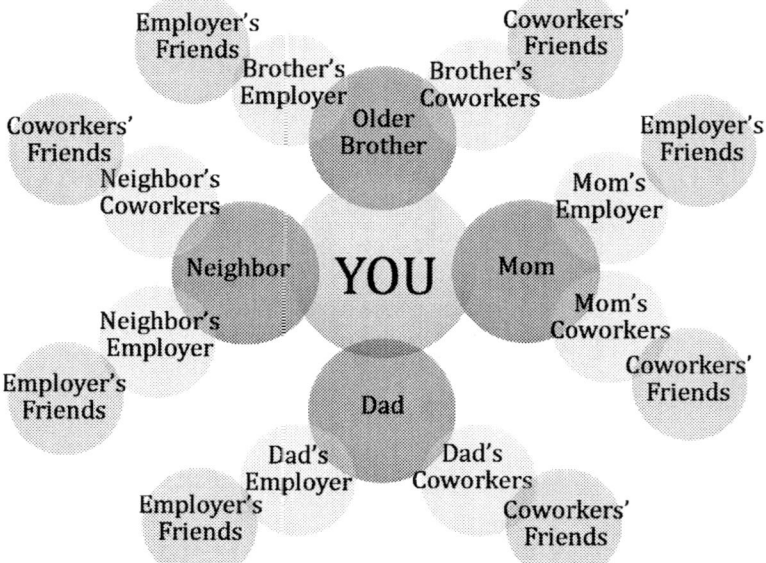

My Turn! Building My Own Network

DIRECTIONS: Let's discover the network you have already! In the blanks below, list both the names and role/relationship of the people in your life who have connections to work or other people who work. Just as in the previous example, these can be family members, neighbors, or friends. Then list the people they know to expand your network. Keep building as many bubbles as you can think of, then complete the reflection questions below.

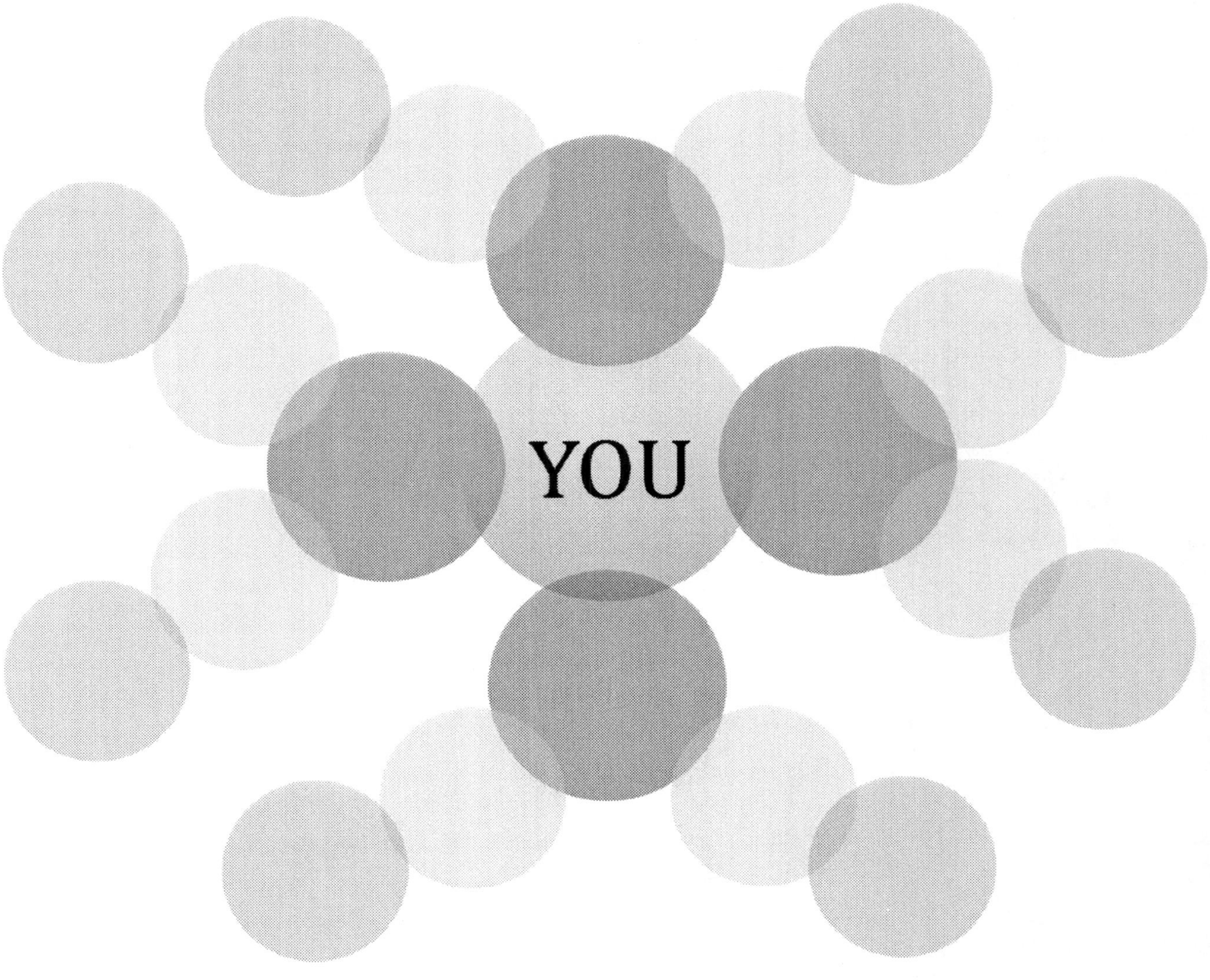

YOU

1. Reflect on the last time that you met someone new. Did you feel like you trusted them? Why? _____

   _____

2. What do you think their first impression of you was? _____

   _____

3. How can that person be an asset to your professional network? _____

   _____

Useful Networking Tips

Making a good impression on adults and peers in your current interactions is important too. You never know for sure just whom you are meeting when you're introduced to someone, even if it's your friend's parents at the grocery store. They could be prominent alumni of, or even hold an important job at the school of your dreams!

Here are some important tips to help you grow a strong and vibrant professional network:

- **Arrive on Time (or Early)!** – You show you care about other people's time – and them – when you show up on time.

- **Ask Questions** – People have tons of interesting things to say. Ask questions and listen closely to their answers. You will surely find something in common!

- **Share Your Passions** – If someone asks you a question, reply openly and honestly. People appreciate your beliefs and can tell when you communicate them with sincerity and conviction.

- **Avoid Hijacking the Conversation** – No one likes a ball hog. Similarly, no one likes to be on the wrong end of a one-way conversation. Wait your turn to speak, avoid interrupting others, and keep your answers clear and concise!

- **Remember to Follow-Up** – If someone asks you to text, call, email or follow up, do it! This is how lifelong relationships begin.

- **Smile** – A smile goes a mile on the way toward making someone feel comfortable with you.

GO! Thank You Notes

After meeting someone new, whether it's for a formal or an informal meeting, send a thank you note for their time. Refer to unit 3 for more information on writing a thank you note.

Conducting a Follow-Up Phone Call

There may be several reasons that you need to call someone. Regardless of why you are reaching out to them, it is important to be professional.

Follow these guidelines for a successful phone conversation:

- Write down the name of the person you are speaking to, so that you can call them by name and/or refer to them if you need to call again.

- Have a plan. What questions do you need answered or what message do you want to relay?

- Make sure you speak clearly and concisely with a strong voice, but do not shout.

- Be polite and courteous to whomever you speak with.

- Smile while you are on the phone because the person on the other end can hear it in your voice.

- If no one answers your call, leave a professional voice message with your name and phone number asking for them to return your call. Do not count on the other person to retrieve your number off the phone.

Virtual Professionalism

In the 21st century, it is remarkably simple to send a message, take a picture, or record a video and publish it online. This is both a blessing and a curse. When you're standing in the checkout line at your local supermarket, take a second to review the newspaper, magazine, and tabloid headlines and pictures. It's truly shocking how quickly and easily a bad picture or misquoted text message can ruin a celebrity's life.

Here's the even more troubling part. The exact same thing can happen to you.

Just as your choices in your physical reality follow you around and affect your life, so too do the choices you make online. It is even possible, in certain situations, that your "virtual identity" can be even more important than your actual identity. People's first impression of you is increasingly taking place on the web.

To help you improve your professional persona and protect your future, this section will focus on the following virtual etiquette areas:

1. Social Media Do's and Do Not's

2. Creating a Professional Email Address

3. Writing a Professional Email

Key Point
Your future employer or college admissions committee could be the audience of your "virtual identity."

Social Media Do's and Do Not's

As of 2016, there are more than 1.5 Billion (that's 1,500,000,000) "friends" on Facebook. That's a lot of people who could view your silly baby pictures or romantic quotes with your significant other. Whether you prefer Facebook, Twitter, Instagram, Snapchat, Kik, Tumblr, or some other social network, follow these Do's and Do Not's to help keep your virtual reputation clean!

Key Point
Follow the Professionalism "Do's" and "Don'ts"; your first impression can make or break whether an employer or admission committee decides to interview or hire you.

Social Media Do's and Do Not's

DO	DO NOT
DO… Use Social Media! It's important to have an online presence to showcase your skills and experience	**DO NOT… Post Inappropriate Material** Colleges and employers are constantly watching you and checking out your online profiles. Posting anything you would be uncomfortable explaining to Grandma is a good rule of thumb in order to avoid embarrassing yourself.
DO… Google Yourself Check every once in awhile to make sure that nothing pops up online that you wouldn't want attached to your name.	**DO NOT… Forget Your Privacy Settings** If you're not careful, people who aren't your friends can see your most personal photos.
DO… Be Careful What You Tweet Anyone on Twitter can read what you post. This is increasingly the case with the newer social networks as well.	**DO NOT… Connect with Everyone** Besides the dangers that come with openly accepting friend requests or "follows" from strangers, it's better for your connections to be made up of strong relationships rather than a large number of people you don't know.

Creating a Professional Email Address

First and foremost, before you email a potential employer or a college you are interested in attending, make sure that you have set up an appropriate email account. Keep your email communications both professional and simple; a general rule of thumb is to use your first and last name in your email address. Remember that your email address will make a first impression on the person or persons it is seen by.

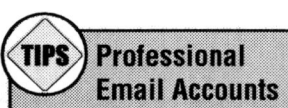

TIPS **Professional Email Accounts**

Create a professional email account specifically for scholarship and college applications.

Employers, scholarship committees, and colleges will not take you seriously if your email is inappropriate or unprofessional. For example, "lilwayne214" or "princess18" will not cut it. Instead, choose an email that represents you positively and professionally such as jose.ramirez, jramirez15, or ramirez2016. If you are considering whether or not you need to make a new account because your current one might be inappropriate, ask your teacher or another adult for approval or create a new account. It's better to be safe than sorry.

When creating your own email address you can use one of the following free email servers:

`www.gmail.com, www.msn.com, www.yahoo.com`

GO! **Create Your New Address**

Your current email address is: _____

A professional email address you could use would be: _____

Once you begin applying to colleges, applying for scholarships, and/or applying to jobs, it is recommended that you set up an alternate email account. By doing this, you ensure that these important email conversations do not get mixed in with your personal emails. Write down your username and password in a secure place that you won't forget!

Writing a Professional Email

You have already learned how to write a professional cover letter, and much of the information for email etiquette is the same in terms of the layout. The main idea is to appear to be professional and responsible.

There are a few specific rules that you should follow:

- Use a meaningful description in the subject line. Give the person you are writing a short summary of the nature of your email, such as "Requesting status update for scholarship submission."
- Address the person to whom you are writing the email in a professional manner. For example, "Dear Dr. Jon Salazar" or "Mr./Mrs. Gomez."
- Do not use slang words or expressions such as "cool" or "whatever."
- Do not write in CAPITALS or include emoticons such as ":)."
- Do not write like you are texting; never use shorthand such as "lol" or "thx."
- Be efficient. Get to the point of your message and be effective with your wording. You are not writing a letter to your friend, so don't include personal information that is not necessary.
- Check your grammar, spelling, and punctuation.
- Make sure you re-read the email before you send it.

Notes

Unit 3: Practice Professionalism

Building A Résumé

The purpose of submitting a résumé is to get an interview. A **résumé** is typically a one-page summary of your past experience and skills. There are many ways to structure your résumé and they will vary depending on your purpose. Look over this section to get an idea of how résumés should look in the future and get an idea of the activities you may want to get involved in to build your résumé. For a great example résumé, see "Exemplar Résumé for Middle School Students" later in the unit.

- Name and contact information
- Education
- Experience (paid and non-paid jobs/internships)*
- Activities/Community Service
- Awards and honors
- Skills
- References

Name and Contact Information

When a recruiter first looks at your résumé, make it easy for them to find your name and contact information. Place this information at the top of your résumé and make your name the largest font (don't go larger than 16-point font). Use a permanent mailing address and phone number you can be reached at. Make sure to include a professional email address on your résumé. A professional email address typically includes your first and last name. No one will take you seriously if your email is krazyness45@hotmail.com.

Education

This section always follows your personal contact information. Here is where you put the name of the high school you are graduating from. Always include your GPA if it is above a 3.0. (to find your GPA, check your high school transcript or talk to your counselor). Including "relevant coursework" is optional. Consider including this if you have taken courses that are related to what you are applying for. For example, if you took AP US History and are applying to a history program, you would definitely want to mention it.

Experience (Paid and Non-paid Jobs/Internships)

If you have had any previous experience that was paid or non-paid, this is where to include those responsibilities and accomplishments. One way to organize this information is to include the exact title of your position, the name of the company/organization, and how long you held this position on one line. Under this information, bullet point your responsibilities and accomplishments to help recruiters understand what you did in this role. If you reference more than one experience, make sure to list it in reverse chronological order, most recent first.

Activities/Community Service

If you are involved in both **extracurricular activities** and community service organizations, it is okay to have separate sections for each. If you held any leadership positions in these activities, don't forget to include them here too. This can be an optional section if you included this information in the experience section.

Awards and honors

If you did not include your awards and honors in the experience section, make sure to list them here. It is always helpful to include a short description of the award/honor and when you received it.

Skills

If you are fluent in a language other than English (you can carry a conversation in Spanish), include it here. This is the place for you to list specific skills that are relevant to what you are applying for. For example, if you are applying for computer jobs, include the programs you are proficient (skilled) in (such as Microsoft Word or PowerPoint). This can be an optional section.

References

Create a **reference** list of three to five people who know you in a professional setting and would be willing to talk about you. A reference will be contacted after an interview, and you want to make sure you choose people who will say good things about you. This can be on a separate page from your résumé. Title the page, "References for _____". If you have had a job before, use your supervisor or boss as a reference. Other references could include teachers, coaches or extracurricular sponsors who know you. Do not include family members or friends. When you list your references, include their full name, exact title, work address, phone number, email address, and their relationship to you. Always make sure you ask your references for permission before you list them, and let them know what you are interviewing for. After the interview, be sure to send them a thank you card for being a reference. Don't burn the bridge with your references; you never know when you will need their help later on.

Formatting your Résumé

Most employers will not spend long looking at your résumé, so make sure that it is easy to read. Here are some common résumé rules to abide by:

- Avoid using the pronoun "I" in your writing. Begin each description with an action verb (see the next page).
- The entire page doesn't need to be filled with text; it is okay to have white space on your résumé.
- To keep your résumé balanced, leave 1-inch margins and take advantage of emphasizing by bolding, italicizing, or capitalizing text.
- Print your résumé on résumé paper or white 8.5" x 11" paper.
- Do not use any paper color other than white or off-white for your résumé, and do not include pictures.

TIPS **Ordering Your Information**

When listing your activities, do so in reverse chronological order. More recent events should come first.

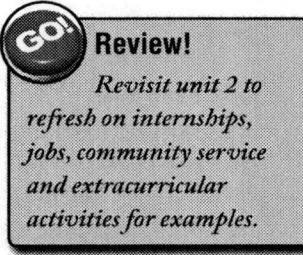

GO! **Review!**

Revisit unit 2 to refresh on internships, jobs, community service and extracurricular activities for examples.

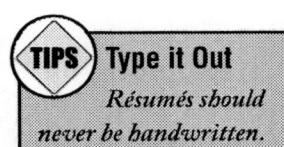

TIPS **Type it Out**

Résumés should never be handwritten.

Unit 3: Practice Professionalism

Action Verbs Word Bank

Below you will find a word bank of action verbs to use in your résumé and cover letters. Using these words will help you stand out. Be sure to use past tense for previously held positions and organizations and present tense for positions and organizations you are currently involved in.

TIPS **Verb Tense**
Pay careful attention to the verb tense you use when describing past and present positions.

Administered	Educated	Organized
Advised	Established	Oversaw
Allocated	Evaluated	Planned
Analyzed	Examined	Prioritized
Assigned	Executed	Produced
Assisted	Financed	Projected
Budgeted	Founded	Recruited
Built	Guided	Reduced
Calculated	Improved	Referred
Clarified	Increased	Represented
Contracted	Influenced	Researched
Consolidated	Improved	Scheduled
Coordinated	Improvised	Shaped
Created	Invented	Solved
Delegated	Maintained	Supervised
Developed	Managed	Supported
Directed	Marketed	Trained
Drafted	Motivated	Upgraded
Edited	Obtained	Wrote

Keeping it Fresh

Below is a list of words that are often overused in writing. Try adding some of these interesting alternatives to separate you from the crowd!

a lot, lots	numerous, multiple, a great deal, often, scores, innumerable, many
also	too, moreover, besides, as well as, in addition to
but	however, yet, still, nevertheless, though, although, on the other hand
delicious	delectable, savory, appetizing, palatable, scrumptious
fun	pleasant, pleasurable, amusing, entertaining
get	receive, obtain, attain, realize
good	excellent, exceptional, fine, marvelous, outstanding, splendid, superb, wonderful
just	there are no alternatives, avoid using this word
look	observe, gaze, glance, glimpse, survey, examine, view, watch, examine
nice	pleasant, charming, fascinating, captivating, delightful, pleasing
tell/say	inform, notify, remark, mention, comment, exclaim, utter, disclose, divulge
then	first, second, next, meanwhile, afterward, later, finally, ultimately, eventually
very	extremely, exceedingly, incredibly, truly, fully, especially, surely, remarkably

Why do you think it would be a bad thing to include "overused" words on your résumé?

_____

_____

Exemplar Résumé for Middle School Students

Résumés change over time as you gain more experience. Notice the changes between a middle school résumé, a high school (applying into college) résumé, and a professional (applying for a job) résumé all look different.

Key Point

Résumés should use correct formatting, grammar, and verb tense. Avoid using the pronoun "I", be 1-2 pages in length, and list experiences in reverse chronological order.

JOE RODRIGUEZ

456 College Way * Boulder, TX 75211 * (456) 789-0123 * joerodriguez@gmail.com

---

EDUCATION

Centennial Middle School, Boulder Valley School District	2013-Present

Weighted GPA.: 85% average (3.4 on a 4.0 scale)
- o Pre-AP Mathematics
- o Pre-AP Language Arts
- o Pre-AP US History
- o Advanced Via Individual Determination (AVID)

Eastfield College, Dallas, TX	Summer 2014
- o Dallas Engineering Camp

EXTRA-CURRICULAR ACTIVITIES

• Academic Activities

o Spanish Club, President	2014-2015
o Math Team	2014-2015
o Knowledge Bowl	2013-2014

• Non-Academic Activities

o Baseball Team, Most Valuable Player	2013-2015
o Church Youth Group, Worship Band Member	2013-2015
o Student Council, Treasurer	2013-2014

COMMUNITY SERVICE

o Boys and Girls Club After School Program, Peer Tutor	2014-2015
o Thanksgiving Canned Food Drive, Volunteer	2013-2015
o Annual Christmas Charity Clothing Drive, Volunteer	2013-2014
o Sunshine Day Care, Reading Time Volunteer	2013-2014

HONORS AND AWARDS

o Perfect Attendance	2014-2015
o Top 10% of AVID Class	2014-2015
o Most Outstanding Math Student	2014-2015

SPECIAL SKILLS AND INTERESTS

- o Bilingual (English and Spanish)
- o Junior Zoo Keeper, Dallas Zoo

ABC Extracurricular Activities

Extracurricular activities are non-classroom activities that students can get involved in at school. They can include activities such as athletics, clubs, student government, recreational and social organizations and events.

Unit 3: Practice Professionalism

*Please Note: *Image is not to scale. Normal résumé files are printed on an 8.5" x 11" sheet of paper.*

TIPS **A Note on Formatting**

Pay careful attention to the spacing of your résumé and make sure it appears clean and consistent.

JANE DOE
123 College Rocks Street * Dallas, TX 75211 * (123) 456-7890 * janedoe@gmail.com

EDUCATION

Sunset High School   June 2015
Overall GPA.: 3.98 on a 4.0 scale
Rank: 1/904, Graduated Summa Cum Laude
SAT Score: 2400 (800 Verbal, 800 Math, 800 Writing)
ACT Score: 33

EXTRA-CURRICULAR ACTIVITIES

Sunset High School Varsity Soccer (Defense)   2011-2015
Varsity Captain   2014
Most Valuable Player   2013, 2014

Sunset High School Junior Varsity Volleyball (Setter)   2011-2013

National Honor Society
President   2014-2015

Student Council   2011-2015
Chair of annual Make-A-Wish fundraising campaign   2013

Dallas Texans '97 Girls Red Competitive Youth Soccer (Defense)   2008-2015
North Texas State Cup Champion   2013

PROFESSIONAL/VOLUNTEER EXPERIENCE

Children's Medical Center of Dallas   Summer 2014
Child Life Intern
• Delivered flowers and gifts to patient rooms
• Planned and executed two weekly activities in the hospital playrooms for ill children

Make-A-Wish Foundation of North Texas   Summer 2013
Public Relations Intern
• Wrote 25+ "wish stories" about children served by the Foundation to be distributed to donors, supporters, and local media
• Translated for Spanish-speaking wish families on a daily basis

HONORS AND AWARDS

Who's Who in Sunset High School   May 2015
• Recognized as one of thirty seniors for outstanding service and leadership

Most Likely to Change the World   May 2015
• Voted by Sunset seniors as student most likely to make a difference in the community, state, or nation

Perfect "A" Honor Roll   May 2014
• Earned all "A's" during junior academic year

SKILLS

• Fluent in Spanish (reading, writing, and speaking)
• Adept at graphic editing using Photoshop and Adobe Illustrator

*Please Note: *Image is not to scale. Normal résumé files are printed on an 8.5" x 11" sheet of paper.*

Exemplar Professional Résumé

AMY DINH TRAN

184 13th Street, Oakland, CA 94601 | amytran510@gmail.com | (510) 448-5210

EDUCATION

University of California, Berkeley| School of Social Welfare
Masters in Social Welfare, Concentration in Management and Planning

Berkeley, CA
May 2016

University of California, Berkeley| College of Letters and Sciences
Bachelor of Arts in Sociology and Mass Communications

Berkeley, CA
May 2011

PROFESSIONAL EXPERIENCE

James Morehouse Project | El Cerrito High School
Individual and Group Counselor, MSW Intern

El Cerrito, CA
Sep 2015 - May 2016

- Prepared and facilitated over 15 weeks of curriculum for a group of immigrant youth to explore identity, culture, & future aspirations
- Built rapport, consulted, and partnered with students, JMP staff, teachers, and school administrators to design and execute a student-centered needs assessment that will continue to inform program planning and resources for immigrant youth
- Counseled high school students ages 14-18 in weekly individual sessions utilizing youth-centered narrative therapy practices
- Collaborated with counseling staff, teachers, and administrators to provide holistic care and support to students

Community Health for Asian Americans
Bilingual Community Engagement Coordinator

Oakland, CA
June 2015 – Aug 2015

- Led and executed data collection project administering health surveys and interviewing nail salon workers to identify workplace issues
- Conducted over 25 nail salon visits and trained owners/workers in green energy efficiency and water conservation practices in salons
- Co-created and facilitated community building events between Vietnamese immigrant nail salon workers and African American clients

African American Studies, University of California, Berkeley
Research Assistant

Berkeley, CA
Aug 2013 – June 2015

- Independently planned and implemented all logistics for a 7-day research trip across Louisiana, visited 9 plantation and museum sites, and conducted 15 interviews with site staff on the preservation of slave cabins and the representation of (or lack of) slave stories
- Executed data collection projects on the representation of race, history, and the formation of collective memory with minimal supervision

Rising Sun Energy Center
Program Planning and Evaluation Assistant, MSW Intern

Berkeley, CA
Aug 2014 – May 2015

- Managed, collected, and analyzed data for a young adult needs assessment to drive program planning, operational efficiency, and impact
- Conducted environmental landscape and program analysis to identify best practices for young adult college and job training programs
- Appraised grants on Grantstation & Foundation Directory databases and supported project management to secure $263,000 EPA grant

COMMUNITY LEADERSHIP

Social Welfare Graduate Assembly | School of Social Welfare
Co-Chair of Operations & Chair of Equity and Inclusion

Berkeley, CA
Jan 2015 – May 2016

- Served as student representative for Masters in Social Welfare student body in administrative meetings with the School of Social Welfare dean, faculty, and staff regarding changes in curriculum, faculty, and the direction of the school
- Planned and implemented anti-oppression workshops for incoming first year students

AWARDS, HONORS, AND SPECIAL ACHIEVEMENTS

- Excellence in Leadership Block Grant Award (2015-2016): $10,000
- School of Social Welfare Department Award (2014-2015): $5,000

SKILLS

- Fluent Vietnamese speaker with basic reading and writing skills
- Proficient in Microsoft Office Suite and Google Suite
- Adept in Adobe InDesign, Salesforce, Asana Task Management System, SmartSheet, and Remark

---

TIPS A Note on Formatting

Years should be aligned from the top of your résumé all the way to the bottom.

Unit 3: Practice Professionalism

---

*Please Note: *Image is not to scale. Normal résumé files are printed on an 8.5" x 11" sheet of paper.*

Exemplar Reference List

References for Jane Doe

Kristen Watkins
High School English teacher/ School Newspaper Sponsor
Moises Molina High School
Dallas ISD
2355 Duncanville Road
Dallas, TX 75211
(123) 456-7891
kristen.watkins@dallasisd.org

I was a student in Ms. Watkins' AP English IV class and worked with her as one of the founding newspaper editors for the Molina Daily Student Newspaper.

Chelsea Johnson
Vice President of Marketing
Roadmap to Success
54321 College St.
Dallas, TX 75211
(987) 654-3210
chelsea.johnson@roadmap2success.org

In the fall of 2011, I interned for Ms. Johnson. I was able to work on the Dallas ISD account and increased sales by 95%. Ms. Johnson also became a mentor and role model for me.

Courtnee Benford
Varsity Soccer Coach
Moises Molina High School
Dallas ISD
2355 Duncanville Road
Dallas, TX 75211
(123) 456-7891

I played three years for Coach Benford and served as team captain for two years.

*Please Note: *Image is not to scale. Normal reference files are printed on an 8.5" x 11" sheet of paper.*

Résumé Fill-In Template Middle School

My Turn! Start Writing My Résumé Today

DIRECTIONS: If you are currently in middle school, use the following two pages as a skeleton résumé to begin outlining your activities. Do your best to fill in as many lines as possible and continue to update this page over time as you gain experience!

NAME: _____
Street Address: _____
City, State Zip: _____
Reliable Phone Number: _____
Appropriate Email Address: _____

EDUCATION

School: _____ Dates of Attendance: _____
GPA.: _____ % Average   (_____ **on a 4.0 scale)**

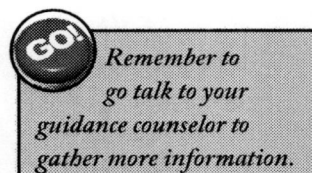

Remember to go talk to your guidance counselor to gather more information.

ACADEMIC ACTIVITIES

List Special Coursework such as Advanced Placement Course (Pre-AP and AP) and Grade Earned.

Course: _____ **(Grade Earned: _____)**
Course: _____ **(Grade Earned: _____)**
Course: _____ **(Grade Earned: _____)**
Course: _____ **(Grade Earned: _____)**

List special programs you've attended (i.e. Engineering Camp, Science Club for Girls)

Name of Program: _____ **Year(s):** _____
Name of Program: _____ **Year(s):** _____

EXTRA-CURRICULAR ACTIVITIES

List both academic (i.e. Math Team, AVID) and non-academic (i.e. Sports, volunteer activities). Also, be sure to list any leadership positions (i.e. President, Captain, etc.) or received recognition (i.e. MVP, Most Committed Team Member, etc.).

- **Sport:** _____ **(Position:_____)** **Year(s):** _____
  Leadership Position: _____ **Year(s):** _____
  Recognition: _____ **Year(s):** _____

- **Sport:** _____ **(Position:_____)** **Year(s):** _____
  Leadership Position: _____ **Year(s):** _____
  Recognition: _____ **Year(s):** _____

- **Club:** _____ **Year(s):** _____
  Leadership Position: _____ **Year(s):** _____
  Leadership Position: _____ **Year(s):** _____

- **Club:** _____ **Year(s):** _____
  Leadership Position: _____ **Year(s):** _____
  Leadership Position: _____ **Year(s):** _____

PROFESSIONAL/VOLUNTEER EXPERIENCE

List any unpaid volunteer experience (i.e. reading at a day care, helping at an animal shelter, helping cook for a community celebration, etc.) when you practiced skills in responsibility, service, and commitment.

- **Company/Organization:** _____ **Year(s):** _____
  Title: _____
  Short Description: _____
  _____

- **Company/Organization:** _____ **Year(s):** _____
  Title: _____
  Short Description: _____
  _____

HONORS AND AWARDS

List any awards or honors you have received (i.e. Perfect Attendance, Outstanding Student of the Month, Outstanding Student in Math).

- **Award:** _____ **Year(s):** _____
  Short Description: _____
  _____

- **Award:** _____ **Year(s):** _____
  Short Description: _____
  _____

SKILLS

Include any special or relevant skills (i.e. language fluency and/or computer skills).

- _____
- _____
- _____
- _____

REFERENCES

Brainstorm teachers, counselors, coaches, and mentors who you would like to list as a reference. Be sure to get their permission to list them as a reference as well as their contact information.

- **Name:** _____ **Job Title:** _____
- **Name:** _____ **Job Title:** _____
- **Name:** _____ **Job Title:** _____

Résumé Fill-In Template High School

My Turn! Start Writing My Résumé Today

DIRECTIONS: If you are in high school, use the following two pages as a skeleton résumé to begin outlining your activities. Do your best to fill in as many lines as possible and continue to update this page over time as you gain experience!

NAME: _____

Street Address: _____

City, State Zip: _____

Reliable Phone Number: _____

Appropriate Email Address: _____

EDUCATION

School: _____ Dates of Attendance: _____

GPA.: _____ % Average   (_____ **on a 4.0 scale)**

Rank: _____/_____

Highest SAT Score: _____ (_____ **Verbal,** _____ **Math,** _____ **Writing)**

Highest ACT Score: _____

ACADEMIC ACTIVITIES

List Special Coursework such as Advanced Placement Course (AP or IB), and grade received in the course, and the assessment score if you have taken the exam.

Course: _____ **(Grade Earned: _____)**

Course: _____ **(Grade Earned: _____)**

Course: _____ **(Grade Earned: _____)**

Course: _____ **(Grade Earned: _____)**

List special programs you've attended (i.e. Engineering Camp, Science Club for Girls)

Name of Program: _____ **Year(s):** _____

Name of Program: _____ **Year(s):** _____

EXTRA-CURRICULAR ACTIVITIES

List both academic (i.e. Math Team, AVID) and non-academic (i.e. Sports, volunteer activities).

- **Sport:** _____ **(Position:_____)** **Year(s):** _____
  Leadership Position: _____ **Year(s):** _____
  Recognition: _____ **Year(s):** _____

- **Sport:** _____ **(Position:_____)** **Year(s):** _____
  Leadership Position: _____ **Year(s):** _____
  Recognition: _____ **Year(s):** _____

- **Club:** _____ **Year(s):** _____
  Leadership Position: _____ **Year(s):** _____
  Leadership Position: _____ **Year(s):** _____

- **Club:** _____ **Year(s):** _____
  Leadership Position: _____ **Year(s):** _____
  Leadership Position: _____ **Year(s):** _____

WORK/VOLUNTEER EXPERIENCE

List any paid work (i.e. dog walking, baby-sitting) or unpaid volunteer experience (i.e. reading at the day care, helping at the animal shelter) when you practiced skills in responsibility, service, and commitment.

- **Company/Organization:** _____ **Year(s):** _____
  Title: _____
  Short Description: _____

- **Company/Organization:** _____ **Year(s):** _____
  Title: _____
  Short Description: _____

HONORS AND AWARDS

List any awards or honors you have received (i.e. Perfect Attendance, Outstanding Student of the Month, Outstanding Student in Math).

- **Award:** _____ **Year(s):** _____
  Short Description: _____

- **Award:** _____ **Year(s):** _____
  Short Description: _____

- **Award:** _____ **Year(s):** _____
  Short Description: _____

SKILLS

Include any special or relevant skills (i.e. language, computer skills).

- _____
- _____
- _____
- _____

REFERENCES

Brainstorm teachers, counselors, coaches, and mentors who you would like to list as a reference. Be sure to get their permission to list them as a reference as well as their contact information.

- **Name:** _____ **Job Title:** _____
  E-mail: _____
  Phone Number: _____

- **Name:** _____ **Job Title:** _____
  E-mail: _____
  Phone Number: _____

- **Name:** _____ **Job Title:** _____
  E-mail: _____
  Phone Number: _____

Unit 3: Practice Professionalism

The Cover Letter

Some colleges and most jobs will require a cover letter as part of your application. A **cover letter** is the introduction to your application. It lets the reader know who you are, what you are applying for and why you are a good fit for the job, or why you would be an excellent student. The purpose of the cover letter is to:

1. Tell the employer what job you want, or let them know you are applying to be a student at their college.

2. Gain interest from the employer in learning more about you.

3. Impress the employer by showcasing your knowledge about the company or school.

4. Show the employer how well you can express yourself.

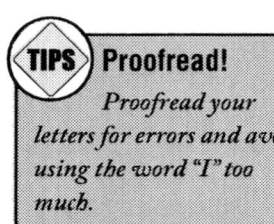

TIPS Proofread!

Proofread your letters for errors and avoid using the word "I" too much.

Key Point

The purpose of a cover letter is to gain interest and encourage follow-up from a college or an employer.

Tips for Getting Started

1. **Address the letter to a specific individual.**

   Call to request the name and title of the person responsible for hiring. "Dear Sir or Madam" and "To Whom it May Concern" are to be avoided. If you can't get a specific name, you can direct the letter to someone with a specific job title, such as Human Resources Representative or Admissions Officer. If these don't fit, simply begin the letter without a salutation such as "Dear _____,"

2. **Write an attention-getting introduction.**

   Remember, you are trying to make the reader want to get to know you better, and ultimately to hire or admit you. Talk about your interest and enthusiasm in the job or school.

3. **State the position for which you are applying and point out your relevant qualifications.**

   Don't just repeat the contents of your résumé. Select specific experiences relevant to the job and discuss them. Fill in the blanks your résumé leaves open. Tell the employer why you are uniquely suited for the job or school. Avoid using "I" to start every sentence.

4. **Tailor your letters to the needs of the company and requirements of the position.**

   How will the company or school benefit from hiring or admitting you? Want ads and college or company publications offer clues about what to focus on.

5. **Provide your contact information for the employer and let them know how to reach you during business hours.**

   Be cautious about initiating contact with the employer. You may wish to contact the employer within a week or 10 days to confirm that they received your application. In some cases, the employer will post on their job announcement "Do Not Call." If this is the case, wait until they contact you.

6. **Don't forget to be positive and confident!**

7. **Write a rough draft and have another person critique it.**

8. **Revamp and refine the letter until you are satisfied that it is warm, personalized, and at the same time, businesslike.**

Cover Letter Format & Contents

Your Street Address
City, State Zip Code

Name of Person & Title
Company/Organization
Street Address
City, State Zip Code

Dear Mr./Ms. _____:

Introduction: The opening paragraph should state **why you are writing** and why you are interested in the organization or school. Name the specific position, or type of work for which you are applying. Mention the resource used in finding out about the job opening/company/college: news media, friend, or faculty.

Body: The second paragraph is where you draw attention to your résumé and highlight specific skills relevant to the potential employer or school. This paragraph is devoted to **explaining how you are qualified and why you are right for the job or school.** Explain why you are interested in working for that employer, or in that field of work, and most importantly what your qualifications are (academic background, work experience, personal skills). Point out achievements that relate to the field and why you enjoy that work. Refer the reader to the enclosed résumé, application, and/or portfolio.

Closing: The closing paragraph is where you summarize your key strengths as a future employee, list your contact information, and express your excitement at the prospect of joining the organization once more. It's also important to thank your reader for taking the time to review your application. If you are also including your résumé and/or references, mention that here and write "enclosure" at the bottom of the page as shown below.

Sincerely,

Sign Your Name

Type Your Name

Enclosure

Key Point

A cover letter should have an introduction, body and closing, be tailored to your passion and the job, and be addressed to the specific person offering the job.

Enclosure

Writing "enclosure" at the end of a cover letter means something is attached to the cover letter, like your résumé or application.

Unit 3: Practice Professionalism

123 College Rocks Street
Dallas, TX 75211

March 20, 2016

Ashley Bryan, Child Life Intern Program
Children's Medical Center of Dallas
1935 Medical District Drive
Dallas, TX 75235

Dear Ms. Bryan:

After speaking with my high school counselor about volunteer opportunities in Dallas, I learned about your Child Life Internship Program at Children's Medical Center. As someone who hopes to attend medical school in the future, I would love the opportunity to volunteer and serve others in need through your program.

My younger sister had heart problems as a baby, and the staff at Children's Medical Center always went above and beyond to make my family feel comfortable and welcome. It was during that time that I realized I wanted to be a pediatrician, and have worked hard towards that goal ever since. I currently hold a 3.98 GPA at Sunset High School and have already taken 23 credits of Advanced Placement courses. Last summer, I was a Public Relations intern with the Make-A-Wish foundation and wrote over 25 "wish stories" about children served by the Foundation. I also served as a translator for Spanish-speaking families on a daily basis. Not only did this experience improve my communication skills, but it also increased my desire to help others suffering from unfortunate circumstances. Along with my intern experience, I also served as the Student Council Chair for the Make-A-Wish fundraising campaign in 2003.

Children's Medical Center's commitment to its patients and reputation for excellence are compelling reasons for joining your Child Life Intern program. My communication style and background would fit well with the youth population I would reach. I also believe that my work ethic and commitment to service are values shared by your staff. Joining the Child Life Internship program would be an outstanding way to serve others and work towards my own goal of someday becoming a pediatrician. That said, I would love to interview with you in person and have enclosed my résumé. You may reach me at (123) 456-7890 or janedoe@gmail.com. Thank you for your consideration.

Sincerely,

Jane Doe
Enclosure

Jane Doe

My Turn! Write a Cover Letter

DIRECTIONS: Whether you plan on applying to school, a job, or just want to practice, use the lines below to see if you can write a superb cover letter that will get you hired!

_____
_____

_____
_____
_____
_____

Dear Mr./Ms._____:

Introduction

_____
_____
_____
_____
_____

Body

_____
_____
_____
_____
_____

Closing

_____
_____
_____
_____
_____

Sincerely,

_____
_____

Enclosure

An **interview** is a formal meeting in person, arranged to determine if you are a good fit for the job or school. This happens between the interviewer (who asks the questions) and the interviewee (the applicant, who answers the questions). An interview is a two-way conversation – it is a great place to showcase your skills and also to learn more about the job or school. There are important things to prepare for each of the three parts of an interview.

DO	DON'T
• Prepare questions that will allow you to learn more and demonstrate that you know what you're applying for.	• Prepare questions about salary, personal questions, or information that can be answered or explained on their website.
• Schedule a mock interview and practice, practice, practice with the feedback given.	• "Wing it" without practicing for the interview many, many times.
• Delete any inappropriate posts or pictures online.	• Post anything you're not sure about! When in doubt, go without.
• Plan on how, when, and with who you are getting to your interview BEFORE that day.	• Figure out directions and transportation the day of the interview.
• Pick your modest, professional outfit BEFORE the day of the interview.	• Pick your outfit the day of the interview and wear casual or inappropriate styles.

Before the Interview

Do Your Homework!

If you are hoping to join this organization or school, you must know as much as you can about it to communicate that you are serious about the position. Take time to search online, ask friends and family, or read brochures about what you are applying for. If it's a college interview, you should know the basics of the school: location, cost, types of degrees/programs, on-campus activities, etc. The time you put in today will help you decide what questions you want to ask the interviewer.

Below are common questions to ask employers in order to help you find out if this job/interview is a fit for you:

- "What are the day-to-day responsibilities for this position?"
- "What do you enjoy most about working with this company/ organization?"
- "What qualities are you looking for in the candidate who fills this position?"
- "I read on the news/organization website that the company has recently..." [this demonstrates you have researched recently and found a news story about them]

Practice with a Mock Interview

Ask a parent, teacher, or counselor if they are willing to help you practice your interview skills by holding a mock interview. A mock interview will allow you to practice for the actual interview and answer possible interview questions. Some school counselors will have mock interviews that you can sign up for. These usually last 30 minutes and are videotaped. After the mock interview, they will review the tape with you and provide constructive feedback. This is a great opportunity to make mistakes before your actual interview so you can improve. Following this section, you will find two blank mock interview templates you can use. Remember – practice makes perfect!

TIPS Informational Interviews

When you contact someone in the field you are interested in to hear about their experience and seek advice, you are conducting an informational interview. Don't forget to prepare questions.

Clean Up Social Media

Do you have Instagram, Facebook, Twitter, or other profiles online? Are there pictures or posts you wouldn't want your employer or professor to see? If so, consider deleting them permanently. Often, when employers review applications, one of their first steps is to look for you on the Internet to find potential red flags. Many employers think the way you present yourself online is an indicator of the way you present yourself in the workplace. Inappropriate pictures or comments online make it much less likely to get hired.

Plan for Transportation

Before the day of the interview, make sure you have mapped out how you will get to the interview. If the interview is in an unfamiliar part of town, make the trip a couple days before so you know exactly where you are going and if you need to avoid any construction. Be sure to arrange another ride if necessary.

Plan Your Outfit

Your interview is often your first chance to make a professional impression. Most interviews will suggest that you dress either business professional or business casual. As a rule of thumb, it is always better to be overdressed (business suit) than underdressed. Below are some suggestions:

- Business Professional vs. Business Casual
  Business professional means that you wear a suit and closed-toed shoes.
  Business casual is similar, but you don't have to wear a suit jacket. When scheduling your interview, you will typically be told what to wear. If you are not told, always assume it is business professional.

- Ladies
  - If you choose to wear a skirt or dress, make sure it is knee length. A good way to measure this is to put your arms straight down at your sides and check whether the skirt goes at least past your fingertips.
  - Blouses or shirts need to have sleeves and not be tight or low cut.
  - Wear closed-toe shoes instead of sandals.
  - Keep accessories and make-up simple.
  - Choose a hairstyle that is neat and that you will not need to adjust during the interview.
  - Avoid heavy perfume.

- Gentlemen
  - Wear good-fitting dress pants, not jeans or shorts.
  - Wear a button-down shirt that is buttoned past your chest and tucked in. Make sure it is not wrinkled and not tight.
  - Consider wearing a tie that matches your shirt.
  - Wear a black or brown leather belt that matches your dress shoes – no sneakers!
  - Be clean-shaven and have an appropriate, simple haircut.
  - Avoid heavy cologne.

What NOT to Wear to an Interview

No matter how much you love your sports teams or your favorite band, do not dress casual for an interview. On the contrary, don't overdress and wear a formal gown/prom dress or tuxedo. Also, no flip-flops!

Ladies

Ladies, if you wear a professional skirt or dress, make sure it goes PAST your fingertips to your knees; make sure it is not too short. This example is not long enough and wearing spaghetti straps is inappropriate for a formal interview. Make sure your shoulders are covered.

Gentlemen

Gentlemen, it is important for you to dress professionally for an interview, as well. The picture shown is inappropriate. Make sure you do not wear jeans, t-shirts, tennis shoes, or wrinkled clothing. Also, it is always advisable to be clean-shaven.

My Turn! How's My Wardrobe?

DIRECTIONS: In the space below, write down an outfit that you already have (or could borrow from someone you know) that you could wear to an interview:

During the Interview

Remember – not every job or college applicant is granted an interview, so this is your time to stand out even more. This is also your first – and maybe your last – impression you will make before hearing back from the employer, so it is important to give it your best effort after all the preparation you have done so far.

- **Arrive 20 to 30 minutes early.** This is important! Many locations have complicated buildings, parking structures, or check-in procedures. You want to arrive relaxed and calm, not anxious and hurried. Arriving early also allows you to walk around and get a feel for the company or school. Walking is a great stress reliever and can help you get rid of any nervous energy you might have.

- **Treat EVERYONE with respect.** You may be greeted by a secretary or assistant. Although they may not be the ones interviewing you, they work for the company and your impression on them is important. Treat everyone in the building respectfully. Even someone in the elevator with you may be your interviewer or work for the company.

- **Give a great handshake.** When greeted by your interviewer, make sure you give him or her a great handshake. Here are some tips:

    - *Be firm.* A firm handshake shows self-confidence and warmth, but don't overdo it and break someone's hand. Weak handshakes make you look timid and not interested in the person you're meeting.

    - *Squeeze quickly.* While shaking someone's hand, give their hand a quick squeeze and then release it. The whole handshake should last 1 – 2 seconds.

- **Make eye contact.** Eye contact is a critical part of social interaction. When you make eye contact, it shows that you are confident. If you don't make eye contact, you make come off as rude, bored, or shy. Making eye contact can be challenging for some people, so here are some tips to make it easier for you:

    - *Listen.* If you're really focused on what someone is saying, making eye contact shouldn't be a problem.

    - *Avoid staring.* You're hoping for a pleasant conversation, so look into the interviewer's eyes in a relaxed manner. Staring can show anxiousness.

- **Posture.** During an interview, you want your posture – the way you are sitting or standing – to show interest but still come off as composed. Here are some tips:

    - *Sit correctly.* Sit up straight during the interview, with your back resting against the back of the chair.

    - *Nod your head.* Nodding at appropriate times is a great way of showing interest in what someone is saying and can also add emphasis to what you are saying.

    - *Do not slouch.* Slouching gives the impression that you are not interested in the job or school and makes you look unprofessional.

    - *Do not cross your arms.* Folding your arms makes you look defensive or angry. Instead, keep your hands clasped together in your lap or on the armrests of the chair you're sitting in.

    - *Don't fidget.* This makes you appear nervous and not confident.

 **More than a Student**

Interviewers not only want to know what you do in class, but what you do outside of class too.

TIPS **Be Friendly**

Always try to smile and make eye contact when interviewing. A smile really can go a mile on the way toward making a strong first impression.

TIPS **The Power of a Thank You Note**

Following the interview, send a handwritten thank you card. This is important and will make you stand out even more.

- **Take notes.** Don't be afraid to take notes during the interview on a notepad or notebook. If the conversation triggers a question you want to ask at the end of the interview, jot it down so you won't forget. Also, don't forget to write down the names of everyone you meet during your interview. This will help you send proper thank you cards following the interview.

- **Be Relaxed.** Just remember you wouldn't have made it this far in the process if the school or job wasn't interested in you. Just relax and show the interviewer who you really are.

- **Be Enthusiastic.** Remember, you want to be a part of this job or school, so show it! Smile and use positive body language to express yourself. Be sure to ask questions at the end of the interview.

- **Be Well-Spoken.** Do not use slang words. Your interviewer doesn't want to hear slang; he or she wants to hear you use the academic language that shows you can speak to clients, managers, professors, and peers. Also, try to avoid verbal ticks when you are talking. A verbal tick is something that you repeat frequently when speaking, such as "like", "um" or "yeah." This can be very distracting in an interview, so think through what you want to say before actually saying it.

After the Interview

Wait for the interviewer's signal to leave. Often your signal will be when the interviewer stands up. Make sure that before you leave you confirm the next steps in the interview process. Thank the interviewer by name for taking the time to meet with you and end with a strong and confident statement. For example, "Mr./Ms., I am ready and excited to be an active part of the incoming class at _____ University. I am confident that I'm ready for the challenge and will not let you down."

Common Interview Questions

Below are common questions employers will ask throughout the interview with tips on ways to craft the right answer. Throughout this section you will find opportunities to practice responding to these questions and exemplar answers to these questions.

What Makes an Exemplar Response to an Interview Question?

When answering a question, follow these general guidelines:

- Explain what you did / what the situation was.
- Explain what you learned from the situation.
- Explain how you plan to use what you learned in the future.

TIPS How to Answer Questions

Always restate the question in your response. For example, if you're asked, "What's your greatest strength?" You should start your reply with: "My greatest strength is..."

Key Point

Interviewers may ask applicants several types of questions, and applicants should be prepared with answers as well as questions of their own.

Personality, Skills and Characteristics		
Question	**Description**	**Example Response**
"Tell me a little bit about yourself."	This is typically one of the first questions interviewers will ask you. They are not looking for your entire life story, so come up with your own personal "brand statement" that explains who you are, your strengths and benefits you can provide their organization. Your response should be 1-3 sentences.	"My entire life, I've known that I wanted to help others who are also in need. I was faced with many challenges growing up, yet still worked diligently to graduate from high school in the top 10% of my class while holding leadership positions in organizations. I am hard-working, persistent, and a team-player who is always striving to improve myself. I am excited to utilize these skills in the _____ position at _____ company/organization in _____ specific ways."
"What are you passionate about?"	This is your opportunity to share what is important to you. It doesn't need to be something related to the company, organization, or school you are interviewing at, but something you truly feel strongly about.	"I am passionate about community service. When I was younger, I enjoyed helping my mom around the house. As I got older I started to volunteer at Habitat for Humanity and truly enjoyed helping build houses for families in need. It is really rewarding to see the impact you can have on others when you take the time to serve."
"What was the last book you read?"	Make sure you have an answer to this question. Your interviewer is looking to see that you have a willingness to learn on your own. Do not pick a book you read for a school assignment.	"The last book I have read was Night by Elie Wiesel. This book really opened my eyes to the inhumane things that happened during the Holocaust. It motivates me to know and understand our world history to help ensure I never contribute to a repeat of those mistakes big or small."
"In a group situation, what role do you typically play?"	Are you the leader? The organizer? The secretary? By answering this question, this gives the interviewer insight into what role you will naturally take at their organization.	"In a group situation, I typically play the role of the organizer. One of my strengths is being able to stay organized and manage my time well, so this allows me to be successful in both completing the task and communicating efficiently with the team. I look forward to working with a team in the _____ position."

"What do you consider to be your strengths and weaknesses?"	This is always one of the easier questions to answer in an interview. When you provide strengths, make sure they relate to what you are applying for. When you provide a weakness, always turn a weakness into a positive characteristic.	*"One of my greatest strengths is my ability to work under a deadline. I do well under the pressure of meeting deadlines on time, and often shoot for reaching the deadline ahead of time. Another strength of mine is time management. In high school, I have been involved in numerous extracurricular activities which have taught me to manage my time so that I can also maintain good grades. One of my weaknesses is that I can be a perfectionist. Over time I have learned to use this to my advantage, because I keep a close focus on details."*

Practice Your Response!

Select a question from those listed previously and practice scripting out your answer on the lines below.

_____

_____

_____

_____

_____

_____

_____

_____

_____

_____

_____

_____

_____

_____

_____

_____

_____

_____

_____

_____

Previous Experience		
Question	**Description**	**Example Response**
"Describe a time when you worked well with others."	The interviewer wants to hear that you can work well with others. Share a specific example that shows you are a "team player."	*"As a member of the Community Service Committee in our school's Student Government, I worked in a team with the six other committee members to plan our annual Spring Break Community Service trip. This required us to work as part of a team to make sure that we planned the project well. Because I have strong organization skills, I helped my team keep track of the various options we discussed in a Word document that included addresses, descriptions, and phone numbers."*
"What extracurricular activities have you been involved in?"	This is your chance to share what you have been involved in outside of the classroom. If you have been involved in multiple clubs and sports, it is okay to reference your résumé, which includes all leadership roles and activities you have been involved in.	*"I am an active member of several extracurricular clubs at my school — all listed on my résumé. One in particular has helped me develop as a learner. In drawing club, I learned it is important to ask for feedback so I can continue to develop my skills to be a better artist."*
"Tell me about some of your past leadership roles."	Begin by briefly explaining the club or organization you have held a leadership role in. Don't assume that your interviewer knows what the organization's acronym stands for. Provide your responsibilities and specific examples of what you were able to accomplish in this role. You can also tell about a skill that you might have improved on while in this role.	*"I am the treasurer of the National Honor Society. My responsibility was to collect membership dues and provide a monthly report to the board about our expenses to ensure we had enough money to follow through with our projects. Last Spring, I was able to convince the board to decrease spending on decorations at our annual Parent-Teacher Dinner, because I learned that many decorations from the year before were reusable, therefore leaving more money for our Service Day activities."*
"What accomplishment are you most proud of?"	Notice the question asked about only one accomplishment. Think of what you are applying for and choose an accomplishment that aligns to the position.	*"My greatest accomplishment was graduating from the top 10% of my senior class of 590 students. It ingrained in me that hard work and goal-setting pays off with the help of mentors along the way."*

Practice Your Response!

Select a question from those listed previously and practice scripting out your answer on the lines below.

_____

_____

_____

_____

_____

_____

_____

_____

_____

_____

Challenges/Obstacles		
Question	**Description**	**Example Response**
"Describe an obstacle and how you overcame it."	This is a question you will find in almost every interview. Be ready to share at least two obstacles/challenges you have worked to overcome. The point of this question is to give the interviewer an insight into how you work through problems. Always include the lesson that overcoming this obstacle has taught you.	*"In National Honor Society, we had planned to hold a fundraising auction to raise money for the women's shelter in our community. Yet, the day of the auction, I realized that the reservation for the caterer had fallen through. After some quick brainstorming with my fellow officers, we came up with a plan. We designated groups within the society to each bring a different dish. We also called a local restaurant, Backyard BBQ, and asked them to bring the meat dishes. Not only did we come up with an alternative plan at the last minute, but we also saved the organization hundreds of dollars, which allowed us to raise more money for the shelter in the end. From this experience, I learned how to be resourceful, creative, and adaptable."*
"How would you resolve conflict in a group situation?"	Interviewers are looking for you to provide one specific example and then walk them through how you solved the conflict. Remember to keep it positive.	*"I tend to be the mediator when there is a conflict in a group situation. I listen to both sides and ensure that everyone's opinion is heard. Then, I work with both sides to come up with some sort of compromise. Regardless of how someone may feel about the decision, I try to make sure that everyone is respected in the discussion."*
"How do you handle stress?"	This is a typical interview question often asked to gain insight on how you manage stress on the job and in your life. Provide a short example about a time you handled stress to help prove you can work in stressful situations or environments.	*"In the past, I have found that I work well under stress and often embrace it because it helps me stay motivated. One way I reduce stress is to run or work out after work or school. I learned it helps clear my mind of unimportant details and refocus the tasks and timeline to complete a project."*

Practice Your Response!

Select a question from those listed previously and practice scripting out your answer on the lines below.

_____

_____

_____

_____

_____

_____

_____

_____

_____

_____

_____

Future, Goals, and the Closing		
Question	**Description**	**Example Response**
"Where do you want to be in five years? Ten years?"	When answering this question, make sure you keep whatever you are interviewing for in mind. If you are interviewing for a college, mention how admisson will help you reach your goal or plan for five (or ten) years down the road. If you are applying for a job, employers don't want to hear that you want to start a family and move – that will not help you.	*"One of the goals I have for myself is to find a company where I can continue to learn and take on additional responsibilities. After I get more experience, I would like to move on from this position to a management position."*
"What can you offer us?"	Make yourself stand out by comparing your goals with those of the organization with whom you are interviewing. Share your past accomplishments and experience, and explain how this will help you succeed in the position."	*"As a Sales Associate, I can bring many of the teamwork skills I've discussed to make sure I work with the other associates to do what's best for customers everyday. I work hard at whatever I do and have learned that asking questions is the best way to learn. I know that if challenges do come up, I have the flexibility and creativity to work with the rest of the team to address them so that we can serve our customers well."*
"Why should we hire you rather than another candidate?"	When asked this question, compare your skills with the responsibilities of the position. Restate your interest in the organization and position and be positive.	*"When I first learned about this position, I thought my experiences as a nursing home volunteer were an excellent match for this position at the Children's Hospital Pediatric Services Internship. I learned from the nurses I worked with at the nursing home how to interact positively with patients and their families and picked up an understanding of proper procedures and protocol. I know I can come into this job with a wealth of experiences already, and I am looking to build on my skillset in the Children's Hospital's supportive setting."*
"Is there anything else I should know about you?"	Don't take this as an open invitation to tell the interviewer everything. If there is something on your résumé or strength of yours you feel like you didn't get the chance to share, here is your chance. Just make sure it can be shared in one to three sentences.	*"I did want to point out that as National Honor Society treasurer, I've built a lot of skills in Microsoft Excel. I know that in this position, we will be looking at information in Excel, and I feel confident in performing a variety of tasks in that program."*
"Do you have any other questions?"	Now it is your turn to ask the questions. Always have at least three prepared.	*"What do you enjoy the most about working with this company/organization?"*

Practice Your Response!

Select a question from those listed previously and practice scripting out your answer on the lines below.

_____

_____

_____

_____

_____

Practice Questions for My Interview

My Turn! Practice My Answers

DIRECTIONS: Read through the questions below. Begin to brainstorm and take notes on the points you would like to make in your responses. Refer back to the exemplar responses written previously to help guide your thoughts.

In order to have the best chance at success, practice answering these questions out loud by yourself, with a partner, and/or in groups before your interview to make sure you are prepared. Use the mock interview template and rubric on the next couple of pages to help prepare.

General
- Tell me a little bit about yourself.
- What are you passionate about?
- What was the last book you read?
- In a group situation, what role do you typically play?
- What do you consider to be your strengths and weaknesses?

Previous Experience
- Describe a time when you worked well with others.
- What extracurricular activities have you been involved in?
- Tell me about some of your past leadership roles.
- What accomplishment are you most proud of?

Challenges/ Obstacles
- Describe an obstacle and how you overcame it.
- How would you resolve conflict in a group situation?
- How do you handle stress?

The Future/ Goals
- Where do you want to be in five years? Ten years?

In Closing
- What can you offer us?
- Why should we hire you rather than another candidate?
- Is there anything else I should know about you?
- Do you have any other questions?

Mock Interview Rubric

My Turn! Practice My Interview Skills

DIRECTIONS: Think of a company or organization you would like to work for in the future and write it in the **company** blank. Next, find a partner and have them write their name in the **interviewer** blank. Write your name in the **interviewee** blank. Give the interviewer your book. Then have your interviewer ask you questions from the previous pages as well as any other questions they would like to ask. Set a time limit of anywhere from 10-30 minutes. The interviewer should take constructive notes throughout the mock interview so you can reference back to them when finished. Finally, at the end of the interview, the interviewer scores your answers to the mock interview on the rubric below. Lastly, switch roles so that you become the interviwer, and write in your partner's book.

	1 Interviewee…	2 Interviewee…	3 Interviewee…
Arrive Early:	…arrived **late**	…arrived **on time**	…arrived **early**
Be Relaxed:	..appeared **nervous** the whole time	…appeared **relaxed some** of the time	…appeared **relaxed** the whole time
Be Enthusiastic:	…**rarely** smiled and used **no** positive body language (arms crossed, frowning, covering mouth with hand, etc.)	…smiled **occasionally** and used **some** positive body language	…**smiled and used positive body language** (facing interviewer, uses hands to explain point, made eye contact, etc.)
Be Well-Spoken:	…uses **numerous** slang words & "verbal ticks" (ex: like, umm, yeah, este, so)	…uses **some** slang words & some "verbal ticks" (ex: like, umm, yeah, este, so)	…uses **no** slang words & "verbal ticks" (ex: like, umm, yeah, este, so)
The Handshake:	…**long (> 3 seconds), limp (like a dead fish)** handshake is given when candidate introduces him/herself	…quick (1-2 seconds), **limp (like a dead fish)** handshake is given when candidate introduces him/herself	…**quick** (1-2 seconds), **firm** (almost hurts hand, but not quite) handshake is given when candidate introduces him/herself
Eye Contact:	…looks **down and away** from interviewer, **rarely** making eye contact	…looks up towards the interviewer, **rarely** making eye contact	…looks up **confidently** at the interviewer, **often** making eye contact
Posture:	…**slouches** in chair, looks down as listening, fidgets hands or feet, & crosses arms	…sits up straight **sometimes, occasionally** nods head as listening, **occasionally** fidgets hands or feet, or crosses arms	…**sits up straight, nods head** in agreement or understanding as listening, does not fidget hands or feet, & keeps arms in open position
Takes notes:	…**forgot** notepad and/or writing utensil, and takes **no** notes or writes **no** questions down	…remembers notepad and writing utensil, and takes **no** notes or writes **no** questions down	… remembers notepad and writing utensil, and **actively takes some notes** or **writes questions down**
Closing:	…leaves too early (**before** interviewer stands or extends handshake) & **forgets to ask questions** or next steps	…leaves **after** interviewer stands or extends handshake, but **forgets to ask questions** or next steps	…leaves **after** interviewer stands or extends handshake, **remembers** to ask questions or next steps

Mock Interview Template

My Turn! Practice My Answers

DIRECTIONS: Utilize the following two pages during your mock interview. The interviewer will write your responses in this template for you to review afterwards. Remember you will only improve with practice!

Mock Interview Sheet

Interviewee: _____

Interviewer: _____

General

- Tell me a little bit about yourself.

  _____
  _____

- What are you passionate about?

  _____
  _____

- What was the last book you read?

  _____
  _____

- In a group situation, what role do you typically play?

  _____
  _____

- What do you consider to be your strengths and weaknesses?

  _____
  _____

Previous Experience

- Describe a time when you worked well with others.

  _____
  _____

- What extracurricular activities have you been involved in?

  _____
  _____

- Tell me about some of your past leadership roles.

  _____

  _____

- What accomplishment are you most proud of?

  _____

  _____

Challenges/ Obstacles

- Describe an obstacle and how you overcame it.

  _____

  _____

- How would you resolve conflict in a group situation?

  _____

  _____

- How do you handle stress?

  _____

  _____

The Future/ Goals

- Where do you want to be in five years? Ten years?

  _____

  _____

In Closing

- What can you offer us?

  _____

  _____

- Why should we hire you rather than another candidate?

  _____

  _____

- Is there anything else I should know about you?

  _____

  _____

- Do you have any other questions?

  _____

  _____

Recommendation Letters and Thank You Notes

What is a Recommendation Letter?

A **recommendation letter** is a letter about you, but not written by you. Instead an adult who knows you well writes it and submits it to the schools that you are applying to. This letter is an extremely important part of getting into a college or university and may also be required for jobs or internships that you apply for.

The letter of recommendation gives schools a chance to determine how other people see you. Given this, a good recommendation letter can really separate you from other students applying to the same school. You want your letter to highlight attributes such as leadership, work experience, academic success, and extracurricular involvement. Make sure that the letter itself is written to match the characteristics the school looks for in applicants. Most importantly, submit the request for your letter in advance in order to give the author plenty of time to work on it; you do not want it to be rushed. Colleges and Universities typically prefer when you waive the right to see the recommendation letter. In waiving the right, the letter becomes confidential and allows the recommender to be completely honest.

Who Should I Ask to Write Me a Recommendation Letter?

You need someone who really knows you and the quality of your potential academic life. This person, usually a teacher, should be able to express clearly your talents, strengths, and perhaps your goals and future possibilities for growth. A wise choice for academic recommendation letters is a teacher who has known you well for over a year and is very familiar with your strong traits as a student, a thinker, and a member of the school community.

Check the instructions on each individual school website to discover how many letters of recommendation you will need, from what sources (such as a core teacher), and what forms you need to download to give to your recommender(s).

What Do I Say to Someone Writing a Recommendation Letter for Me?

Saying "thank you" is an excellent start – whoever is writing the letter for you will appreciate your gratitude and write a better letter as a result.

Once you've decided who's going to write your recommendation letter, make sure you let them know what you're looking for in the letter. Tell them which schools and programs you're applying to and mention which of your attributes and experiences you want them to focus on. Supply your recommenders with your résumé as well as any forms required by the college or university, with your factual information already filled in at the top. If the application requires you to mail the letter, provide the recommender with a stamped and addressed envelope.

Build Relationships!

Start building positive relationships with potential recommenders early. The more genuine and personal your relationship, the better things they'll have to write about you!

Be sure to write your recommender a handwritten thank you card, and keep them updated on your school decisions. They will be more than happy to help again in the future if you are polite and professional.

TIPS Say Thank You!

Send the person who wrote your letter a hand-written thank you card.

What Should a Recommendation Letter Look Like?

A good letter of recommendation should be between 1-2 pages long. It doesn't need to be a 25-page biography, but it should be a thorough, detailed letter that explains why you would be a good fit for the school you're applying to.

There should be an opening paragraph, about 3-4 body paragraphs discussing your academic talents and successes, your contributions and leadership, your ability to work hard, and your good character, then a closing paragraph.

My Turn! Brainstorm Recommenders

DIRECTIONS: Who could write a recommendation letter for you? Remember, you want to ask someone who can speak very highly on your behalf. Write down at least three people who come to mind to start the wheels turning on this very important part of the process!

Who Would Recommend Me?

Name of Person, Title	Relationship to You	What Would They Say?
1. Mr. Rodriguez, Former Head Soccer Coach	Coached me in soccer for three years	I'm a strong leader and team player
2.		
3.		
4.		
5.		

TIPS Rec Letters for Jobs

If you are requesting a recommendation letter for a job, not for acceptance to a college or university, most of these facts still apply. However, in that case, your recommenders can be people other than teachers such as previous bosses, coaches, city officials, and principals to name a few.

Unit 3: Practice Professionalism

My Turn! Recommendation Reflections

DIRECTIONS: Write your responses to each question in the box below it.

What do you think your teachers, or employers, would say about you in a recommendation letter?

Are you happy with that response? Why or why not?

If you aren't sure that there are any adults you could ask who would know you well enough to have positive things to write in a letter of recommendation, what can you start doing now to change this? Are there adults who you would like to have a better relationship with? What steps could you take to grow a relationship with them?doing now to build more positive relationships with adults?

If you think you would have a great recommendation letter, what are you doing to help build those positive relationships?

Writing a Thank You Note

One of the most under-appreciated, and often neglected, aspects of professionalism is the simple exercise of saying "thank you" and sending thank you notes to people who deserve to hear it. Some people believe that sending thank you notes is old fashioned, but they can do wonders. It shows the person you are sending the note to how truly grateful you are for their help.

The best news? Writing a genuine thank you note is not hard to do! Follow these simple steps and you'll be sure to send a great message every time!

1. **Address Your Note** – "Dear _____,"

2. **Start With the Message** – Start off by thanking them right away.

3. **Be Specific** – Add concrete details of how their contributions helped you out.

4. **Be Genuine** – Write from the heart, both honestly and sincerely. Remember to keep the card about them.

5. **Sign Off** – Phrases such as "Sincerely," or even just "Thank you," are always a safe choice.

TIPS A Special "Thank You"

Write your notes on card stock or stationery. This little effort helps a ton!

My Turn! Practice Writing a Thank You Note

DIRECTIONS: Let's practice writing a thank you note! In the space below you will find an example thank you note from a student, Alex, to her teacher Ms. Fadley. Please read that note and try and write an even better note on the blank lines below to someone who has impacted your life in a way you're thankful for. The only requirement regarding who you write your letter to is that he or she needs to be an adult. After you're finished, cut out the card and deliver it to the recipient.

TIPS Stationery

In the future, write thank you notes on stationery or cardstock (aka: nice paper).

Dear Ms. Fadley,

Thank you so much for writing a college recommendation letter for me. Your words and confidence in me continue to be encouraging as I complete the application process. I hope to one day join you as a "Horned-Frog" alum of TCU. Again, thank you so much for your help. You will be the first to know when I hear back!

Sincerely,
Alex

CUT HERE

- -

Thank You!

_____

_____

_____

_____

_____

_____

_____

_____

_____

Notes

UNIT 3 Summary: Practice Professionalism

It is not always easy to stand out in a crowd, but the actions you take as a middle and/or high school student can separate you from the pack. You must be active in your community and participate in school clubs and/or activities to build your résumé. You must take challenging courses, do well academically, and develop good study habits in order to increase your GPA. Always speak and dress professionally and positively represent yourself online because first impressions are extremely important. Do not forget to send a thoughtful thank you note to the individuals who interviewed you as well as those who provided any assistance during the application process. Success does not happen by accident! You must be focused, motivated, and work hard. Don't settle for good enough; always strive to be the best!

My Turn! 3-2-1... Practice Professionalism!

List THREE things YOU should do in an interview to make a good impression:

-
-
-

List TWO things you should be mindful about when using social media:

-
-

List ONE action you will take this school year to enhance your résumé:

-

UNIT 4
EXPLORE CAREER PATHS

DIRECTIONS: In reflection of the information you learned in this unit, draw an emoji of how you feel now.

DIRECTIONS: Read the topics of this unit on the roadmap. Draw an "emoji" of your emotions about this content as you start the unit.

What is a major? How should I choose the major and career for me?

What are my options after high school?

What makes each type of school different?

Associate's Degree	Dissertation	Online Courses	Resident (In-State Tuition)
Bachelor's Degree	Doctoral Degree	Out-of-State Tuition	Soft Skills
Career Aptitude Test	In-State Tuition	Non-Resident (Out-of-State Tuition)	Trade School
College	Graduate Student/ School	Postgraduate	Undergraduate
Community/ Junior College	Major	Private College/ University	University
Credit Hour	Master's Degree	Public College/ University	
Degree	Minor		

DIRECTIONS: In the space below, select several unfamiliar words from the vocabulary word bank. Then, define each word using the glossary or a dictionary. Last, create an original sentence for each of the selected words.

Vocabulary Word	Definition	Your Original Sentence

Options After High School

You have heard about the power of reaching higher levels of education after graduating from high school. There are a variety of options to choose from – it's a matter of selecting one that will help you explore and achieve your career goals.

Imagine a forest with a variety of trees. The different types of trees represent the different types of schools you can attend to further your education – each one has different characteristics that make it unique.

College/University   **Community College**   **Trade/Vocational School**

(ABC) College

An institution of higher education that gives out degrees and certificates. The term is also used to refer to the different parts of a large university such as the College of Education or the College of Engineering.

You will often hear the words "college" and "university" used interchangeably. There's a difference between the two terms. Imagine a very large tree full of branches and leaves. A **university** is a large institution with many **colleges** inside of it – just as a large tree has many branches.

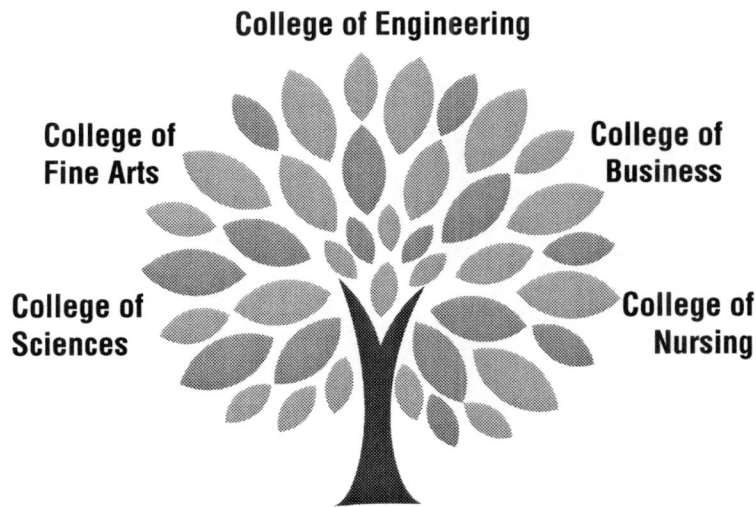

College of Engineering

College of Fine Arts

College of Business

College of Sciences

College of Nursing

The University of Texas

(GO!) *Remember to go talk to your guidance counselor to gather more information.*

In the following pages, you will explore the variety of paths you can take after high school. At times, having so many options can be intimidating. That's okay; the variety of choices is a good thing. Without a doubt, there's a post-secondary option for everyone to find success and realize their dreams.

The University of Texas   **Austin College**   **ITT Technical Institute**   **Brookhaven College**   **Stanford University**

Even if you do not think you will attend college at this point in your life, it is important to note that almost every career you want to pursue will require at least a high school diploma. However, please consider that having only a high school diploma* will put you at the "bottom of the ranks" in these career fields, so a college education is still recommended. Some examples are listed below.

Joining the Military or Armed Forces

Divisions of the military include the Army, Navy, Air Force and Marines. After you turn 18, you can join the military if that is the career path you choose. If you are considering joining the military straight out of high school because you cannot afford college, there is a great option for you. The Registered Officer Training Program, or ROTC, is a tuition program in which the military pays your way through college. In return, you will be required to do limited military service while you are receiving your college education as well as full-time service for a predetermined amount of time post-college graduation. Even if you do not join ROTC while in school, as an active duty soldier/marine/sailor/airman or veteran, you have access to a G.I. bill to get free college credit.

Becoming a Public Service Worker:

Police officers, paramedics, emergency medical technicians, and firefighters are some examples of public service workers. The kind of education and training necessary to pursue a career in the public service field varies depending on which position you are interested in. Some of the careers require completion of a college degree, while others may require only a high school diploma followed by a specialized training academy. However, if this is a field that interests you, speak with your guidance counselor or contact public service agencies to inquire about their application process and their requirements beyond high school graduation.

*Disclaimer: *You may have heard of a GED, or General Education Diploma, which is a group of tests that students who do not finish high school can take. It is not recognized as a high school diploma by most colleges and universities and will lead to lower status employment opportunities (if any at all) in the fields listed above. However, with a GED, there are stronger employment and education opportunities than without the high school diploma.*

Four-Year Schools and Other Options

Traditional Four-Year Schools

- **Public College/University**— Public universities such as the University of Arizona, the University of Colorado, or Texas A&M University are schools that receive public money. These schools are labeled public because the state and local government pay for part of their budget. If you attend one of these schools in your home state, assuming you have been a **resident** to that state for several years prior to applying to college, you are usually eligible for "in-state tuition," meaning you get to pay less to go to school. If you choose to go to a public university outside of your home state, you will likely pay "out-of-state tuition," since you will be considered a **non-resident**, which can cost just as much as the most expensive schools in the country. The quality of public universities can be as strong as private schools and offer nearly every major a student could desire. In terms of size, public schools are generally the largest in the country. They often have over 15,000 students and some approach close to 100,000. As a result, some classes can be very large (with over 300 students) and taught by graduate assistants rather than professors.

- **Private College/University**— Private universities such as Baylor, Vanderbilt, and Vassar College charge more because they rely on tuition and fees from their students to pay for many of their expenses. Private schools are also usually more prestigious, more selective, and also have smaller student populations compared to public schools. While the higher price tags can be discouraging, private colleges often offer very generous scholarships. For example, 23% of students attending Vassar College are recipients of the Pell Grant making attendance more affordable for low-income students. Many students believe the more personalized attention they receive makes these schools well worth the additional cost.

Unique Four-Year Schools

- **Minority-Serving Institutions (MSI)** - Minority Serving Institutions are colleges/universities that focus on serving historically underrepresented students of color by offering an environment rich in tradition and pride, cultural immersion opportunities, and unique support for first generation college students. They do so with diverse faculties & staff and by providing opportunities that significantly enhance student learning and leadership skills. Today, MSIs continue to demonstrate their value by boasting high graduation rates and awarding a high number of degrees in the STEM field to students of color. Some well-known examples are Spelman College, Howard University, and The University of Texas at El Paso.

  These institutions are known as:

  - Historically Black Colleges and Universities (HBCUs)
  - Hispanic-Serving Institutions (HSIs)
  - Tribal College or Universities (TCUs)
  - Asian American and Native American Pacific Islander-Serving Institutions (AANAPISIs)

ABC) In-State Tuition

A student who meets residency requirements, usually meaning they have lived in the same state as the college or university they are planning to attend to for several years prior to enrolling, will pay a lower tuition rate than those who are from other states.

Key Point

Public and private colleges have different funding structures and often differ in tuition and size.

ABC) Out-of-State Tuition

Out-of-state tuition applies to students who are applying for a college or university that are not located in their home state and typically have to pay more to attend school there.

Key Point

Large public universities tend to offer more majors and degree options than smaller universities.

- Alaska Native-Serving Institutions
- Native Hawaiian-Serving Institutions
- Predominantly Black Institutions
- Native American-Serving Nontribal Institutions

Each type of MSI can vary in cost, size, selectivity, and number of majors offered. Students are offered the same types of financial aid as traditional four-year schools. An applicant is not required to be a part of or identify with a specific ethnicity/race to apply.

- **The Ivy League**— The Ivy League is perhaps the most famous group of private schools in America, if not the world. The eight schools in the Ivy League are Brown University, Columbia University, Cornell University, Dartmouth College, Harvard University, Princeton University, the University of Pennsylvania, and Yale University. While many schools compete with the Ivy League in some programs, these institutions are widely considered to be the strongest schools in the country. However, these schools typically have the highest tuition rates. Most ivy leagues have need-based and need-blind financial aid. If students from low-wealth households are admitted into these schools, the university offers 100% of the difference between what tuition and fees are and what the FAFSA says that their family can afford to pay.

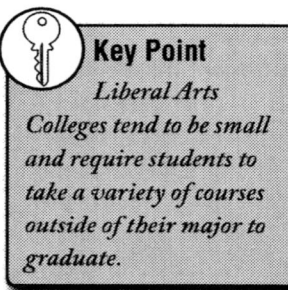

Key Point

Liberal Arts Colleges tend to be small and require students to take a variety of courses outside of their major to graduate.

- **Liberal Arts Schools**— Liberal Arts schools are the exception to the naming rule when it comes to "colleges" and "universities." Often the word "college" is in the name, but liberal arts colleges function as a university would, having colleges within the umbrella college. The vast majority of the time, they are privately funded. Some well known Liberal arts schools are Occidental College and Whittier College. These are smaller schools, usually under 5,000 students in total. One nice benefit of this is that classes tend to be small and personal, unlike some larger universities. Liberal arts schools offer a broad range of courses in the humanities (English, History, etc.), social sciences and sciences. However, highly specialized degrees may not be offered at a smaller liberal arts college, so always check which degrees are available before enrolling.

My Turn! Traditional Four-Year Schools

DIRECTIONS: Fill in the blanks in this chart below. Use the content on the previous page to locate the missing information.

Type of School	Are many or few majors offered?	What is the selectivity? (highly selective, selective, moderately selective, open)	Would you need to travel far for this type of school?	What generally is the size of this type of school?	Generally, what is the cost of this type of school?	Is this a fit for you? Yes or no?
Public School	Many majors	Varies, generally selective	Varies			
Private School	Many majors		Varies			
Ivy League	Many majors		Varies	10,000 or less		
Liberal Arts Schools		Varies	Varies		Moderately expensive	
Minority Serving Institutions	Many majors		Varies			

Other Options

Up to this point, the types of colleges described have all been four year schools that culminate in students receiving a Bachelor's Degree. While the majority of college students start out in one of these collegiate settings, not every successful person has followed this path. In the lists below, you will find some solid choices that can be used as a stepping-stone into a traditional four-year university setting or, with hard work and commitment, a reliable career.

- **Community or Junior Colleges**— These schools offer technical programs that prepare students for careers in a wide variety of fields and provide students with the foundational knowledge they may have missed in high school to be successful in a traditional school setting. Tuition prices in these settings are also usually lower. After two years, students can graduate with special certificates, diplomas, or associate's degrees with access to jobs such as becoming a paralegal, dental hygienist, or broadcast technician among others.

- **Trade Schools (Also called Vocational or Technical Schools)**— Trade, vocational, or technical schools are where you go to learn a set of specific skills and knowledge related to a particular job or career field. In these schools, you learn hands on skills, become an apprentice, and/or shadow a professional,

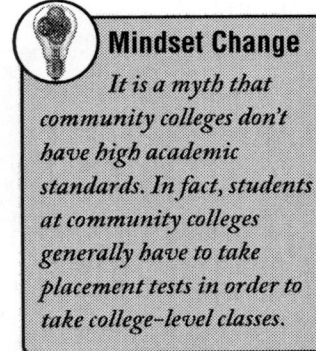

Mindset Change

It is a myth that community colleges don't have high academic standards. In fact, students at community colleges generally have to take placement tests in order to take college-level classes.

in that specific field. These schools are intended to lead to immediate employment upon graduation. Examples of jobs after trade school include; cosmetologist (beautician), plumber, air traffic controller, dental assistant, barber, culinary artist, carpenter, welder, as well as many more. While you will have less flexibility to enter fields unrelated to your school's expertise, many people find this option to lead to comfortable lives and careers they enjoy.

If you are interested in this type of education, begin the process by talking to your guidance or career counselor. Some high schools have specific trade academies that offer specialized elective courses for students to explore. Consider these schools when you are choosing your high school. Some academies prepare students to complete a certification or license in their field by the time they graduate high school. Additionally, ask if your school has a job-shadowing program where you can spend a day (or part of a day) with someone in a career field that matches your interests.

- **Online Options**— Two options exist for students who would like to attend school online while working full time. First, many traditional schools offer excellent **online courses** that allow you to engage with the same professors and receive the same degree as traditional universities. Second, some schools completely exist online. But be careful! The credibility of degrees issued by these solely online schools can be questionable. As with any college choice, research before enrolling!

TIPS **Transferring**

*Many students start out their college career at Community or Junior Colleges and then **transfer** to traditional four-year schools. This allows them to save money on tuition during their early years. But, keep in mind, if you do choose to transfer, you will want to make sure as many of your college credits as possible transfer with you. Otherwise, you may be forced to take classes over again.*

My Turn! Other Options

DIRECTIONS: Fill in the blanks in this chart below. Use the content above to locate the missing information.

Type of School	Are many or few majors offered?	What is the selectivity?	Would you need to travel far for this type of school?	What generally is the size of this type of school?	Generally, what is the cost of this type of school?	Is this a fit for you? Yes or no?
Community College/ Junior College		Open	No	Small		
Trade School (Vocational/ Technical School)	Few	Open	No	Small		
Online Schools	Many	Varies	No	N/A	Varies	

My Turn! Charting Post-Secondary Options

DIRECTIONS: In the circles below, write a short phrase to describe the schooling option mentioned. Use the previous pages about post-secondary options to help make your selections. After filling in all of the outside circles, answer the questions below.

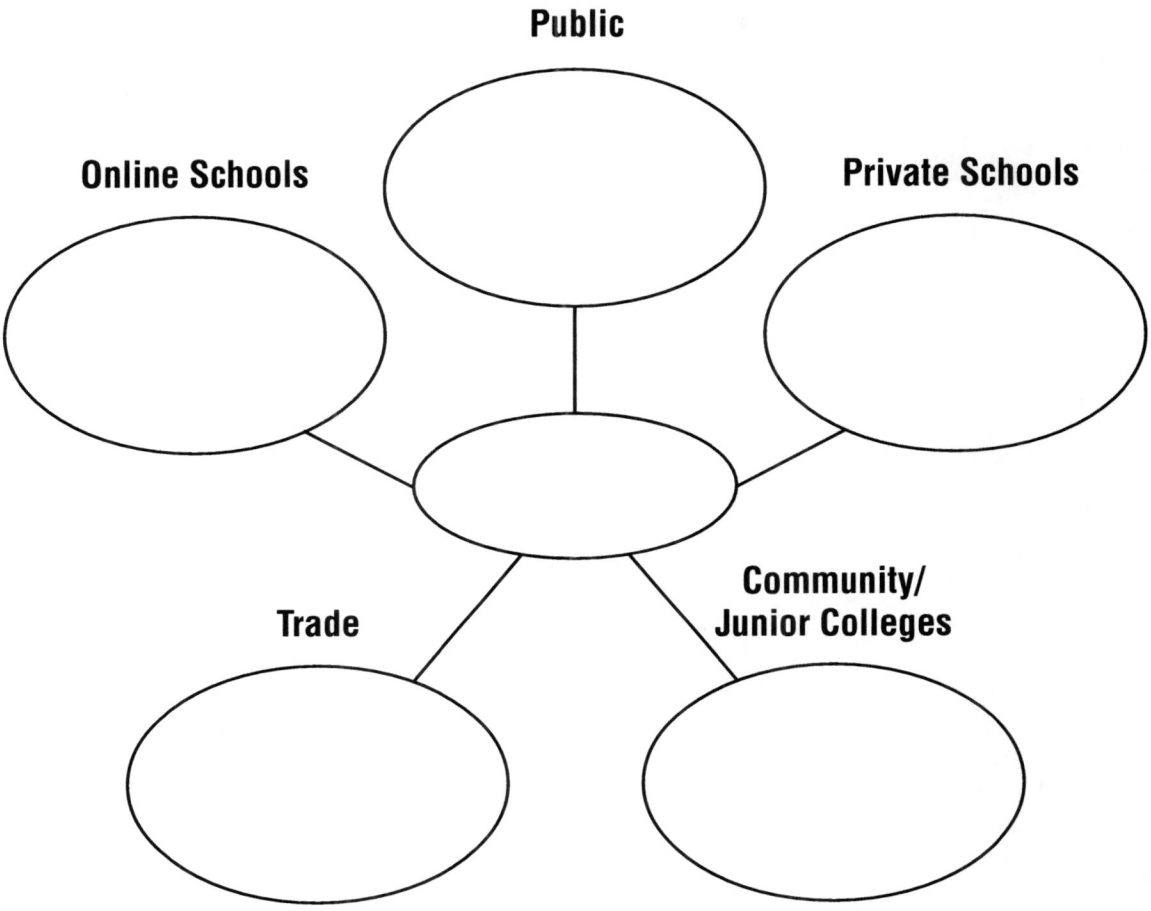

Public

Online Schools

Private Schools

Trade

Community/
Junior Colleges

1. Based on the information in the graphic organizer, what do you think is the best title to go in the center? Please write your answer in the central circle.

2. Which option written above is the most appealing to you?

   _____

3. Why is this option appealing to you?

   _____
   _____
   _____

4. How do you feel about this option? (Circle all that apply)

   Intimidated   Excited   Seems too easy   Not sure what it takes

Notes

Why Go To College

Now that you know there are multiple options for your future in education, get excited for the possibilities! Setting goals is an important part of your journey. Knowing the direction you're headed and why you're heading there will help guide you along the way. Similar to how a map guides you to your destination.

MY Turn! Set Goals for Your Education

PART 1 DIRECTIONS: STEP 1: Fill in the center box of the chart with one reason why YOU want to go to school. **STEP 2:** Fill in the other boxes with reasons other people want to go to college, or other reasons you have besides the one you wrote in the center.

	I want to continue my education because...	

PART 2 DIRECTIONS: Making the decision to continue your education beyond high school is a big deal! A group of adults who attended college mentioned these reasons for why they attended school now that they are finished and have a career. Circle the one that resonates with you the most.

I attended college to...

    Gain Independence   **Develop Myself Personally**

    Create Social Connections   **Gain Knowledge to Pursue My Passions**

Using the statement you wrote in the chart above and the phrase you circled, write a 1 sentence goal explaining your reasons for continuing your education past high school.

Example: I want to go to college to gain knowledge about the education field and learn how I can contribute to the future generations of students in my community as an educator.

_____

_____

_____

_____

Before starting the college application process, you need to figure out which type of degree you are interested in. There are five main types of **degrees**:

Associate's Degree/Technical Training
(Approximate Median Salary: $41,000)

This degree requires about 60 **credit hours,** or 2 years. If you were going to attend a community or junior college, this is the type of degree you would receive. Some examples of careers that require an associate's degree or technical training are: plumber, beautician, sound engineer and mechanic. In many cases, the class credits you earn as part of an associate's degree can also be applied towards a bachelor's degree (see below). Because of this, many students who complete an associate's degree program transfer into a bachelor's degree program, which is recommended.

Bachelor's Degree
(Approximate Median Salary: $57,000)

The **bachelor's degree**, also known as an **undergraduate** degree, is the most popular of all degree programs. When people say "I'm going to college," this is the degree they are probably going to earn. Students who receive a bachelor's degree must complete around 120 credit hours, or about 4 years. Students pursuing professions ranging from business administration, to computer services, to journalism, to education as well as most other careers need this degree.

- **Bachelor of Science vs. Bachelor of Arts: What's the Difference?**
  Most colleges offer both Bachelor of Science (B.S.) and Bachelor of Arts (B.A.) degree programs. The differences between the two vary from school to school. For a general comparison of the degrees, see the table below.

Bachelor of Science	Bachelor of Arts
• Specialized	• Academic and Research Focused, General
• Labs, Hands-on Practice, Experience Based Learning	• Theory, Reading, Writing
• Focus on Math and Science	• Focus on Arts and Humanities
• Requires More Classes in the Major, Less Classes in Electives	• Requires Less Classes in the Major, More time for Electives, Double Majors/Minors

Note: Some colleges offer both options while others only offer one.

- Universities usually offer either a B.A. or a B.S. for a particular major. Sometimes, a student can decide on a major, then choose the track that they prefer. The B.A. track will provide more freedom to take electives and students will receive a broader education on the subject. A B.S. track will, on the other hand, provide a more technical education on the subject.

My Turn! Bachelor's of Arts or Science?

DIRECTIONS: Below are two brief descriptions about two college students, Paris and Andy, and their academic interests. In the space provided, please write whether you believe they are most likely on track to receive a B.A. or a B.S. based on the descriptions of their coursework.

1. Paris wants to pursue a degree in physics. She is particularly interested in the physics of sound and how humans interpret sound. Based on this, would Student A more likely attain a Bachelor's of Arts or a Bachelor's of Science?

   _____

2. Andy is an award winning violinist and is also interested in music history. She is hoping to be a music teacher one day and to write a book on her favorite musician. Based on this, would Student B more likely attain a Bachelor's of Arts or a Bachelor's of Science? _____

> **(ABC) Graduate School/ Student**
>
> *Colleges and universities around the country offer graduate programs for students who want to study a subject area in further depth beyond their undergraduate studies. A student who is enrolled in this type of a program is described as a graduate student.*

Graduate Degrees

Master's Degree
(Approximate Median Salary: $69,000)

Before you earn a master's degree, you need to earn a bachelor's degree. **Master's degrees** typically take one to two years to obtain, and require the completion of a thesis. The master's degree allows students to go more in depth in a specific area of study such as business, science, history, etc. Having this type of degree makes you much more attractive to potential employers because it shows you have a deeper knowledge of a certain subject area.

> **🔑 Key Point**
>
> *A Master's degree (1-2 years), Doctoral degree (3-5+ years) and Professional degrees (1-4+ years) are the three types of graduate degrees earned following the completion of your Bachelor's degree.*

Doctoral Degree
(Approximate Median Salary: $83,000)

Before you earn a doctoral degree in an academic field such as psychology (also known as a PhD), you need to earn a bachelor's degree and (usually) a master's degree. A **doctoral degree** is considered to be the highest level of degree a person can earn. Typically, it takes about five years to complete a doctoral degree. In order to receive this degree, students must write a publishable **dissertation** (see glossary), complete their own original research, and complete a course of study. Doctoral degrees usually lead to jobs as university professors, public policy experts, psychologists, and science researchers.

My Turn! Which Degree is for Me?

DIRECTIONS: In the space below, please write at least two complete sentences answering this question: "which type of degree do you want to pursue and why?"

_____

_____

_____

Professional School and Postgraduate Programs

(ABC) Postgraduate = After College

The phrase "postgraduate" literally means post(after) graduating from college. Every lawyer, doctor, and specialized professional had to earn their bachelor's degree first.

Have you ever dreamed of becoming an architect, a doctor, a dentist, or maybe a lawyer? Even though this decision is a long time away, it is important to understand the steps you must take to enter certain professions. First, before you can attend any sort of professional school in the United States, you have to get your bachelor's degree. This is why it is called a **postgraduate** program; you start it after you have graduated from college with a bachelor's degree. Once you have earned your bachelor's degree, or you are on track to complete it, you can begin to research and apply to professional schools. Professional schools are designed to prepare you for a career in a specific field such as law or medicine. Keep in mind that requirements for professional schools vary from country to country, and not every school is the same. Below, you will find examples of three of the most common postgraduate programs, but remember that there are many other postgraduate programs available.

(TIPS) Step by Step

Once you have earned your bachelor's degree... you can begin to research and apply to professional schools.

Becoming a Lawyer

Law School is a postgraduate program that typically lasts 3 years. In order to apply to law school, a prospective student must take the Law School Admissions Test (LSAT), maintain a high GPA throughout college, and have a minimum four-year bachelor's degree in any major. Once you complete law school, you will earn a Juris Doctor (J.D.). Law degree.

Becoming a Doctor

Mindset Change

"If I'm a 'Pre-Med' Major doesn't that mean that I'm already in medical school?"

This can be confusing, but the answer is actually no. Being a pre-med major in college is not the same thing as going to medical school.

Medical school applicants must complete several prerequisite (required) courses as an undergraduate. Your college will be able to tell you which specific courses you need to take. Prospective students must also take the Medical College Admissions Test (MCAT) and maintain a high GPA throughout college. The standard curriculum for medical school is 4 years long including classes, rotations with patients, and clinical settings. After completing the 4-year program, students earn their Doctor of Medicine (M.D.) or a Doctor of Osteopathic Medicine (D.O.). Next is optional residency training, which is a supervised training period of three to seven years that prepares medical students for specific specialty areas. Becoming a doctor is not easy, but can be accomplished in the long run if you work hard in science courses and you are willing to go to school for a total of seven years or more.

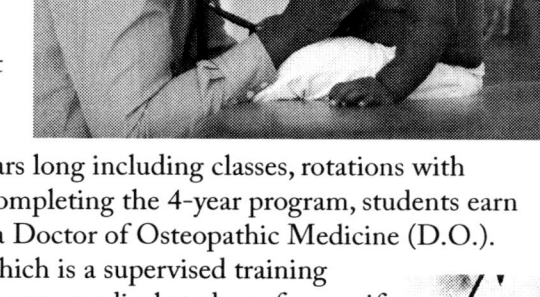

Becoming a Veterinarian

In the United States, a general veterinarian program takes approximately four years to complete. This is also a postgraduate program that students apply to after they earn their bachelor's degree and have taken the appropriate science-oriented classes. After completing the program, students earn a Doctor of Veterinary Medicine (DVM), or a similar degree and are able to practice medicine on animals.

Education Pays, Continued

The Trend Between Level of Education and Level of Earnings

As you already know, the level of education that you attain will impact your yearly salary. In a recent study by the National Center for Education Statistics, they found the data in the table to the right.

Level of Education Completed	Approximate Median Salary in 2014
Less than high school completion	$25,000
High School diploma or equivalent	$35,000
Associate's Degree or trade certificate	$41,000
Bachelor's Degree	$57,000
Master's Degree	$69,000
Doctoral Degree	

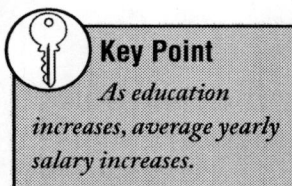

Key Point

As education increases, average yearly salary increases.

My Turn! How Much Does Education Pay?

DIRECTIONS: Using the information in the table, complete the bar graph below. Assuming that the trend will continue, make an educated guess for the median earnings of someone with a Doctoral Degree. Insert your guess into the table above and into your bar graph. Once done, answer the question below.

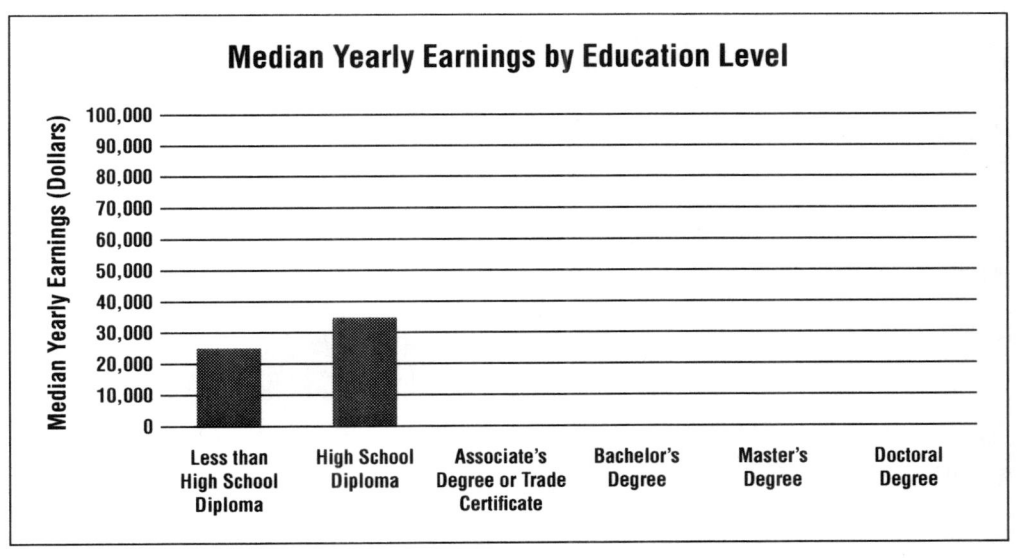

In at least three complete sentences explain the relationship between educational attainment (the highest degree someone earns) and median yearly income.

_____

_____

_____

_____

The Power of Money Over Time

The power of reaching higher levels of education, and making more money, actually increases over time. Take a look at the graph below.

According to this graphic, individuals who obtain a Bachelor's Degree make more than twice (2x) the amount of money that someone with only a high school diploma makes each year. Those workers with an Advanced Degree make roughly three times (3x) the money than workers with only a high school diploma.

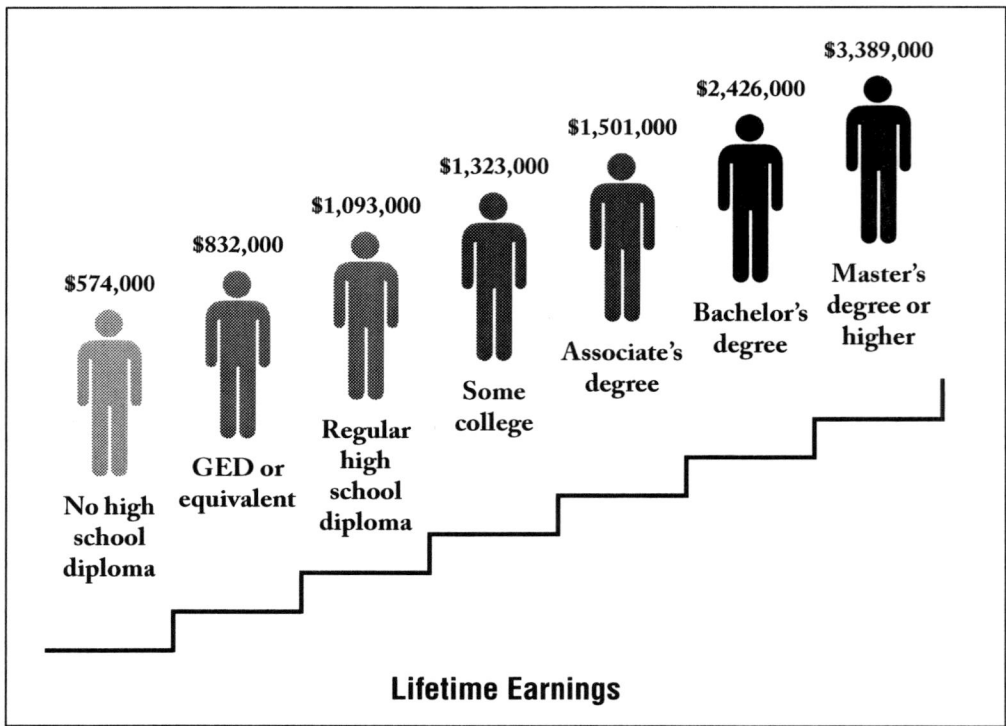

Surn, A., & Khatiwada, I. (2012, November). *High school dropouts in Chicago and Illinois and their persistent labor market problems*. Chicago: Center for Labor Market Studies, Northeastern University. Reflects 18 to 64 year olds.

My Turn! Time to Crunch Some Numbers

DIRECTIONS: The power of money over time can be a tricky concept to completely understand at first glance. To practice, complete the table below and watch how the gap in the total amount of money each worker earns can widen over as short as four years!

Do the Math!	Total Earned After Year 1	Total Earned After Year 2	Total Earned After Year 3	Total Earned After Year 4
High School Dominick	$34,000 (Actual Salary)	$68,000 (=Year 1 Salary x 2)	(=Year 1 Salary x 3)	(=Year 1 Salary x 4)
Bachelors Degree Sean	$51,000 (=$34,000 x 1.5)	(=Year 1 Salary x 2)	(=Year 1 Salary x 3)	(=Year 1 Salary x 4)
Advanced Degree Teresa	$102,000 (=$34,000 x 3)	(=Year 1 Salary x 2)	(=Year 1 Salary x 3)	(=Year 1 Salary x 4)

Comparing Unemployment Rates to Weekly Earnings Based on Level of Education, 2015

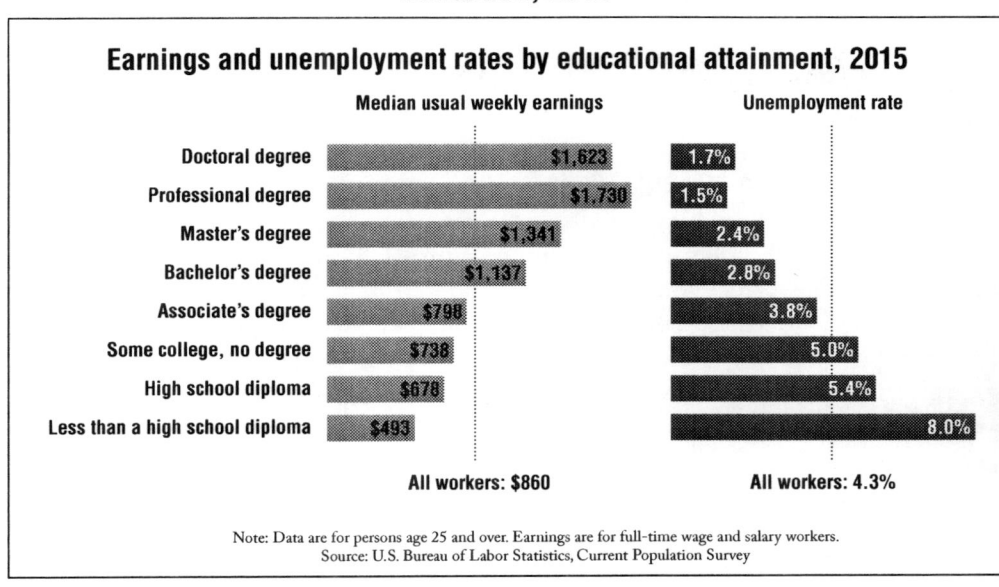

Earnings and unemployment rates by educational attainment, 2015

	Median usual weekly earnings	Unemployment rate
Doctoral degree	$1,623	1.7%
Professional degree	$1,730	1.5%
Master's degree	$1,341	2.4%
Bachelor's degree	$1,137	2.8%
Associate's degree	$798	3.8%
Some college, no degree	$738	5.0%
High school diploma	$678	5.4%
Less than a high school diploma	$493	8.0%
	All workers: $860	All workers: 4.3%

Note: Data are for persons age 25 and over. Earnings are for full-time wage and salary workers.
Source: U.S. Bureau of Labor Statistics, Current Population Survey

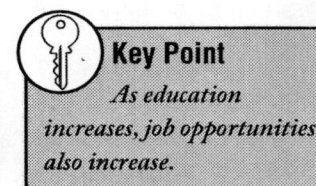

Key Point

As education increases, job opportunities also increase.

My Turn! Does Education Keep Me Employed?

DIRECTIONS: Use the chart and the table above to answer the three questions below.

1. What trend do you notice in this graph? _____
_____
_____

2. Explain the relationship between the level of education someone receives and their chances of being unemployed. _____
_____
_____
_____

3. Explain the relationship between the level of education someone receives and their average weekly earnings. _____
_____
_____
_____

Choosing a Major

(ABC) Major

A major is a student's area of study in college and is the degree a student earns upon graduation.

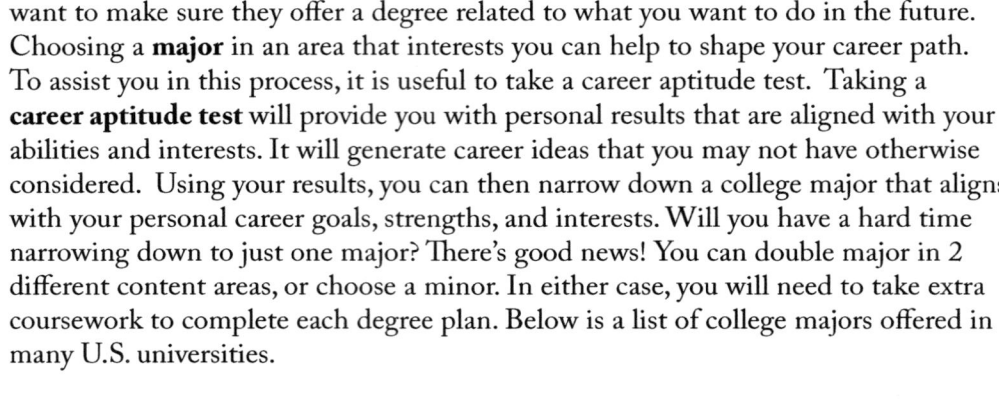

Mindset Change

"Can't I take whatever classes I want to when I get to college?" While it is true that you have a lot more flexibility over your course selection in college, many colleges will ask you to take a placement exam in core subject areas. These tests will determine your class schedule, particularly over your first two years.

GO! Take a Career Aptitude Test!

Having a hard time choosing? Are you scared of picking the "wrong" major?

Take a career aptitude test! While the science behind them is not perfect, they can help focus your selection on a major or career that could be the best fit for you. And remember, no matter what the results, you still have all the power in choosing what you end up doing.

Before making a final decision on the college or university you will attend, you want to make sure they offer a degree related to what you want to do in the future. Choosing a **major** in an area that interests you can help to shape your career path. To assist you in this process, it is useful to take a career aptitude test. Taking a **career aptitude test** will provide you with personal results that are aligned with your abilities and interests. It will generate career ideas that you may not have otherwise considered. Using your results, you can then narrow down a college major that aligns with your personal career goals, strengths, and interests. Will you have a hard time narrowing down to just one major? There's good news! You can double major in 2 different content areas, or choose a minor. In either case, you will need to take extra coursework to complete each degree plan. Below is a list of college majors offered in many U.S. universities.

My Turn! What Majors Interest Me?

DIRECTIONS: Flip through the following pages that list nearly every major offered at universities in the United States. After you've glanced around, go back once more and circle any major that interests you and/or you believe can help you reach your future goals and aspirations. If you have never heard of a major, do not be afraid to ask or look it up yourself. When you're finished, answer the questions at the end of this list.

Agriculture, Food, and Natural Resources

Agricultural Business and Management

Agricultural Economics

Agricultural Journalism

Agricultural Mechanization

Agricultural Technology Management

Agriculture

Agronomy and Crop Science

Floriculture

Forestry

Horticulture

Livestock Management

Natural Resource Conservation

Soil Science

Wildlife Management

Arts and Science

Adult Developing and Aging

African Studies

African-American Studies

American History

American Literature

American Sign Language

Ancient Studies

Anthropology

Applied Mathematics

Applied Physics

Aquatic Biology

Asian-American Studies

Astronomy

Astrophysics

Biblical Studies

Biochemistry

Bioethics

Biology

Biopsychology

Botany/Plant Biology

Cell Biology

Chemical Physics

Chemistry

Child Care and Development

Arts and Science Continued...

Chinese
Comparative Literature
Counseling
Creative Writing
Criminal Justice
Developmental Psychology
East Asian Studies
Educational Psychology
English
English Composition
English Literature
Environmental Science
Ethnic Studies
French
Genetics
Geography
Geology
Geophysics
German
Government
Graphic Design
Hebrew
Hindi
Hispanic-American Studies
History
Industrial Psychology
Islamic Studies
Italian
Japanese

Jewish Studies
Journalism
Korean
Land Use Planning and Management
Latin American Studies
Linguistics
Marine Biology
Marine Science
Materials Science
Mathematics
Microbiology
Military Science
Molecular Biology
Molecular Genetics
Native American Studies
Neurobiology
Neuroscience
Oceanography
Optical Sciences
Paleontology
Pastoral Studies
Pathology
Philosophy
Photojournalism
Physiological Psychology
Planetary Science
Playwriting and Screenwriting
Political Science

Portuguese
Pre-Law
Psychology
Rehabilitation Counseling
Religious Studies
Romance Languages
Rural Sociology
Social Psychology
Social Work
Sociology
Southeast Asian Studies
Spanish
Speech Pathology
Sport and Leisure Studies
Surveying
Technical Writing
Theology
Urban Planning
Urban Studies

ABC Capped Majors
Some majors are "capped," meaning the school will only admit a certain number of students into the program each year because they are so competitive. Talk to an admissions officer or search online so you can plan ahead.

GO! *Remember to go talk to your guidance counselor to gather more information.*

Key Point
Not all colleges offer all majors.

Business

Accounting
Actuarial Science
Advertising
Business Administration
Communications Studies
Digital Communications and Multimedia
Economics
Entrepreneurship
Ethics
Finance

Hospitality
Human Resource Management
Industrial Management
International Business
Management Information Systems
Managerial Economics
Marketing
Master of Business Administration
Merchandising and Buying Operations

Operations Management
Organizational Behavior Studies
Public Administration
Public Policy Analysis
Public Relations
Radio and Television
Risk Management
Sports Management
Statistics

ABC Minor
You can also receive a minor in most subjects, which requires less credit hours and is a great addition to your résumé.

Computers

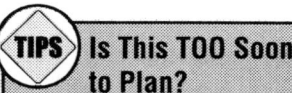

Key Point

It is important to research colleges and universities to make sure they offer the major you are interested in.

Animation

Artificial Intelligence and Robotics

Computer and Information Science

Computer Graphics

Computer Systems Analysis

Gaming

Graphic Communications

Graphic Design

Network Design and Administration

Web Design

Webmaster and Web Management

Education

TIPS **Is This TOO Soon to Plan?**

Don't worry about picking the "right" major at this point. You're way ahead of the game by looking at this list already.

Business Education

Early Childhood Education

Education

Elementary Education

Physical Education

Secondary Education and Teaching

Special Education

Teacher Education

Engineering and Architecture

Acoustical Engineering

Acoustics

Aerospace Engineering

Architecture

Architectural Engineering

Automotive Engineering

Biomedical Engineering

Chemical Engineering

Civil Engineering

Computer Engineering

Electrical Engineering

Engineering Design

Environmental Engineering

Geological Engineering

Industrial Design

Industrial Engineering

Interior Architecture

Landscape Architecture

Mechanical Engineering

Mineral Engineering

Nuclear Engineering

Petroleum Engineering

Fine and Performing Arts

Apparel and Textile Marketing Management

Art

Art Education

Art History

Ceramics

Cinematography

Costume Design

Dance

Illustration

Jazz Studies

Lighting Specialist

Music

Music History

Music Management

Musical Theater

Painting

Photography

Piano

Sculpture

Theater

Medicine, Nursing, and Health Professions

Anatomy
Art Therapy
Biometrics/Biostatistics
Biomedical Science
Biotechnology
Chiropractic
Community Health and
    Preventive Medicine
Dental Hygiene
Dietitian
Health Administration

Kinesiology
Massage therapy
Medical Radiologic
    Technology
Medical Sonography
Music Therapy
Nursing
Nutrition
Occupational Therapy
Optometry
Pharmacology

Pharmacy
Physical Therapy
Physician Assistant
Pre-Dentistry
Pre-Medicince
Public Health
Radiation Therapist
Toxicology
Veterinary Medicine

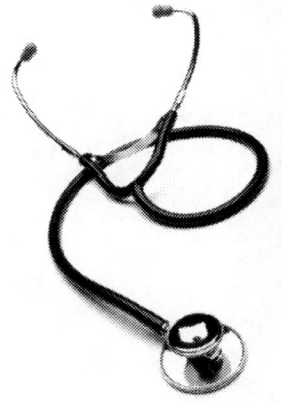

Trade, Technical, and Vocational School

Automotive Mechanic
Carpentry
Commercial Pilot
Computer Programmer
Chef
Data Management Specialist

Dental Hygienist
Electronics Repairer
Massage Therapist
Medical Sonographer
Medical Technician
Paralegal

Welder

TIPS Trade School Requirements

Remember, vocational and trade school majors also require a high school diploma or GED.

My Turn! What are My Top Choices?

DIRECTIONS: Now that you have seen a variety of the majors available at colleges nationwide, make a list of potential majors you may be interested in pursuing. Next, research specific information about the majors you are interested in and complete the following questions.

1. Potential Majors:

    A. _____ B. _____ C. _____

2. How many months/semesters/years does it take to complete the major/program? ____
    _____

3. Does the major or program include on-the-job work experience (e.g. work study or internships)? _____
    _____

4. Which type of qualification do you receive after completing the program (e.g. bachelor degree, associate degree, certificate)? _____
    _____
    _____

Exploring the Career for Me

Mindset Change

While you should absolutely study what interests you, it is highly recommended that you keep an eye on the employment opportunities for after college. It is simply a real-world reality that some majors/career paths will have more job opportunities than others based on market trends.

In the "major cards" below, three majors are spotlighted: Computer Engineering, School Psychology and Economics. Each card previews a description of the degree as well as lists (1) helpful high school courses, (2) typical major courses, and (3) some potential related careers that are available to graduate with that major. It makes sense that different majors can lead you toward different career paths, but you can start preparing yourself for success in that field today by taking specialized classes in addition to your regular course load. Wouldn't it be nice to arrive at college with knowledge and skills that can already put you ahead of your peers?

COMPUTER ENGINEERING
Degree: B.S. in Computer Engineering
Description: Computer engineering students learn how computers work and learn how to make machines smarter, faster, and better than current technology. Through math and science, students learn how to make computer hardware, software, and applications (apps). If you're interested in technology and like to solve problems, computer engineering might be the major for you.

Helpful High School Courses	Typical Major Courses	Potential Related Careers
AP Calculus	Calculus	Aerospace Engineer
Electronics	Computer Architecture	Computer Hardware
Chemistry	Physics	Engineer
AP Computer Science	Programming languages	Computer-Repair Tech
AP Physics	Digital-logic design	Software Developer

Key Point

Career aptitude tests can help determine what major/career may be the best fit for you based on your skills and interests.

SCHOOL SOCIAL/EMOTIONAL COUNSELING
Degree: B.A. in School Psychology
Description: School social/emotional counselots use intentional individual or group conversations to help students in the school setting. Becoming a licensed school counselor requires more than a four-year bachelor's degree. Many school counselors start with a psychology major and continue their education to become a school counselor.

Helpful High School Courses	Typical Major Courses	Potential Related Careers
AP Psychology	Group Dynamics	School Counselor
AP English Language	Personality Theories	Rehab Counselor
Statistics	Social Psychology	Clinical Psychologist
Biology	Child Psychology	Youth Counselor
AP Physics	Psychology of Personality	Youth Program Director

Consider This!

Do the classes required for the major you want to pursue actually line up well with your academic strengths and interests?

ECONOMICS
Degree: B.A./B.S. in Economics
Description: Economics majors learn about how resources such as land, labor, and raw materials are produced, sold, bought, and used. Economics students research, analyze, and develop important solutions to solve business or social problems.

Helpful High School Courses	Typical Major Courses	Potential Related Careers
AP Macroeconomics	Microeconomics	Economist
AP Calculus	Macroeconomics	Lawyer
World History	Finance	Financial Advisor
U.S. History	Business Economics	Politician
Foreign Languages	Statistics	Real Estate Agent

My Turn! Exploring the Career for Me

DIRECTIONS: Based on your current interests, select 2 or 3 additional careers that you are interested in. Complete the Major Cards below after researching online and/or speaking with someone with that particular career.

Challenge Yourself: Go a step further and estimate/research the average salary for each of the 3 careers mentioned on the "Exploring the Career for Me" page and the 2 that you chose for this page.

Career: _____

Degree: _____

Description: _____
_____
_____
_____

Helpful High School Courses	Typical Major Courses	Potential Related Courses
_____	_____	_____
_____	_____	_____
_____	_____	_____

Career: _____

Degree: _____

Description: _____
_____
_____
_____

Helpful High School Courses	Typical Major Courses	Potential Related Courses
_____	_____	_____
_____	_____	_____
_____	_____	_____

Additional Career Options or Notes

Choosing Education as a Career Path

Mindset Change

You could work in your dream job, have a positive impact on students in your community, AND make as much or possibly more money than you could outside of the field!

The Education Field is a dynamic, growing industry with countless opportunities. Graduates who hold degrees in education, as well as in many different specialties, find impactful careers in education. Not everyone who works in education is a teacher or principal! Below are five generalized buckets of career paths within the education workforce. As you can see, several career paths are represented. Think about your career aspirations and which bucket it would fit in.

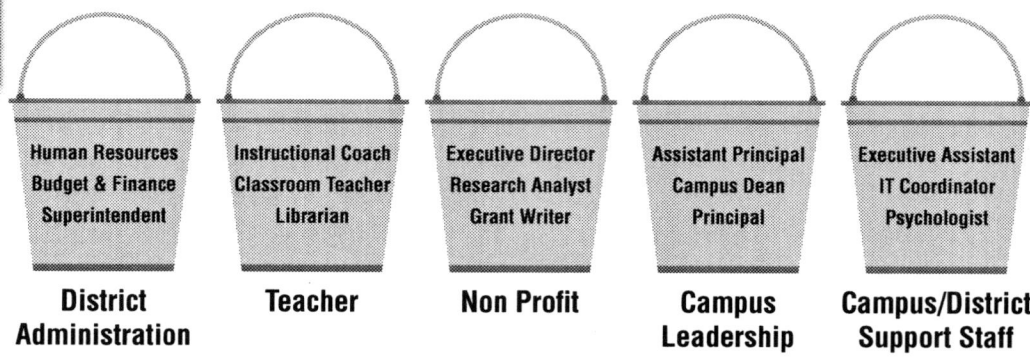

District Administration	Teacher	Non Profit	Campus Leadership	Campus/District Support Staff
Human Resources Budget & Finance Superintendent	Instructional Coach Classroom Teacher Librarian	Executive Director Research Analyst Grant Writer	Assistant Principal Campus Dean Principal	Executive Assistant IT Coordinator Psychologist

My Turn! Dream Jobs in Education

My dream job is... _____

Which "bucket" in the education field could your dream job fit into?

_____

Education Field Salaries

Often people assume that the salaries in education are not as high as other fields. The salaries in education are comparable to, or in some cases higher than other fields. Take a look at the average salaries of common careers in education in the graph.

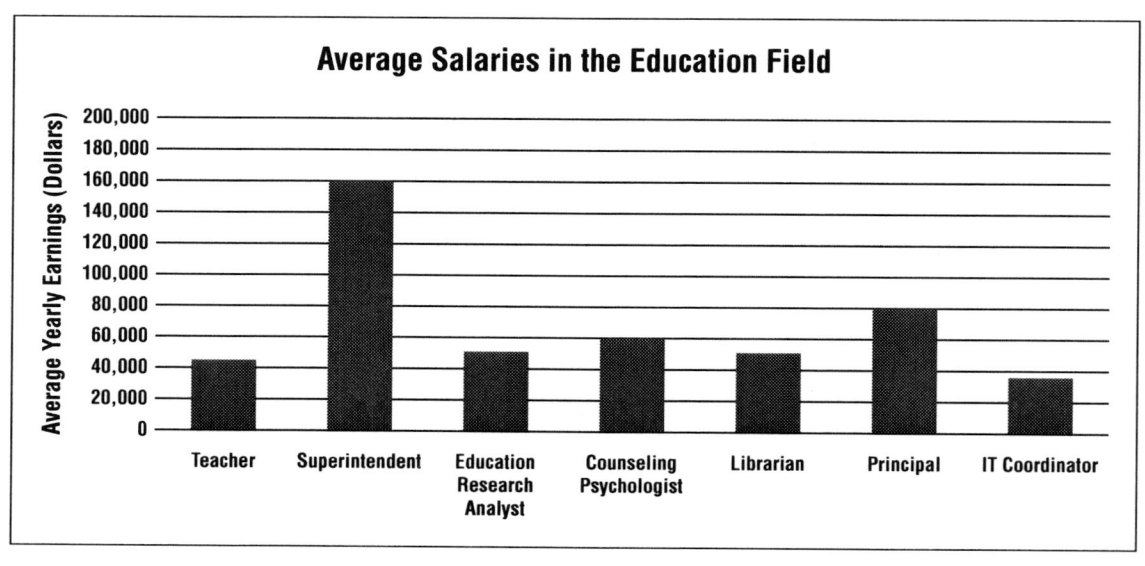

Average Salaries in the Education Field

My Turn! Let's Compare

DIRECTIONS: Using the information that you already know about your dream job and have now learned about the education field, complete the details below. Note: This likely will require additional research online.

Career Details

1. What major would you pursue for your dream job? _____
2. What is the average salary for that role within the field of education? _____
3. What is the average salary for that role outside of the field of education? _____
4. Why is this pathway interesting to you? _____
   _____

Becoming A Teacher

If you would like to become a teacher, there are two different pathways for you to become a fully certified teacher. Teachers on a particular campus often came to the classroom from many different backgrounds—some majored in education while others decided to change careers later in life.

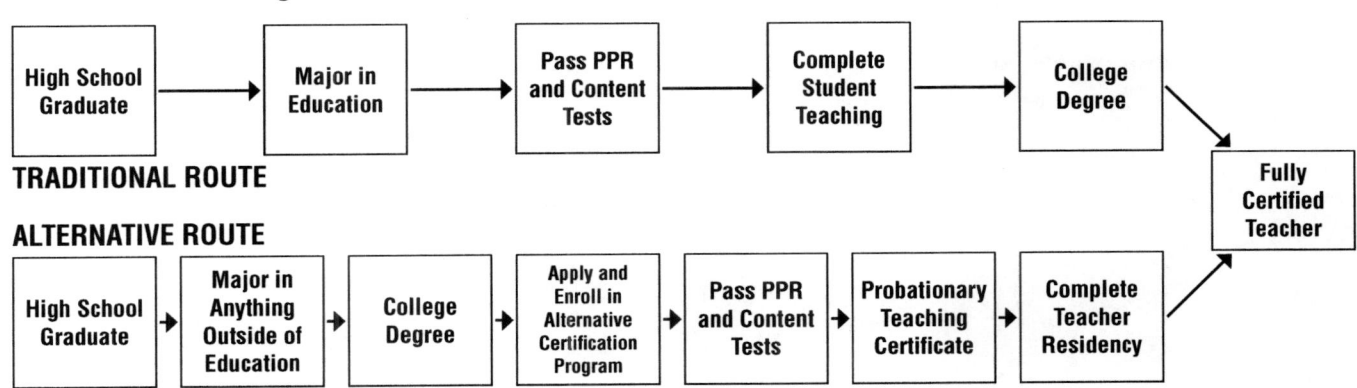

In most states, the pathways are called a "traditional route" or "alternative route". Traditional route teachers attend college, major in education and are fully certified upon college graduation as long as all steps along the way are passed. An alternative certification program is an option for aspiring teachers who hold a bachelor's degree, but do not have a degree in education. For example: a science teacher who holds a degree in Biology. These teachers complete the necessary steps to become fully certified while working another job.

My Turn! Talk to A Teacher

DIRECTIONS: Passionate people, hoping to make a positive impact on the next generation, often make the choice to work in the field of education or service. Take some time to talk with a teacher or education leader about her/his path to working in the field. In the space below write a brief summary of what you found memorable or interesting about her/his pathway.

_____

_____

_____

Soft Skills

In college, you will be in classes that will give you the background information to prepare you for the career of your choice. Although you will be learning hard skills – information necessary to do a job – almost all careers value employees who have soft skills. **Soft skills** are abilities that characterize your relationships with other people. They include abilities like communication, leadership, and managing others.

ABC Soft Skills
Soft skills are abilities that characterize your relationships with other people such as communication, leadership, and managing others.

Many people may be qualified for one job. Employers value applicants who have soft skills that make them pleasurable and productive to work with. For example, Abby and Celestino may both be graduates from a college with an excellent engineering program. They have had the same internships and same training for a position as a junior engineer. Celestino, however, writes strong emails, is a great listener, and works in teams very well. Abby still struggles in communicating with others and it is often difficult to work with her on a team. Although they have the same education, Celestino's soft skills set him apart.

My Turn! What are My Soft Skills?

DIRECTIONS: Reflect on your own soft skills by rating yourself from 1 to 10 on each one below. 1 means you never display this skill; 10 means you always display this skill. Then, share with your ratings with a partner and ask if he or she agrees.

Soft Skill	Rate Yourself
Strong work ethic	
Dependable	
Positive attitude	
Self motivated	
Team oriented	
Organized	
Works well under pressure	
Effective communicator	
Flexible	
Confident	

1. What soft skills did you and your partner agree you do very well?

   _____

2. What soft skills do you or your partner feel you do not do very well?

   _____

3. Which soft skills do you want to improve on? Why do you feel like you rated yourself low on those skills?

   _____

   _____

Playing a Sport While in College

If you are exceptionally committed and skilled in a particular sport during high school, colleges may recruit you to play that sport at their school. Research on the Internet which schools offer athletic scholarships or financial aid in a sport you are interested, exceptionally skilled, and experienced in. Talk to your coaches about opportunities for recruitment and scholarships. Also go on to the College Board website to check what level of academic performance the colleges and universities are expecting from their applicants. Keep in mind that athletes must go through the same admissions process as all other applicants to a college or university.

College sports are sponsored by the NCAA (National Collegiate Athletic Association). More than 1,100 colleges are a part of the NCAA with over 460,000 student-athletes participating. The NCAA sponsors the following sports:

Fall Sports

Cross Country (Men & Women)	Football (M)	Water Polo (M)
	Soccer (M & W)	
Field Hockey (W)	Volleyball (W)	

Winter Sports

Basketball (M & W)	Ice Hockey (M & W)	(M & W)
Bowling (W)	Rifle (M & W)	Indoor Track and Field (M& W)
Fencing (M & W)	Skiing (M & W)	
Gymnastics (M & W)	Swimming and Diving	Wrestling (M)

Spring Sports

Baseball (M)	Softball (W)	Volleyball (M)
Golf (M & W)	Tennis (M & W)	Water Polo (W)
Lacrosse (M & W)	Outdoor Track and Field (M & W)	
Rowing (W)		

Emerging Sports (soon to have full support)

Equestrian-Horseback Riding (W)	Rugby (W)	Squash (W)
	Sand Volleyball (W)	

Mindset Change

Many students believe that they will go to school on a sports scholarships and go pro. If you are exceptionally talented and work hard in a sport, it is absolutely possible. However, very few students make it to pro. Depending on the sport, only between 1 and 10% of athletes make it to the professional league.

Mindset Change

In order to compete in the professional league of sports, you must compete in college sports first. Competing in college is also a competitive process, only 6% of athletes compete in college sports.

NCAA Divisions

The NCAA is divided into three divisions that offer different levels of competition and different scholarships levels.

Division 1 (D-1):

These are the teams you hear about a lot. Some examples of Division 1 schools are: The University of Texas, the University of California Berkeley, and the University of Colorado-Boulder. Division 1 schools can offer full scholarships to student-athletes, meaning they pay for your books, tuition and living expenses. There are over 300 Division 1 schools in the U.S. These schools have the highest level of competition and therefore expect the highest level of commitment and evidence of talent and experience from their student athletes.

TIPS **Student Athlete**

Being a good high school athlete, but having poor grades, will not result in you receiving scholarship offers. Do not neglect your studies.

Division 2 (D-2):

Division 2 schools are similar to Division 1 schools in that they can also offer scholarships. However, they offer fewer scholarships than Division 1 schools. Student athletes in Division 2 schools will often have their tuition paid for, but they must pay for living expenses through other means (other scholarships, government loans, etc). There are almost 300 Division 2 schools in the United States. The University of Central Washington, the University of Charleston, and Kentucky State University are examples of Division 2 schools.

Division 3 (D-3):

Division 3 schools cannot offer scholarships to their athletes, though they are more likely to admit someone who will be on one of their teams. Division 3 student athletes still compete at a very high level but do not have the same time commitment as Division 1 student athletes, leaving more time for school and other extracurricular activities. There are over 430 schools that compete at the Division 3 level. The University of Chicago, Amherst College, and New York University are all examples of Division 3 schools.

What College Coaches Look For

Once you have decided that you want to play a sport in college, you need to start researching colleges that match your talent level and find a program that would accept you onto their team. High school coaches and athletic directors are outstanding resources in this area. They can serve as your "agent" and help you communicate with college coaches. Your high school coaches know your skill level, leadership qualities, and dedication better than anyone and can help convey these skills to college recruiters. College recruiters look for many things:

1. **Talent Level:** Competing in college is a big step up from high school. All of the athletes are the best of the best from their high schools. College coaches will look at game films from high school or may even come to personally watch you practice and play. They know what it takes to be successful at their schools and will make sure that you match up to their standards.

2. **Personality and Dedication:** Playing a sport in college is a huge time commitment. Coaches will talk to you personally and talk to your high school coaches and teachers to determine if you can handle it. If you decide to play sports in college, chances are that you will be living on your own for the first time. College coaches need to know that you will be able to excel and take personal responsibility for your education and athletic development. They also need to know that you will work well with their current players.

3. **Academics:** College academics can be challenging. They become even more challenging when trying to juggle games and practices throughout the week. College coaches see your high school academic achievement as a reflection of your overall work ethic. Are you constantly striving to be the best in everything or are you content doing the bare minimum? Before you are even eligible to play in college you must meet the requirements of the NCAA Clearinghouse. The NCAA Clearinghouse mandates what courses you need to have completed in high school as well as the minimum standards for your GPA and ACT or SAT scores. The NCAA requires that you take the following 16 core courses in order to play Division 1* sports in college:

- 4 years of English
- 3 years of math (Algebra 1 or higher)
- 2 years of natural or physical sciences (including one year of lab science if offered by your high school)
- 1 extra year of English, math, or natural or physical science
- 2 years of social science
- 4 years of extra core courses (from any category above, foreign language, or philosophy)

*__Note:__ *Division 2 course requirements are different. Check* collegeboard.com *for more information.*

> **TIPS** **Work Hard, Get Noticed**
>
> *If you want to be attractive to a college recruiter, you must demonstrate that you can rise to the challenge and that you are willing to work hard, be a leader, and sacrifice for your team.*

> **TIPS** **Make Time**
>
> *It's all about time management. Make the time to accomplish all of your goals both on and off the field.*

Benefits of Sports in College

In addition to improving your odds of getting into the school of your choice, as well as scholarship opportunities, being a college athlete has other benefits. Taking on the challenge of playing sports in college can be very rewarding. When you arrive on campus in the fall, you will already know your teammates and be instantly connected with people who share a common interest with you. You will also be able to continue to play a sport that you love and truly become the best you can be at it. Finally, sports in college will build off of skills that you already developed in high school, including: leadership abilities, time management, commitment, dedication, and teamwork abilities.

> Sports talent can help you be admitted to a college and pay for your education...

There are many different paths for you to choose from after high school graduation. It is extremely important to research your options starting today. Some key things to consider are: the selectivity of the colleges or universities you are interested in, the career you hope to pursue based on your interests and skills, the major required for that career, how much money you would like to earn annually, and the likely employment rates for various level of degrees and careers. Remember, those who attain advanced degrees, or learn a specialty, will earn considerably more money during their lifetime than those with only a high school diploma. It is indeed true; hard work does pay off.

Start your research process now. This will only help inform you further and bring you that much closer to the great things that await you in your future.

My Turn! 3-2-1... Explore Career Paths!

List THREE different types of degrees you can earn after graduating from high school. Include the number of years required to earn each degree:

-
-
-

List TWO trends about salary and availability of jobs that occur as your level of education increases:

-
-

List ONE major you hope to obtain and why:

-
-

UNIT 5

PURSUE FINANCIAL AID

What are the differences among grants, loans, and scholarships?

DIRECTIONS: In reflection of the information you learned in this unit, draw an emoji of how you feel now.

What is financial aid and how do I apply for it?

How do know if a financial aid package is right for me?

DIRECTIONS: Read the topics of this unit on the roadmap. Draw an "emoji" of your emotions about this content as you start the unit.

How expensive is college?

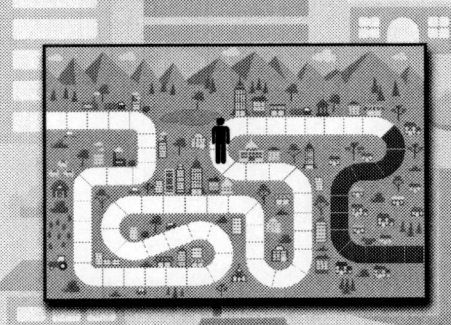

Cost of Attendance (COA)	Expected Family Contribution (EFC)	Interest	Student Activities Fee
College Scholarship Service Profile (CSS Profile)	Free Application for Federal Student Aid (FAFSA)	Loans	Subsidized Loan
		Room and Board	Tuition
Compound Interest	Financial Aid	Satisfactory Academic Progress (SAP)	Undocumented Student
DACA Student	Full-Time/Part-Time Enrollment	Student Aid Report (SAR)	Unsubsidized Loan
Dormitory			Work-Study
	Grants	Scholarship	

DIRECTIONS: In the space below, select several unfamiliar words from the vocabulary word bank. Then, define each word using the glossary or a dictionary. Last, create an original sentence for each of the selected words.

Vocabulary Word	Definition	Your Original Sentence

Financial Literacy

Let's face it – money can be scary. Making money, spending money, saving money, and budgeting money are all sources of stress.

At this point, you may or may not have a job, but you will soon have things to spend money on – especially when you go to college! It's never too early to launch your life on the path toward financial security. The three habits that are focused on in this lesson are:

1. **Saving** – Why it's important, and three simple saving tricks to help you get started!

2. **Bank Accounts** – Why placing your money in the bank is smart, safe, and beneficial.

3. **The Power of Compound Interest** – A great way to make your money grow effortlessly.

My Turn! Saving

DIRECTIONS: Imagine it's your birthday and you have received $200 total in cash and checks from your friends and family. Now that it's yours, you have three choices of how to use it. Take about 30 seconds and circle the choice below that you think you would most likely make:

1. Spend it all   2. Save it all   3. Spend some and save some

Most Americans will spend all, or almost all, of the new income they make. It's hard not to. Advertising companies are successful because they are excellent at marketing their products and making you want to buy them.

The secret about saving is that even the smallest effort will produce big gains. Consider if you save $5 a week every week for a year? Since there are 52 weeks in the year, you just saved $260 with very little effort! With good saving habits, you can always have a little extra cash to spend on a snack at school, go to the movie theater, have money for an emergency, donate to charity, or buy a home someday!

Savings Tips

Here is a list of some helpful tips to get you started!

1. **Separate Your Accounts-** Wherever you keep your money (we recommend a bank), divide your money into two separate accounts labeled "Spending" and "Saving." Many banks will already do this for you. Contribute to BOTH accounts regularly and DO NOT transfer dollars from one account to another unless it's absolutely necessary – emergencies, big purchases you've been saving for, etc.

2. **Set Goals-** If you really want something, set a goal to buy it and save a little bit each month until you can afford it. Don't buy something you cannot afford!

3. **Save First-** Whenever you make some money, make sure the first thing you do is put that money into your savings account. This will protect you from making impulse decisions and it will make saving much easier.

Key Point

It's never too early to begin saving money and establish strong financial habits.

Save More, Spend More

If you want to make big purchases that are important to you, you must save to make it happen!

Key Point

An FDIC bank is the safest location to keep your money because your money is always secure and available to you anytime, in addition you earn interest for lending the bank money so they can lend larger amounts of money to other people.

TIPS Is it Affordable?

How can you tell if you can afford something? Well, if the purchase requires you to spend more money than you have in your account, that's a big sign not to buy it. Also, be wary of monthly subscriptions – even $9.99 per month can add up very quickly!

Bank Accounts

Banks are safe places to keep your savings and spending accounts. Banks have security systems and your money is insured by the U.S. government. You can access your money easily from an ATM or with a debit card. A debit card allows you to spend the money you have in the bank without having to use cash.

Most banks usually require $25 - $50 to open your first savings account. If you're not 18, your parents can open a bank account for you – as soon as today! Your parents will "jointly own" the account with you and will be ultimately responsible for any problems that may come up.

My Turn! A Little Bit Goes A Long Way

DIRECTIONS: Calculate the possible outcomes of the following scenario.

You work a part-time job after school and make $400 each month. You hold this job all through high school and college – a total of 8 years. At the end of those 8 years,...

1. How much money would you have if you **saved all** of it?

2. How much money would you have if you **spent half and saved half**?

3. How much money would you have if you **saved $100** each month?

> In the long run, even small differences in spending and saving make a BIG impact!

The Power of Compound Interest

Another great reason to save your money in a bank is because they pay you for every single dollar you keep with them. Seems crazy, right? But it's true.

Banks pay YOU money – called **interest** – on your savings account. The money you put in your savings account is called a deposit. For example, if you deposited $100 in the bank at a 5% interest rate and your money stayed in the bank for the entire year untouched, you would have $105. That's right, that $5 is free money!

Even better, banks today pay interest on the total amount in your account, including any interest you've already earned! This is called **compound interest**. This means next year, your bank will be calculating the 5% based on the $105 that is already in there.

Now, at the end of Year 2, the bank is going to pay 5% interest on the $105 you have in your account. You will end Year 2 with $110.25 – and you did not have to do anything for that money to grow!

To see the potential of compound interest, turn to the table on the next page. Remember: if you do not set up a bank account, your money will not grow hidden in your shoebox!

Great Resource!

There are many great resources online to help you learn more about ways to put your money to work for you. A great one is The Mint. You can visit **www.themint.org** or search "mint for kids" online.

My Turn! Regular vs. Compound Interest

DIRECTIONS: The table below helps to explain the banking tips on the previous pages. It shows the difference in the growth of your money over time depending on whether you have a bank account with a regular interest rate or a compound interest rate. To help express this point, take some time to review this first example and answer questions 1-3 below.

TIPS A Note on the Numbers

In order to try and keep the math simple, a 5% interest rate is used as the example here. However, it should be noted that finding a bank with a 5% interest rate would be rather hard. But the point still holds: interest helps your money grow!

Interest Rate of 5%	Amount Deposited	Years in the Bank				
		1	2	5	15	25
Regular Interest	$100.00	$105.00	$110.00	$125.00	$175.00	$225.00
Compound Interest	$100.00	$105.00	$110.25	$127.63	$207.89	$338.64

1. (Circle Your Answer). Based on the table, what type of interest rate should you choose for your bank account?

   Regular Interest   or   **Compound Interest**

2. After 25 years, how much more money would the bank account with compound interest make compared to the bank account with regular interest? _____

   _____

3. In two sentences, describe what happens to your money the longer it stays in the bank regardless of whether you have a regular interest or compound interest account?

   _____
   _____
   _____
   _____
   _____
   _____

Are YOU ready to start saving?

My Turn! Saving $100 with Compound Interest

DIRECTIONS: It's clear that compound interest is even more powerful at growing your money than regular interest, but how much does the amount of money you invest matter? The table below shows the difference in the growth of two bank accounts at the same compound interest rate of 5 percent. The difference this time is that one smart saver has chosen to deposit money each year, instead of just one time. Once again, please review the table and then answer questions 1 and 2 below.

Compound Interest of 5% for Both	Amount Deposited	Years in the Bank				
		1	2	5	15	25
$100 Once	$100.00	$105.00	$110.25	$127.63	$207.89	$338.64
$100 Each Year	$100.00	$105.00	$215.25	$580.19	$2,265.75	$5,011.35

1. (Circle Your Answer) Does saving a little bit each year make a difference?

    Yes   or   **No**

2. After 25 years, how much more money would you make if you deposited $100 into your account each year vs. $100 just once? _____

Notes

Unit 5: Pursue Financial Aid

Calculating the Cost of College

How much do you think an average public (in-state) college costs per year?

a. $100+
b. $1,000+
c. $10,000
d. $20,000 - $30,000

Enrique's Story

Enrique received $400 for his birthday from his family. He is so excited to spend his money, but he takes a couple of days to think about and research what he really wants to buy. Plus, he has saved $100 from mowing the neighbor's yard all summer, so he has a total of $500.

What Enrique really wants is an iPhone 6 Plus. After doing research, there are a few different models to choose from. He can go with the (1) 16GB iPhone 6 for $549, (2) the 64GB iPhone 6 for $649, or (3) the 16GB iPhone 6 Plus for $649. The problem is that he doesn't have quite enough money to buy any of them.

He has to think about what he wants to do. He could ask his mom if he can borrow some money to make up the difference. He could wait and mow more lawns in order to make money. Or, he could settle on getting a 16GB iPhone SE for $399. He has enough money for that.

My Turn! Weigh The Options

DIRECTIONS: With a partner, or adult, discuss each of Enrique's options. In the chart below, fill in the pros (positives) and the cons (negatives) of each of his three choices. Enrique must also consider that he:

- Will need an Internet connection to keep his iPhone working; his family may ask him to contribute to the Internet bill each month.
- May want to buy some accessories like better headphones, apps and music.
- Is nervous to settle for the cheaper iPhone SE because he will be wishing he had gotten the iPhone 6 or iPhone 6 Plus every time he uses it.

Option 1: Borrow Money from Mom*		Option 2: Mow a few more lawns to get the iPhone 6 or iPhone 6 Plus		Option 3: Buy the Cheaper iPhone SE	
Pros	Cons	Pros	Cons	Pros	Cons
•	•	•	•	•	•
•	•	•	•	•	•

***NOTE:** If Enrique chooses to borrow money from his Mom, he has to pay her back. If he doesn't pay her back within one month, she will take the iPhone away.*

1. Which iPhone would you choose if you were Enrique? Which option would you use to pay for it? _____

2. Why do you feel most comfortable with this decision? _____
_____

3. Please list the factors that influenced your decision: _____
_____

How Much Does College Cost?

As you've probably heard before, college can be expensive. You will definitely spend more money than the **tuition** price listed on your school's website over the years that you attend. Yet you should also remember that many forms of financial aid are available. In this section, you will learn how much college can cost in addition to ways that you can pay for your college education.

In college, you will have to pay for the following costs (see glossary for any terms that are new to you):

- Course Fees/Tuition
- Room and Board
- Textbooks and other supplies
- Student Activity Fees
- Student Health Insurance
- Parking
- Personal Spending

Below is an example of how much it might cost to attend a Public Two-Year Community College (in-state) over the course of two years. This example shows how much it will cost if you live in a **dormitory**, buildings on college campuses that students live in, for one year. Of course financial aid will make a difference in helping you pay.

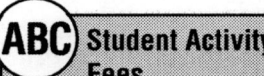

Key Point
College costs include course fees (tuition), room and board (housing and meal plan), textbooks and supplies, student activity fees, student health insurance, parking, and personal spending.

ABC **Student Activity Fees**
Student activity fees are fees paid to support student organizations, student activities, intramural sports, and other events on campus.

Key Point
Fees are different at different colleges.

ABC **Room and Board**
The amount of money it costs for housing in dorms and meals in the dining halls, or cafeterias, per semester.

Public Two-Year Community College (In-State)

Fee	Cost per Semester	# of Semesters	Calculations	Total
Courses	$1,500	4	$1,500 x 4	$6,000
Room & Board (on-campus)	$6,000	2	$6,000 x 2	$12,000
Room & Board (off-campus)	$4,000	2	$4,000 x 2	$8,000
Textbooks/Supplies	$600	4	$600 x 4	$2,400
Student Activities	$750	4	$750 x 4	$3,000
Health Insurance	$450	4	$450 x 4	$1,800
On-campus parking	$300	4	$300 x 4	$1,200
Personal	$450	4	$450 x 4	$1,800

Total for 2 Years: $36,200

My Turn! Calculating the Cost of College

DIRECTIONS: Two sample colleges are listed below. Using the numbers provided and referencing the sample on the previous page, calculate the cost of attending a Public Four-Year University (In-State).

Public Four-Year University (In-State)

Fee	Cost per semester	# of semesters	Calculations (cost x semesters)	Total
Courses	$4,500	8		
Room & Board (on-campus)	$5,000	2		
Room & Board (off-campus)	$3,000	6		
Textbooks/Supplies	$600	8		
Student Activities	$750	8		
Health Insurance	$450	8		
On-campus parking	$300	8		
Personal	$450	8		

Total for 4 Years: $_____

DIRECTIONS: Next, research the course fees (a.k.a. tuition) and room and board costs of a Public Four-Year University (Out-of-State) or a Private University of your choice. Insert the cost per semester in the appropriate boxes in the chart below. Calculate the cost per fee for all four years. Finally, calculate the overall cost of college for four years.

Public Four-Year (Out-of-State) School <u>or</u> Private School

Fee	Cost per semester	# of semesters	Calculations (cost x semesters)	Total
Courses		8		
Room & Board (on-campus)		2		
Room & Board (off-campus)		6		
Textbooks/Supplies	$600	8		
Student Activities	$750	8		
Health Insurance	$450	8		
On-campus parking	$300	8		
Personal	$450	8		

Total for 4 Years: $_____

Consider Enrique's Decision Once More...

Now that you have calculated the cost of various types of colleges, you may realize choosing and paying for a college is similar to Enrique's decision. Except, of course, that the dollar amount is significantly higher.

DIRECTIONS: Using a pencil, draw lines to connect the terms from Enrique's Story to the related college term. The bold words in the box on the left have an exact match to a word in the box on the right. For the remaining words, there may be more than one correct connection. Just be sure that, if asked, you can defend and explain your connection.

Enrique's Story Terms	College Terms
• **16GB iPhone 6 Plus** • **64GB iPhone 6** • **16GB iPhone 6** • **16GB iPhone SE** • Borrowing money • Working for more money • Gift from family members • Selecting the iPhone SE instead of the iPhone 6 • Headphones • Case • Apps • Music • Internet connection	• Ivy League college • Student loans • Books • Work study & deferred acceptance • Public university • Health care • Monthly rent/housing costs • Scholarship • Entertainment (movies, etc.) • Choosing a more affordable college option • Private university • Community college • Food/groceries

1. What are two ways to save money on college costs? (Hint: consider the cost of tuition for each type of college and the cost of room and board based on where you choose to live). _____

   _____

2. Recall the iPhone decision you made earlier. Looking at the type of college it matches up with, would you also choose that same schooling option? Why or why not? _____

   _____

   _____

3. In your opinion, would it be beneficial to save up for the most expensive type of college if it's your dream school? Why or why not? _____

   _____

   _____

4. Do you feel there are options to help you pay for your dream school outside of you saving up your own money? Why or why not? (Hint: there is no wrong answer for this question) _____

   _____

   _____

Paying for College

Key Point

Financial aid is money that federal, state, college and private sources offer students to help pay for college.

Mindset Change

There is a belief among many students that they can't afford college. However, in truth, there are many different types of funding available to help you pay for college.

ABC FAFSA

The FAFSA is an application for financial aid, including loans, grants, college work-study and other federal and state funding. It is often required before a student can be considered for scholarships.

TIPS *You should never have to pay to find scholarships that you can easily find yourself!*

Key Point

Scholarships and grants do not need to be paid back, while loans DO need to be paid back (typically with interest).

For most students, paying for college is a major concern. If you have this fear, you are not alone. However, there are various types of **financial aid** that you can receive in order to support your college education.

One of the first steps that you should take is to visit The College Board website in order to research college funding available at a specific college. You can find out exactly how much scholarship money and financial aid students have received in previous years based on demonstrated family need or personal merit. This information is a great starting point in figuring out the resources available to pay for college.

In general, there are four different types of funding available to help pay for your college education. They are explained in detail below.

University Scholarships/Grants

Once you are accepted to a university, you may be offered **scholarships** or **grant** money from that particular school. These do not need to be paid back! The amount awarded will be based on your application and/or your **FAFSA** (which you will learn about later in this Unit) and probably won't be offered until the spring of your senior year of high school.

Private Scholarships

There are a variety of private scholarships offered each year by corporate, professional, civic, religious, and other organizations. If you receive a private scholarship, you can use it at whichever college you decide to attend! Like the category above, private scholarships do not have to be paid back. Typically, to be considered, you must meet the eligibility requirements specified by the sponsor and fill out an application, which will almost always include an essay question. For example, some scholarships may only be for students who are Latino, going into the U.S. Army, or have minimum 3.5 GPAs, etc. A good starting point to find these scholarships is to search for "Private Scholarships" online, but you should never pay to do so. If you qualify for a scholarship, print out the application information. Keep all of your scholarship applications in sequential order (by date) based on which ones are due first. Complete and submit them early in order to avoid being rushed or missing deadlines.

You may be asking, "Is there a difference between a scholarship and a grant?" Generally speaking, the answer is no because you do not pay either of them back. However, the term **scholarship** is primarily used when referring to academic merit (which means good grades), or for something you have achieved (being an all-star athlete). This is not always true as there are needs-based scholarships available as well.

Government Loans

Government **loans** are important because they help pay for anything that private or university scholarships

do not cover. Some people are afraid to take out loans and go into debt because you have to pay them back. Instead, they take a semester or two off of school to work, or go to a cheaper college. Generally speaking, this will lengthen the number of years it takes for a student to earn their degree. Taking a small loan from the government now will allow you to get a good education and make much more money later on in life! Put it this way – it's easier to pay back government loans when you're earning $60,000 a year as a college graduate than trying to save up the money by working a minimum wage. Consider a loan as an investment in your future, but borrow only the amount you need for your education!

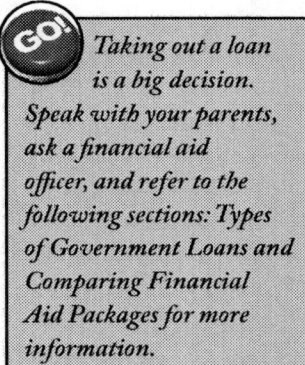
Taking out a loan is a big decision. Speak with your parents, ask a financial aid officer, and refer to the following sections: Types of Government Loans and Comparing Financial Aid Packages for more information.

My Turn! Pros and Cons of Financial Aid

DIRECTIONS: You have read a ton of information about the benefits of financial aid and the various forms it comes in. In order to double check your understanding, review the information once more from the previous pages and fill out the chart below. At the bottom, be sure to list pros and cons about each of these types of financial aid.

	Government Loan	Grant	Scholarship
Where does the money come from?			
Does the money have to be paid back?			
Does interest for fees accumulate on the money you receive? (Meaning you have to pay back more than you received)			
Does a student need to fill out the FAFSA (see next section in manual) to get this award?			
Are there limits to the amount of money you can get?			
Can only US citizens get money?			
PROS (+)			
CONS (-)			

Apply Early
College funding and financial aid are usually distributed on a first come, first serve basis. Do the necessary paperwork ASAP!

Be Cautious
According to the Consumer Financial Protection Bureau, student debt in the US has reached over $1 Trillion! Be cautious when accepting loans and ONLY accept what you absolutely need.

Work-Study Positions

Once your FAFSA has been evaluated, the government may recommend that you participate in a work-study program to cover additional tuition costs. **Work-study** allows students to have a paying job on campus, sometimes related to one's major. College work-study wages cannot be less than minimum wage, and students typically are not allowed to work more than 20 hours per week during one semester.

Over 3,000 college campuses in the United States have work study programs. To determine your eligibility to participate in work-study, the government looks at a student's **Expected Family Contribution** (or EFC, which will be discussed in detail later in this section). However, some work-study positions are also available to students who do not qualify for work-study in their financial aid packages. Be sure to check with your university's requirements!

Working While in School

Many students are employed workers during the school year. Often students have a job to pay off student loans, pay rent and grocery expenses, or to have some extra spending money. Having a part time job can be a great way to earn income, prove your time management skills, and gain critical job skills. Some common jobs for college students include:

- Retail (a store selling clothing or other merchandise)
- Waiter/Waitress
- On Campus Office or Professor Assistant
- Intern for a Company or Organization
- Babysitting or being a nanny

Part-Time Versus Full-Time Student

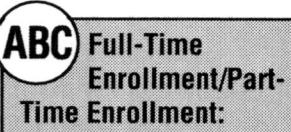
It is important to note that there are two statuses you can have as a student! A **full time student** is the most common, meaning you have to take at least 12 credit hours per semester. However, some students choose to be a **part-time student**, which is any commitment under 12 credit hours per semester. While this may seem like the better option, keep in mind that being a part time student can affect your financial aid status.

Remember: Do not overcommit yourself! While in college, school should be your first priority.

My Turn! Paying for College Research Activity

DIRECTIONS: Research the different costs of your favorite college and fill the information in to the charts below. Be sure to find the costs for an entire year, not just a semester.

Goal College Name: _____

Current total cost of attendance: _____

Tuition Cost:	
Room & Board Cost:	
Books Cost:	
Extra Fees:	
Total Cost of Attendance:	

Average amount of yearly financial aid given by university:	
Expected amount of family contribution (How much do you think your family can pay per year?):	
Total Aid and Family Contributions:	

_____ - _____ = _____
Total cost of attendance   **Total Aid and Family**   **Left over need**
(including room & board)   **Contributions**

TIPS **Great News!** *Keep reading below to discover ways to cover your left over need.*

_____ - _____ = _____
Tuition cost only   **Total Aid and Family**   **Left over need**
    Contributions

Options for covering the remaining amount you need to pay:
- Get a summer job and start saving now!
- Apply for scholarships not offered by the University. (YMCA, private donors, large stores, etc.) Ask your guidance counselor at school about some of these options.
- Talk to family members about starting a family savings plan for your college. There are savings accounts that will accumulate interest as your money sits in the bank account. Talk to a local bank about your options.
- Keep in mind that you can still attend college by only paying the tuition and student fees. If you live at home, you do not have to pay for room and board/ rent or a meal plan on campus.
- Keep reading the following pages to learn more specifics about Loans and Scholarships!

As you read earlier in this section, loans are a type of financial aid that you will eventually have to pay back. Before you accept or decline any loans you are offered in your financial aid package, you need to understand the different types and specific details of each of them.

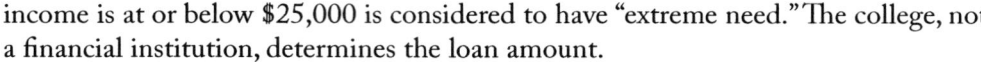

Perkins Loan

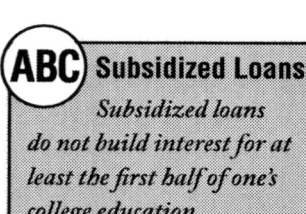

The Perkins Loan is a federal low-interest loan that does not have to be paid back until after graduation. Students can receive a Perkins loan from any one of the 1,800+ college institutions in the United States, especially if those students demonstrate "extreme need." What is "extreme need"? Generally, any student whose family income is at or below $25,000 is considered to have "extreme need." The college, not a financial institution, determines the loan amount.

Benefits of a Perkins Loan

- The interest rate is low - only 5%. This means that you will only have to pay an additional 5% of the original loan amount. For example, if you accept a loan of $5,000, you will have to pay an additional $250 (or 5% of $5,000) as you pay it back.

- There is a nine-month grace period after graduation until you have to start paying it back. Most loans only have a six-month grace period. This means that you will have an extra three months to get settled with a new job after graduation before you have to worry about starting to pay back your loan.

- There are ways you can become eligible for loan cancellation (meaning you would no longer have to pay your loans back). Some include teaching, military work, working for the Peace Corps, or working in law enforcement.

Stafford Loan

The Stafford Loan is another federal loan that does not have to be paid back until after graduation. So what's the difference between a Stafford Loan and a Perkins Loan? Stafford loans may be offered as either subsidized or unsubsidized loans.

ABC Subsidized Loans

Subsidized loans do not build interest for at least the first half of one's college education.

Subsidized vs. Unsubsidized

A **subsidized loan** is the best choice for a student because of its low interest rate. These loans are based on financial need and do not build interest while you are in school for at least half of the time (which means less money you will have to pay back!). They are called subsidized loans because the government "subsidizes" (or pays back) any interest that builds for at least the first half of your college education.

An **unsubsidized loan** is federally granted and NOT based on financial need. Interest builds as soon as you begin school and the government does not pay any of it for you.

Benefits of a Stafford Loan

- **Subsidized Loan**

    - Interest rates could be as low as 4.29%

    - No payments required while in school

    - No interest accrued (or built) for at least the first half of education

- **Unsubsidized Loan**

    - Can borrow up to $7,500 as a dependent student and up to $12,500 as an independent student per year, all depending upon the number of years in school. (dependent means that a parent or caregiver is claiming you as a dependent on his/her taxes.

    - Fixed interest rate of 6.8% ("fixed interest rate" – will always remain at 6.8% until changed by law)

    - No payments required while in school

State Specific Loan Programs

In addition to federal loans, states also have loan programs. Programs will vary from state to state. Research your state's Department of Education by visiting their website for details about state-specific loans available at the school you plan to attend.

PLUS Loan

A PLUS loan is one borrowed by a parent on behalf of a student to help pay for tuition and other expenses. For a parent to take out a PLUS loan, the student must be enrolled in at least part time education, and the parent or guardian must go through a credit check. PLUS loans are not need-based and have a fixed interest rate.

PLUS Loan Benefits

- Fixed interest rate of 6.84%

- Can fund up to the total cost of a student's education minus other aid received

- Have up to 10 years to repay loan

The College Scholarship Service (CSS) Profile

The **College Scholarship Service (CSS) Profile** is another application students may fill out to receive nonfederal student aid. Over 500 colleges, universities and scholarship programs in the United States use the information on the CSS Profile to determine student aid packages. Once you register for the CSS Profile online, you will be sent a personalized application based on your particular needs and your financial situation. You should fill out this application as soon as you know where you will apply for aid. This should be, at a minimum, two weeks before the earliest scholarship or college priority deadline.

Unlike the FAFSA, the CSS is not a free application – it costs $25 for the application and initial school report and $16 for every scholarship or college program you wish to attend. **But fee waivers are available!** So why use the profile? Some colleges require the FAFSA and the CSS. On the other hand, in many cases, the

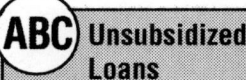

ABC) Unsubsidized Loans

Unsubsidized loans are federally funded and not based on financial need therefore interest begins to build on the loan as soon as the student borrower starts college.

TIPS) Is Your Loan Enough?

If not, you can find additional loans through banks if your financial aid package does not cover all of your unmet need.

Unit 5: Pursue Financial Aid

GO! Always Apply for Fee Waivers!

Fee waivers are like free passes to apply for scholarships or financial aid. Save your money for college, if you can.

TIPS) CSSP

The College Scholarship Service Profile is another application students may fill out to receive nonfederal student aid.

CSS is not necessary to fill out. Therefore, you need to research colleges you are thinking about applying to and see whether they need one, or both.

My Turn! Student Loan Basics

DIRECTIONS: Talk to your parents! Complete this chart to help guide conversations about loans with your parents as well as help you understand types of loans!

	Perkins	Stafford Subsidized	Stafford Unsubsidized	State Loan Program	PLUS Loan
Interest Rate (Include fixed or variable)					
How do you qualify?					
When do you start paying the loan back?					
When do interest payments start?					
Other special information					

Searching for Scholarships

You have already learned that scholarships and grants are types of financial aid that do not have to be paid back. You may be wondering where you find them or how to navigate the various kinds. While there are several different types of grants and scholarships, for practical purposes we can boil them down into four categories: (1) Government Grants, (2) Well-Known Scholarships, (3) Local/Regional Scholarships, and (4) Scholarships for Minority Students.

1) Government Grants

The first category includes federal and state scholarships and grants available to students who fill out the FAFSA. Listed below are the most commonly offered financial aid packages. Government grants and scholarships often come directly through the financial aid office of an individual campus on the basis of successful application to the college and submission of the FAFSA.

Federal Pell Grants

These are considered to be the foundation of financial aid, but you should be aware that the amount can change yearly based on decisions or laws enacted by the U.S. Congress. For the 2016–17 award year (July 1, 2016, to June 30, 2017), the maximum award is $5,815. The amount you receive will depend on: your financial aid need, cost of attendance, status as a full-time or part-time student, and plans to attend school for a full academic year or less.

Federal Supplemental Educational Opportunity (SEO) Grant

The Federal SEO Grant program provides grants to low-income undergraduate students. Priority is given to students with the most need (or with the lowest EFCs) and grants are awarded after a student completes a FAFSA. These grants range from $100 to $4,000 per year, with an average of just over $700 per year.

State Grants

Almost every state in the United States offers grants for undergraduate students. Be sure to search online for grants that may be available to you in your state.

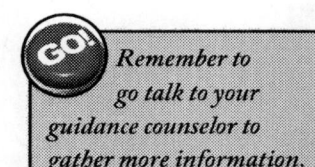

Remember to go talk to your guidance counselor to gather more information.

2) Well-Known Scholarships

The secondary category consists of well-known scholarships, the kind that will show up if you go to a scholarship listing website. This is where you'll find the major national scholarships and some of the better-known state scholarships. The advantage of these scholarships is that they are pretty easy to find. Just go to a scholarship website, enter your information, and a list will appear. The disadvantage is, because these scholarships are easier to find, more people apply. Therefore, they may be harder to earn.

How To Find These Scholarships:

It's simple, so don't feel stressed. To get started, all you need to do is find a scholarship website online, enter your information, and see what comes up. Then follow the application instructions for the scholarships, submit them, and wait to hear back. Here are a few scholarship websites and forms that you should definitely check out online:

- `The College Board Scholarship Search`
- `Fastweb`
- `CSS/Financial Aid PROFILE from the College Board`

3) Local/Regional Scholarships

The third category consists mostly of local/regional scholarships that are less well known and are usually only open to people who live in a certain geographic area such as a city, neighborhood, or school district. The advantage of this category is that fewer people apply for these scholarships. The disadvantage is that finding out about these scholarships may be a little more difficult and they may not be for large amounts of money. However, some money will still go a lot further than no money!

How to Find These Scholarships:

Check with your school's counseling office or district administration to see what kind of scholarship website or information sheets they make available for students. Many regional/local scholarship offers come through the district itself or are sent to school professionals for distribution.

4) Scholarships for Minority Students

The fourth category consists of scholarships that are open only to people of a certain minority status determined by race, ethnicity, gender, religion, or various other categories. For example, there are many Hispanic and African American scholarships available.

How to Find These Scholarships:

There are some excellent resources for finding minority/heritage/experience specific scholarships. Some can be found on the scholarship listing websites mentioned in the "well-known scholarships" section. In addition, here are a few that are especially worth investigating. As a starting point, it is recommended you search online as well as visit the websites of the following scholarship organizations:

- Black Excel: The College Help Network
- United Negro College Fund
- Congressional Hispanic Caucus Institute Regional Scholarships
- The Hispanic Scholarship Fund
- Latino College Dollars
- Free Hispanic Grant Offers:
  - `www.collegescholarships.org/`
- American Indian College Fund
- Native American Rights Fund
- Catching the Dream
- Asian & Pacific Islander American Scholarship Fund
- The Gates Millennium Scholars Program

- Educators for Fair Consideration (E4FC) New American Scholars Program
- The Dream US Scholarship (for **DACA** eligible youth)
- Point Foundation: College Scholarships for LGBT Students
- Girl Inc. Lucile Miller Wright Scholars Program
- The Islamic Society of North America (ISNA)
- The Islamic Scholarship Fund

"Most often a college or university has a separate application for financial aid and may request extra essays"

TIPS **Look Everywhere!**
Also look for minority scholarships specific to your state or district.

Note: *Please remember that the above list is intended to help your scholarship search, not to be the only list of scholarships you research and apply for. There are a surplus of scholarships available. The organizations referenced above are meant to help you as a starting point, but be sure to search online, talk to your teachers, and talk to your counselors to find more resources.*

Record the **scholarships** that you find below, and good luck on your applications!

My personal list of potential scholarships that I am eligible for:

1. _____
2. _____
3. _____
4. _____
5. _____

Important Note Regarding Scholarships

Colleges and universities, private businesses, and generous individuals have the privilege of establishing any criteria they want when they offer scholarships to students. Campuses list on their individual websites all of the scholarships offered by that university and what guidelines they have established for various kinds of financial aid. Typically, a college or university has a separate application for financial aid and may request extra essays. Most insist that the student and family have filed a FAFSA before the maximum amount of financial aid can be granted. Private sources such as civic clubs, businesses, and church groups may ask for a wide variety of application materials, including a transcript, a photograph of the applicant, a short essay, letters of recommendation, and/or an interview. This information is usually posted with the school, the district, or on the web.

My Turn! Organize My Scholarship Apps!

DIRECTIONS: Using your personal list of potential scholarships that you are eligible for, fill out this template for each scholarship you are considering. This will allow you to better understand the eligibility requirements, keep yourself organized, and prioritize the scholarship due dates. Also, you can create a soft copy version to save on your computer.

_____

(Scholarship Name)

_____

(Due Date)

Requirements: (Check all that apply)

- ☐ GPA
- ☐ SAT
- ☐ ACT
- ☐ Transcripts
- ☐ US Citizen
- ☐ Major Specific
- ☐ Community Service
- ☐ Letter of Recommendation
- ☐ Essay
- ☐ Ability to reapply
- ☐ Other _____

Scholarship Amount: _____

Time Line:

- Due to High School Counselors _____
- Due to Scholarship Committee _____

Submission Details:

Website: _____

Address: _____

_____

_____

_____

Scholarship Essays

Do not be intimidated if the scholarship application asks for an essay. You can and will write an amazing essay if you write several drafts and take the time to eliminate errors as well as unclear remarks. Show your work to an adult with good writing skills or to a friend who does very well in English. Bear in mind that the people reading your essay are more interested in what you have to say rather than the size of your vocabulary, but they will be expecting good command of grammar and clear, organized paragraphs. Here is some general advice on writing strong scholarship essays.

Practice Your Writing Skills

Remember that practicing your writing skills is important! It will strengthen your ability to tell your story in your scholarship essays!

Adapt Existing Essays

As you apply for scholarships, you will notice that many of the essay topics are quite similar. This allows you to adapt ideas and concepts from an essay you have already written (for example, a college application essay) rather than starting from scratch. Do not feel bad about doing this, as this is a good writing technique. However, keep in mind that the essay you are adapting needs to be good. Trying to adapt a bad essay to an entirely new topic is going to result in an even worse piece of writing.

Address the Essay Topic

Every scholarship essay will give you instructions. Follow them. If they want you to talk about community service, do not spend two pages describing your love for soccer. If they want to know about your heritage, do not write an essay about how much you want to be a dentist. If you blatantly fail to address the topic the scholarship asked for or have clearly just copied an existing essay, you definitely will not be the strongest candidate that you could be.

TIPS Be Confident!

Writing scholarship essays can be tough. It can be hard to write about yourself. Don't let this discourage you from applying to as many scholarships as possible. Remember, you can't get the scholarship if you don't apply!

Be You

Scholarships exist to give money to students who need it, who deserve it, and who might not be able to afford college without it. They do not exist to give money to perfect people from perfect homes in perfect neighborhoods, and they can tell when you're pretending to be that person. Do not write the essay you think "they" want to hear. Just be you.

Things to Highlight in My Scholarship Application Essay

It is important to avoid simply listing your accomplishments in your essay. Instead, focus on traits about your character that show you are hardworking, dependable, focused, and able to take advantage of opportunities. You can write an excellent essay showing how "I am a very _____ person." This trait has led to your success as a leader in school, in extracurricular activities, or at a job. You can even write about how that characteristic has

helped create your unique character or led to your individual goals and dreams.

Leadership Abilities

Examples of leadership abilities are being captain of a sports team, president of a school club, or starting a new organization, as well as opportunities you have chosen outside of school in church, scouts, or other group activities. This type of experience shows you're not afraid to take on challenges and will help convince schools that you can handle high level academic work and will be active in extracurricular activities while you're in college.

Academic Success

Market your successes. If you scored in the top 10% on the ACT or have a high GPA, it's worth letting schools know. Particularly focus on how you have accomplished your academic success. Be proud of the characteristics that make you a good student and a good candidate for a scholarship.

> "Colleges love to admit students with leadership experience."

Extracurricular Activities

TIPS **No Excuses!**
Having a job and working during the school week, while difficult, should not be used as an excuse to have poor grades or missing assignments.

College is all about balancing extracurriculars and academics. Schools love to see that you were involved in many different things in high school. They love it even more, though, if you devote your time to those activities that best showcase your talents and interests. If you were involved in high school athletics, you can write an excellent essay about how you successfully balanced sports and school. Similarly, if you did a lot of volunteer work, you can focus on how your unique interest led you to volunteer at your church, a homeless shelter, etc.

Work Experience

TIPS **Well Balanced**
Colleges love students who have work experience prior to applying to school, especially if the student maintained a solid GPA.

Jobs show that you have discipline and a good work ethic. In addition, a job gives students a set of skills that others who have never had to work simply won't have. Let the colleges know what skills and self-discipline you have picked up that you can use at college. If you have a construction job over the summer, let the colleges know. If you work after school, make sure you talk about it. This will help colleges understand why you haven't been more active in extracurricular activities, sports, and community service. However, it is important to note that colleges will frown upon a student who thinks a 30 hour work week replaces having good grades and academic focus. If you have to work so many hours to contribute to your family, colleges will respect that and will want to know that. On the contrary, if you are working to pay for your personal extras, like cars and electronics, cut back on the work hours and focus on school.

Character

You have amazing qualities as a person, and the colleges you are applying to want to know what they are. If you have experienced hardship, colleges want to know how you overcame it. Do not get carried away exaggerating your accomplishments, but a few examples or real life scenarios

showcasing how hard you work, your persistence, and your problem-solving skills won't hurt.

Goals and Dreams

It's great to be transparent, so let the places you're applying to know where you want to go in life. In addition to explaining how attending this college will help you accomplish your goals, emphasize activities and talents in your past that match well with your dream.

Schools love to see that you were involved in many different things in high school, but are especially interested in your having devoted extra time and energy to a few activities that reflect your interests and talents.

Financial Aid: The FAFSA

The bad news is that financial aid is possibly the most complex part of applying to college. The good news is that there is a ton of money available for students who spend the time to figure the system out. In some cases, you can even get paid to go to college!

My Starting Point: The FAFSA

To be eligible for ANY federal financial aid, you must fill out the **Free Application for Federal Student Aid (FAFSA)** when you're applying to college AND every year you are in college. Why? FREE MONEY! The FAFSA is a snapshot into your family's finances and helps schools and the government determine what amount of money they will provide in aid. Filling out the FAFSA will automatically make you eligible for many scholarships, grants, and loans. On the other hand, not filling out a FAFSA will mean you won't be able to get many scholarships. Even if you don't get enough scholarship money to pay for everything, the FAFSA is still useful because you may be eligible for loans to help pay for college.

How do I fill out the FAFSA

The FAFSA can be submitted online. There are several tips to keep in mind to successfully complete it:

1. Prepare your documents and involve your parents

Because the FAFSA collects information on your family's finances, there are a few documents you should pull together to make the process as smooth as possible:

- Your social security number
- Driver's license (if you have one)
- W-2 form (if you have a job)
- Your parents' tax forms (try really hard to get this!)

2. Start EARLY!

Every year, the FAFSA application opens on October 1st. The money is distributed on a "first come, first served" basis, so be sure to start as soon as it becomes available! You may have many questions along the way, and getting started early will ensure those questions won't slow you down to getting FREE MONEY!

If you want to preview the form before October 1st, search for "FAFSA4caster" online. This website takes you through many similar questions so you and your family can discuss these together.

> "The good news is that there is a ton of money available for students..."

3. Submit online

Find the FAFSA at www.fafsa.gov or call 1-800-4-FED-AID. Once you have the documents, search online for "five minute FAFSA" for a video that guides you through the document step by step to help you submit online.

DON'T FORGET TO FILL OUT YOUR FAFSA EACH YEAR OF COLLEGE! You must reapply each year to continue to receive financial aid.

Frequently Asked Questions about FAFSA

1. "How does the government determine my financial aid?"

The government uses a basic equation to determine student need. This equation is:

$$\textit{Cost of Attendance} - \textit{Expected Family Contribution} = \textit{Financial Need}$$

Any aid that does not cover your financial need is called "unmet need."

2. "What does Expected Family Contribution (EFC) on the FAFSA mean?"

This is an extremely important part of the FAFSA. It is the government's way of determining your financial need based on the amount of money that your family will contribute to your college education. Basically, the less your EFC, the more money you can expect to receive. Many things go into calculating your EFC – family size, current earnings, number of family members in college, and family savings.

3. "As an undocumented student or DACA student, am I eligible for federal student aid?"

No. Undocumented students, including DACA students, are not eligible for federal student aid. However, you may be eligible for state or college financial aid. Most states and colleges use information collected on the FAFSA to determine whether you are eligible for aid.

If you have a social security number, you may complete the FAFSA. Most undocumented students are not eligible for a Social Security number; thus, they cannot complete the FAFSA. However, DACA students with Social Security numbers can complete the FAFSA.

4. "As an undocumented student, am I eligible for state financial aid?"

Yes, but only in California, Connecticut, Illinois, Kansas, Maryland, Nebraska, New Mexico, New York, Oklahoma, Rhode Island, Texas, Utah, Washington, and Wisconsin. For example, in Texas, you can fill out a Texas Application for State Financial Aid (TASFA). The TASFA is for students who are ineligible to complete the Free Application for Federal Student Aid (FAFSA) but are eligible for state residency. TASFA is for state aid. TASFA is only for public universities within the state of Texas. For more information, search for "TASFA" online.

(ABC) Cost of Attendance (COA)

The estimated cost of a full-time student completing one full year of his or her college education at a given school including tuition, room and board, student fees, books and supplies, and transportation costs.

Key Point

Every school has resources to help students complete the FAFSA, ask your guidance counselor for help or refer to any website ending in ".gov" for additional assistance and to complete your FAFSA.

(ABC) DACA Student

A DACA student has received deferred action under the Deferred Action for Childhood Arrivals process. Most DACA students are also granted work authorization; and if a student has work authorization, the student may be eligible to obtain a Social Security number.

Unit 5: Pursue Financial Aid

5. "As an undocumented student or DACA student, am I eligible for in-state tuition?"

As of January 2015, undocumented students may be eligible for in-state tuition in the following states: California, Colorado, Connecticut, Florida, Hawaii, Illinois, Kansas, Kentucky, Maryland, Michigan, Minnesota, Nebraska, New mexico, New York, Oklahoma, Oregon, Rhode Island, Texas, Utah, and Washington.

DACA students are eligible for in-state tuition in the states mentioned above and in some schools in Arizona, Massachusetts, Missouri, New Hampshire, Ohio, and Virginia. For more information about tuition equity, search "United We Dream" and "DREAM Educational Empowerment Program."

6. "Can I fill out a FAFSA if I'm a U.S. citizen but my parents are not?"

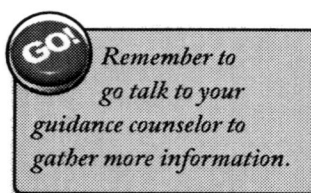

Remember to go talk to your guidance counselor to gather more information.

If your parents are not U.S. citizens, or even if your parents have criminal records, you can still fill out the FAFSA, but you will definitely want to start the application process as early as possible. Your parents will still be required to sign the application to verify its authenticity, and this form must be mailed in physically.

Before you print the form, ensure that you check the box indicating that your parents are NOT U.S. citizens. Enter your parents' social security numbers as 000-00-0000. Do not make one up or use a fake one – this will likely mean your FAFSA will be rejected!

7. "I'm a U.S. citizen but I don't have a social security number. What do I do?"

Go to a social security administration office in your city; they can help you out. Here's their website – `http://www.ssa.gov`. Use this as a resource for detailed application steps as well as a list of required documents.

8. "How do I answer the questions about taxes if I (or my parents) don't pay taxes?"

- For tax questions, answer "Will Not File"

- This will take you to another question, which will ask for information regarding income earned from work.

- Enter any money earned from a job that is listed as taxed on a W-2 form.

- From that point forward, answer only those income questions that apply to you based on this information.

9. "If my parents are divorced or don't live together, whose information do I report?"

Think about the last 12 months. Which parent have you lived with more? Which parent claims you on their taxes? That is the parent that you should provide information for. If you split the time pretty equally, list the one who provided you with more financial support (i.e. paid for more stuff).

10. "What if I have a major life change after filing my FAFSA (parent lost job, passed away, etc.)?"

You need to contact the Federal Student Aid Office and update your FAFSA. If you've already received your financial aid reward packages, you should contact the financial aid offices at the colleges in which you were accepted.

TIPS **Student Aid Report**

If you would like to send your SAR to a school that wasn't listed on your FAFSA, do so immediately so that you don't miss opportunities or deadlines!

11. "Do I have to fill out the FAFSA online?"

You may complete the application online or you may print it out and send it.

12. "What happens after I fill out the FAFSA?"

The Student Aid Report (SAR)

After you have filed your FAFSA, the government will send a **Student Aid Report (SAR)** to you and the colleges you filed on your application. After you have been accepted to a few colleges, they will send a financial aid package based on your EFC from the SAR. You should apply to multiple schools in order to determine the best financial aid package for you. Wait until you receive all of your financial aid packages before accepting any, yet make sure that you accept your offers before their deadlines pass. Remember, finding money for college can be difficult – but it's not impossible!

13. "Can I lose my financial aid package?"

Yes, you can lose your financial aid package, but you would know about it in advance and have an opportunity to fix the issue(s). Some reasons you can lose your financial aid package are: changing from a full-time to a part-time student, leaving or being expelled from your campus, deciding not to attend the school, or your GPA falling below an acceptable standard (deemed by the provider). A federal aid accountability system called **Satisfactory Academic Progress (SAP)** states that students receiving financial aid under federally supported programs must follow certain standards to continue receiving aid. These standards include holding a certain GPA and completing a minimum number of credit hours per semester.

14. "Unmet Need"

Some financial aid packages will not cover all of your financial needs. If this is the case, you will have to pay for any "unmet need" on your own (in addition to your family contribution). If your unmet need is too large for you to afford, you may want to consider going to a different college.

My Turn! FAFSA Debrief

DIRECTIONS: The FAFSA, filling it out, and keeping track of all of the information is one of the most complicated parts of the college-going process. Please answer questions 1-4 below to confirm your understanding of this tricky, but essential, process.

1. In your own words, what is the FAFSA?_____

_____

_____

2. Where do you access the FAFSA? _____

_____

_____

3. Who should you ask to help you fill out the FAFSA? _____

_____

_____

4. How many times do you have to submit the FAFSA? _____

_____

_____

Notes

_____

_____

_____

_____

_____

_____

_____

_____

_____

_____

_____

Comparing Financial Aid Packages

Comparing Aid Packages

If your aid packages have met almost all of your financial needs, you should focus on the following before making a decision on which award to accept:

- **Grants and scholarships are best.*** You do not have to pay these back.

    - ***Note:** Pay close attention as to whether your scholarships are **renewable** or **non-renewable**. If they are **renewable**, be sure to meet the scholarship requirements each year so that you can continue getting the scholarships. If they are **non-renewable**, you only get it for a year and do not have a chance of getting it the following year.*

- Loans are not as good. You have to pay these back. However, federally subsidized loans are not as bad because the government pays the interest while you are fully enrolled, and the interest rates are low once you begin repaying after graduation.

- <u>You don't have to accept loans</u> if you can find another way to pay for your tuition (such as a scholarship or part-time job). Before deciding that you don't want any loans, consider the size of the loan and the college offering the loan. If it's a relatively small loan or if it's a college that you're most excited to attend, it may make more sense to accept it.

Key Point

Financial aid packages include grants and scholarships as well as loans and work study, all of which you can accept or decline.

Unit 5: Pursue Financial Aid

Make a Decision and Don't Miss Deadlines!

Follow your head and your heart. You won't be successful in college solely because one school is cheaper than another, so don't base your decision only on money. On the other hand, remember that borrowing a ton of money to attend your dream school might not be the best idea. If you aren't satisfied with any of your financial aid packages, you do have a choice to appeal for more money by contacting the financial aid office and writing a letter of appeal.

My Turn! Decision Point

DIRECTIONS: On the following pages you will find three sample financial aid packages from three example universities:

- Roadmap Public University
- Achievement Community College
- Success Private University

Read the profiles of each university to get to know them and the opportunities on their campus. Then, read their financial aid offers closely to find out what they are really offering you!

Roadmap Public University Profile

Located in Roadmap, USA (one of America's best college towns), Roadmap University is an exceptional top-tier public university offering an array of over 300 majors, talented professors, and top-notch facilities. All of these characteristics allow students more opportunities to explore, grow, and succeed. Roadmap Public University has a student population of 30,000 graduate and undergraduate students, yet the 500+ student organizations and programs on campus make it easy for students to find their "place" and feel at home. It is only one of five universities nationwide that offers law, medicine, veterinary medicine and a nuclear reactor research facility on one campus. It is currently ranked as a top 75 school by U.S. News and World Report.

What Are They **Really** Offering?

DIRECTIONS: Answer the following questions to help determine the strength of Roadmap Public University's offer:

1. Find the "Unmet Need" line. If you accept the entire award package, will you have any unmet need left to pay? CIRCLE (Yes / No)
   - *If you do have "Unmet Need," how much of your need is unmet?*

   $_____

2. Take a closer look at the Award Package. Are they offering you Grants? Scholarships? Loans? Work Study? Calculate the total amount of money of each type of aid offered:
   - "Free" Money = (Grants + Scholarships + Awards)

     $_____
   - Money to be paid back later = (Loans)

     $_____
   - Other Awards = Work Study

     $_____

Roadmap Public University

Office of Financial Aid

Jayda Batchelder   March 25, 2019
321 Tulane St.   Award Year: 2019-2020
New Orleans, LA 70118   SN: 123-45-6780

Notice of Financial Aid Offer

After reviewing your Student Aid Application, the financial aid committee is pleased to provide you with the following offer. To accept this award, please complete, sign, and return a white copy of this form within two weeks. This award is subject to cancellation if not returned by this date.

Please place a check mark next to "**A**" for Accept or "**D**" to Decline.

AWARD PACKAGE

The following amounts will be awarded for both the Fall and Spring semesters of 2017-18.

		A	D
Public University Award	$1,500	( )	( )
Federal SEO Grant	$500	( )	( )
Federal Pell Grant	$2,650	( )	( )
State Grant	$1,000	( )	( )
Federal Perkins Loan	$1,000	( )	( )
Federal Sub. Stafford Loan	$2,500	( )	( )
Federal Work Study	$1,000	( )	( )

SEMESTER TOTAL   **$10,150**
YEARLY TOTAL   **$20,300**

Family Resources

Parents' Contribution	$ 0
Student's Contribution	$ 2,580
Total Contribution	$2,580

SUMMARY

Estimated Cost of Attendance	$22,880
(LESS) Family Contribution	$ 2,580
Financial Need	**$20,300**

(LESS) Financial Aid Offer	$20,300
Unmet Need	**$ 0**

---

3. This university expects you to make a $2,580 contribution on your own. Is attending this university worth the effort to fill this financial gap to you? Please explain why with at least two pieces of evidence.

_____

_____

_____

_____

_____

_____

Achievement Community College Profile

Achievement College is a wonderful community college located in the South County suburb of Achievement, USA. Whether a commuter or an on-campus resident, students at Achievement College thoroughly enjoy the "Achievement" lifestyle. There are approximately 3,500 students enrolled, all of who are working on completing their Associate's Degree. Achievement College takes pride in preparing students to make the full-time transition to a traditional four-year university. Achievement College currently offers approximately 50 degree programs and has over 50 student organizations. It is currently ranked as a top 500 school by U.S. News and World Report.

What Are They <u>Really</u> Offering?

DIRECTIONS: Answer the following questions to help determine the strength of Achievement Community College's offer:

1. Find the "Unmet Need" line. If you accept the entire award package, will you have any unmet need left to pay? CIRCLE (Yes / No)
   * *If you do have "Unmet Need," how much of your need is unmet?*

   $_____

2. Take a closer look at the Award Package. Are they offering you Grants? Scholarships? Loans? Work Study? Calculate the total amount of money of each type of aid offered:
   * "Free" Money = (Grants + Scholarships + Awards)

   $_____
   * Money to be paid back later = (Loans)

   $_____
   * Other Awards = Work Study

   $_____

Achievement Community College

Office of Financial Aid

Kristen Watkins   March 25, 2019
123 Jayhawk Rd.   Award Year: 2019-2020
Lawrence, KS 66045   SN: 000-98-0123

Notice of Financial Aid Offer

After reviewing your Student Aid Application, the financial aid committee is pleased to provide you with the following offer. To accept this award, please complete, sign, and return a white copy of this form within two weeks. This award is subject to cancellation if not returned by this date.

Please place a check mark next to "**A**" for Accept or "**D**" to Decline.

AWARD PACKAGE

The following amounts will be awarded for both the Fall and Spring semesters of 2017–18.

		A	D
Achievement Scholarship	$1,500	( )	( )
Federal SEO Grant	$1,100	( )	( )
Federal Pell Grant	$4,200	( )	( )
Federal Stafford Loan	$2,600	( )	( )

SEMESTER TOTAL	**$9,400**
YEARLY TOTAL	**$18,800**

Family Resources

Parents' Contribution	$	0
Student's Contribution	$	0
Total Contribution	$	0

SUMMARY

Estimated Cost of Attendance	$19,800
(LESS) Family Contribution	$ 0
Financial Need	
$19,800	

(LESS) Financial Aid Offer	$18,800
Unmet Need	**$1,000**

---

3. This college doesn't expect your family to make a contribution in order to attend. But you have at least $1,000 in unmet need that you will need to find a way to fill. Is attending this college worth the effort to you? Please explain your answer with at least two pieces of evidence.

_____

_____

_____

_____

_____

_____

Success Private University Profile

Nestled in the brisk northeast, Success Private University is one of the top private schools in the country. It is highly selective, and to be offered admission to the undergraduate program is an elite honor. Students, faculty, and alumni from Success Private University are world renowned for contributions in a variety of fields, including politics and business. Because the quality of applicants is so strong and the value of education is so high, Success Private University does not award merit-based scholarships. While the price tag is high, it has been consistently ranked as a "Top Ten" school in U.S. News and World Report for the past decade.

What Are They <u>Really</u> Offering?

DIRECTIONS: Answer the following questions to help determine the strength of Success Private University's offer:

1. Find the "Unmet Need" line. If you accept the entire award package, will you have any unmet need left to pay? CIRCLE (Yes / No)
   - *If you do have "Unmet Need," how much of your need is unmet?*

   $_____

2. Take a closer look at the Award Package. Are they offering you Grants? Scholarships? Loans? Work Study? Calculate the total amount of money of each type of aid offered:
   - "Free" Money = (Grants + Scholarships + Awards)

     $_____
   - Money to be paid back later = (Loans)

     $_____
   - Other Awards = Work Study

     $_____

Success Private University

Office of Financial Aid

Sean Planchard   March 25, 2019
123 Buffalo Rd.   Award Year: 2019-2020
Boulder, CO 80302   SN: 987-65-3210

Notice of Financial Aid Offer

After reviewing your Student Aid Application, the financial aid committee is pleased to provide you with the following offer. To accept this award, please complete, sign, and return a white copy of this form within two weeks. This award is subject to cancellation if not returned by this date.

Please place a check mark under "**A**" for Accept or "**D**" to Decline.

AWARD PACKAGE

The following amounts will be awarded for both the Fall and Spring semesters of 2017–18.

		A	D
Need-Based Scholarship	$7,500	( )	( )
Federal SEO Grant	$5,500	( )	( )
Federal Subsidized Loan	$5,250	( )	( )
Federal Perkins Loan	$2,600	( )	( )

SEMESTER TOTAL	**$20,850**
YEARLY TOTAL	**$41,700**

Family Resources

Parents' Contribution	$	0
Student's Contribution	$	0
Total Contribution	$	0

SUMMARY

Estimated Cost of Attendance
$41,700

(LESS) Family Contribution	$ 0
Financial Need	**$41,700**

(LESS) Financial Aid Offer	$41,700
Unmet Need	**$ 0**

---

3. While this university has met all of your financial aid obligations, it appears you will be required to take out a significant amount of loans in order to attend. How comfortable are you with this decision? Are the loans worth it to you to attend? Please explain your answer with at least two pieces of evidence:

_____
_____
_____
_____
_____
_____

My Turn! Weigh My Decision

DIRECTIONS: Now that you've had a chance to look at each financial aid offer in depth, it's time to weigh the pros (positives) and the cons (negatives) of each of the three options offered. Remember, there is no one right choice for everyone. Where you will be happiest and find the most success in college is truly up to you! Use the questions below to help you weigh your decision. Keep in mind, these financial aid packages only cover 1 of 4 years in college.

Unit 5: Pursue Financial Aid

Roadmap Public University		Achievement Community College		Success Private University	
Pros	**Cons**	**Pros**	**Cons**	**Pros**	**Cons**
•	•	•	•	•	•
•	•	•	•	•	•
•	•	•	•	•	•

Questions to Consider as You Make Your Choice

1. Which financial aid package offers the most grants/scholarships? Even if they offer more grants/scholarships, is it enough to completely cover your cost of attendance?

    _____

    _____

2. Which financial aid package offers more loans? Which loans would you rather pay off and why?

    _____

    _____

3. Really consider the university profiles (descriptions). Do you feel like the financial aid award offer (and each of their pros and cons) matches your level of interest to attend that school? Why/Why not?

    _____

    _____

My College Choice Is: _____!

Surveys show that the biggest obstacle facing college bound students is money. Remember that the "sticker price" for the college of your choice is not necessarily the price you will have to pay. You can help lower the costs of college by living off campus, earning college credit in high school, or finding a part time job. College can be very expensive, but as you have learned, there are many different options available to help you finance your education. The first step is filling out a FAFSA. You will need your parents' help and input to complete this time-consuming, but necessary, task. There is a huge amount of free money available, so apply for financial aid even if your finances are stable. Start a savings plan as soon as possible, and put aside every penny you can spare. Always spend your money wisely, and separate what you may need from what you want. Do not let money be the reason you fail to pursue your dreams. College can be affordable for everyone!

My Turn! 3-2-1... Pursue Financial Aid!

List and explain THREE different types of financial aid:

-

-

-

List TWO factors that influence the amount of federal aid you can receive to attend college:

-

-

List ONE task you MUST complete in order to receive any federal financial aid, and whose help you will need in order to complete it:

-

UNIT 6
APPLY TO COLLEGE

What are the steps for applying to college?

DIRECTIONS: Read the topics of this unit on the roadmap. Draw an "emoji" of your emotions about this content as you start the unit.

Unit 6 Vocabulary
page 188

College Selectivity
page 189

Types of College Admission
page 192

Choosing A School
page 195

My College Research
page 197

Whose help do I need in the application process?

The College Application Process
page 198

DIRECTIONS: In reflection of the information you learned in this unit, draw an emoji of how you feel now.

What are the SAT and ACT? Are there any tips for scoring well on them?

About the SAT and the ACT
page 200

The College Application Essay
page 207

College Application Tracker
page 218

Practice College Common Application
page 219

Unit 6 Summary
page 226

Unit 6 Vocabulary

Acceptance/ Admission	Candidates Reply Date Agreement (CRDA)	Early Action	Regular Admission
Admissions Committee	The Common Application	Early Admission	Rolling Admission
Binding Application		Early Decision	SAT/ACT
		Personal Statement	Transcript

DIRECTIONS: In the space below, select several unfamiliar words from the vocabulary word bank. Then, define each word using the glossary or a dictionary. Last, create an original sentence for each of the selected words.

Vocabulary Word	Definition	Your Original Sentence

College Selection

Before you can choose which colleges to apply to, you should be aware of the different levels of 'competiveness' or 'selectiveness' of potential schools. There are four categories: (1) Highly Selective, (2) Selective, (3) Moderately Selective, and (4) Open. Bear in mind that these are very broad categories – for example, some schools in the highly selective category will be easier to get into than others. However, you can only apply to so many schools, so it is useful to try and match yourself to schools that you will have a good chance of getting into in terms of your GPA, class rank, SAT or ACT scores, and affordability. That said, you should also be ambitious. Take a chance and apply to your dream school, it won't hurt. Lastly, talk to your school counselor about which schools are realistic for you.

Since college applications take time and money, it doesn't make sense to apply to every school in the country. Here is a suggested list of the types of schools you should apply to as a senior.

1-2 "Safe Schools"	Safe schools are ones that you have a VERY good chance of being admitted to.
3-4 "Moderate Schools"	Moderate schools are ones that you have a decent chance of admission, but not a guarantee.
1-2 "Dream Schools"	Dream schools are ones that you may have a hard time being admitted to, but are always worth a shot!

Keep in mind; some schools that are reach schools are moderate schools for other students, and vice versa. It's good to have a spread between safety and ambition; because you never know what can happen or what financial aid you will receive!

Highly Selective (Very Competitive)

These are the hardest colleges to get into. In most cases, you will need to have good grades, high SAT and/or ACT scores, lots of extracurricular involvement, strong college essays and recommendation letters, and sometimes a personal interview. These schools typically accept less than 17% of applicants. Examples of highly selective colleges include: Harvard, Yale, Stanford, and Northwestern.

Selective (Competitive)

These are colleges that are quite challenging to get into, but not quite as tough as the highly selective ones listed above. While these schools are selective, their application process isn't quite as rigorous. These colleges tend to accept fewer than half of the students who apply. Examples of selective colleges include University of Texas – Austin, Tulane University, New York University, College of William and Mary, and Notre Dame University.

Moderately Selective (Moderately Competitive)

These colleges make up the largest pool, with the majority of colleges falling into this

TIPS **Are You a Match?**
The perfect school is out there for you. You need to find the right fit! Spend the time it takes to compare your GPA, class rank, and test scores to find the best school for you!

Key Point
Schools range in their selectivity: highly selective, selective, moderately selective, and open enrollment.

Key Point
There are no colleges that accept all students; all schools consider grades, test scores, and extracurricular activities when determining admission.

"Take a chance and apply to your dream school, it won't hurt."

Unit 6: Apply to College

Visit School Websites!

Generally, colleges post their expectations for prospective students on their school website. Take advantage of this information.

category. While good grades and extracurricular involvement are a must, the SAT/ACT scores and good grades are not necessarily a cutoff. These colleges' "selectivity" typically range from acceptance rates of 50%-75%. Examples of moderately selective colleges include University of North Carolina at Chapel Hill, University of Nebraska – Lincoln, Baylor University, Georgia Tech, Indiana University – Bloomington, and Virginia Tech.

Open (Actively Seeking Students)

This is the easiest category of schools to get admitted to. However, it's worth noting that this doesn't mean you are by any means guaranteed acceptance. Students with weak grades, few extracurricular activities and low SAT and/ or ACT scores will still find it challenging to get into these schools. These colleges often admits students in the bottom half of their class, but still have guidelines and requirements. Examples of open colleges include University of Texas – Arlington and community colleges.

Below is a table that loosely sorts a sample of schools and organizes them according to these four levels of selectivity. Remember, college admissions is not a hard and fast science, and there are thousands, if not millions, of stories of students getting into schools they never thought they could reach and vice versa.

Schools Organized by Relative Selectivity

School Type	Highly Selective	Selective	Moderately Selective	Open
Representative Enrollment Community	♟	♟♟♟	♟♟♟♟♟	♟♟♟♟♟♟♟♟♟♟
Ivy League Examples	• Harvard • Yale • Princeton • Brown • Dartmouth • Columbia • University of Pennsylvania • Cornell			
Private School Examples	• Juilliard • Stanford • Duke • Vanderbilt • Northwestern	• Wake Forest • University of Southern California • Boston University	• TCU • Samford • Clemson University	
Public School Examples	• University of California - Berkeley	• University of Virginia • University of North Carolina - Chapel Hill	• Oklahoma University • University of Arkansas • Michigan State University	
Community College Examples				• Grossmont College (CA) • El Centro College (TX) • Bunker Hill Community College (MA) • Front Range Community College (CO)

A Note on College Selectiveness

Most schools have already established guidelines for the students they hope to accept in a given year. Research and take advantage of this information. They make their expectations known to prospective students on their website and in college research materials. College acceptance rates vary from year to year. Do your research to learn how selective your colleges of interest are.

Check the Rankings

When choosing your college, compare academic ranking! `http://colleges.usnews.rankingsandreviews.com/best-colleges`

College Rankings

In the same way that seniors graduating from high school are given a class rank, colleges and universities are ranked in areas ranging from cost to academic quality. These should play a role in your decision about where to go to college; future employers would rather hire a graduate of a top ranked college than a graduate of a low ranked college. While there are many sources for these rankings, one of the most commonly referenced is U.S. News & World Report, which can be accessed online or at a bookstore. It supplies lists of schools in different categories such as small liberal arts colleges or large state universities.

My Turn! College Selectiveness

DIRECTIONS: Using the information on the previous pages, fill out the chart below with different facts that you have learned about colleges and their relative levels of selectiveness. Once finished, use the information from the table to answer the questions below.

College Selectiveness	
Highly Selective	**Selective**
Fact 1:	Fact 1:
Fact 2:	Fact 2:
Example School:	Example School:
Moderately Selective	**Open Admission**
Fact 1:	Fact 1:
Fact 2:	Fact 2:
Example School:	Example School:

1. What type of college is the most difficult to get into?

   A. Selective   C. Highly Selective

   B. Open Admission   D. Moderately Selective

2. Put an X on the factors that a college would NOT consider.

   ○ Grades   ○ Hometown   ○ Clubs/Organizations

   ○ Friends   ○ Test Scores   ○ Age

3. What is one reason that a student would attend a college that is highly ranked in academics? _____

Types of College Admission

TIPS Applying Early Helps!

Applying early does significantly increase your chances of getting accepted to the university of your choice.

ABC Binding Application

A binding application binds the student to that particular college or university that they are applying. This means that if they are accepted to that college or university that they applied for they must attend there the following semester.

TIPS Priority Deadline

Regardless of the admission you choose, do not miss the Priority Deadline. The priority deadline is the date by which your application — whether it's for college admission, student housing or financial aid — must be received to be given the strongest consideration.

There are three types of **admission** you can apply for as a student: early, regular and rolling. In many cases colleges offer more than one. For example, a college may offer early admission if you apply by a certain date, but still offer regular admission past that date. However, the different types of admission influence your chances of getting admitted, so you should investigate which types of admission the colleges you would like to apply to offer. Once you know this, pick the one that is going to maximize your chance of getting in. Most importantly, familiarize yourself with the deadlines for application and financial aid requests at each of your potential colleges or universities.

Early Admission

Some schools, generally private colleges and universities, offer **early admission**. The overall idea is quite simple – you apply earlier in the year. Applicants choose to do this because, generally, you have a better chance of being admitted since the university knows you are sincerely interested in attending. There are typically two types of Early Admission.

Early Decision (ED) programs are commonly binding. **Binding** means that the applicant must attend the school if their application is accepted. Early decision applicants are expected to submit only one early decision application to one school. However, you need to be positive that you want to attend a specific university before you commit to the considerable work it will take to do a strong admissions packet early in your senior year.

Early Action (EA) programs are non-binding. Students get an early response to their application but do not have to make a decision immediately. This allows students the opportunity to consider other colleges and compare financial aid packages.

Although a school can decide to move your file from the early admission consideration to a later deadline consideration, you can only apply once.

Regular Admission

Regular admission is the type of admission that most schools offer. There is a set deadline by which an applicant has to submit their application. After this, all of the college's admission decisions are usually sent out around the same time. You can apply for regular admission to as many schools as you want and, once you receive your offers of admission, you can pick whichever school you would like to go to. Most of the time you will want to apply for regular admission, although you can turn in your materials long before the deadline if they are thorough and polished.

Rolling Admission

Rolling admission, which means the college will accept applications year round, is not as common as having a specific deadline; however, some schools do offer it. The easiest way to understand rolling admission is to view it as the opposite of regular admission. Regular admission has a specific deadline for applications, and acceptances are often sent out to all students on the same date. Rolling admission means that a college will assign a large window (up to six months) during which applicants can submit an application at any time until the college has filled all of its freshman class. Similarly, admission decisions are not sent out all at once – they are given out whenever the college makes a decision on whether or not they want the applicant to be a student there. Keep in mind, financial aid may be less available for students applying during their senior year at the end of a rolling, late spring, or summer deadline.

TIPS **Plan Ahead**
Don't miss the deadline for the college of your choice!

My Turn! So, What's the Difference?

DIRECTIONS: Go back through the text one more time and pull out what makes these admission processes unique. Record your answers in the chart below.

Early Decision	Early Action
Regular Admission	**Rolling Admission**

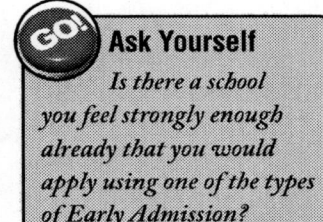

GO! Ask Yourself
Is there a school you feel strongly enough already that you would apply using one of the types of Early Admission?

You may be asking yourself, "What happens after I am admitted to the college(s) of my choice if I didn't apply Early Decision?"

Once you are accepted, many colleges follow the **Candidates Reply Date Agreement (CRDA)**, which gives applicants until May 1 to accept or decline offers of admission. This will give you, as the student, time to get responses from most of the colleges you have applied to before choosing one. Then accept the one that is right for you!

Notes/Drawings

Choosing A School

My Turn! Prioritizing College Characteristics

There are roughly 4,000 colleges and universities in the United States. As a result, deciding where to apply can sometimes seem overwhelming for students. This section is designed to help you narrow down the list to around 5-10 schools you feel you might apply to. However, make sure you go further than just this section – always make sure to _thoroughly_ research schools before you apply.

You can consult the free website for _The College Board_ at `www.collegeboard.org` to find the most recent statistics each college and university has posted on the SAT scores of their recently accepted applicants, the average class ranks and GPA of current students, as well as costs and current statistics regarding how much financial aid has recently been given.

TIPS **Do Your Research!**
You should never blindly apply to a school without researching it first. If you do, you are likely going to waste a lot of time, energy, and money, too.

DIRECTIONS: For each characteristic, place a checkmark under "Not Very Important", "Somewhat Important", or "Very Important". When you are done, look at the characteristics you marked as "Very Important". These will help you narrow down the most important factors to you in choosing a college or university.

Key Point
It is important to consider personal fit when choosing a college, including majors offered, selectivity, location, size, and cost.

GO! _Remember to go talk to your guidance counselor to gather more information._

College Characteristic	Importance Rating		
	Not Very Important	Somewhat Important	Very Important
1. Variety of majors offered			
2. Selective and well-known reputation			
3. Distance from home			
4. Size of the student body			
5. Cost of attending			
6. Guidance and personal attention to students, especially first generation college students			
7. Extracurricular activities			
8. Good sports program			
9. Diverse student body			
10. Job and graduate school placcement			

Unit 6: Apply to College

Go Further

After completing the chart, you can start an initial search. If you want to stay in-state, or know you would like to attend college in a particular state, check out colleges on either the U.S. News & World Report or The College Board website. On these sites, you can access a school's information quickly in order to search and compare schools and programs.

Family Visit!
Involve your family in the college visit process and make a trip out of it.

Visit Schools

Visiting schools is the next step. You should visit as many schools as possible, even if you have little interest in attending some of them. This is the best way for you to get an overall feeling about the school alongside with the rankings, majors and extracurricular activities available. Have a student guide, or current student, give you a tour of the campus to further help you make an informed decision.

Ask Your Student Guide(s):

- Do people have an easy time transitioning from high school to this school?
- What do the professors expect of students?
- What tutoring resources are available to me as a freshman? Do a lot of freshmen need tutoring support when they start here?
- What is it like for students socially?
- What types of clubs/groups/activities do freshmen usually join?
- What else do you think might be a good idea to ask your guide?

Ask Yourself:

- How close do my GPA, class rank, and SAT/ACT scores match the average statistics for students recently admitted to this campus?
- What do I really like and dislike about the campus?
- Do I feel comfortable here?
- If I had the chance, would I come here to study after high school?

My Turn! What Else to Ask?

DIRECTIONS: You know yourself better than anyone else. What other questions do YOU think would be important to ask on a college visit?

- _____
  _____
- _____
  _____
- _____
  _____

My College Research

My Turn! College Research Template

DIRECTIONS: As you research new universities and colleges, use these questions below as a template (a.k.a. a guide). It will help you learn more about the school and whether or not it will meet your needs as a college student.

Basic Information

1. Is it Public or Private? _____

2. Located in: _____

3. Founded in the year: _____

4. School Mascot/ Team name: _____

5. Number of students: _____

6. Traditions:

Investigate!

Remember, the list of questions to the left is like a trampoline – it's a great jumping off point. Ask as many questions as you feel necessary in order to find the school of your dreams!

7. How well is it ranked? Does it offer the major you're looking for?

8. How can you apply? Do they accept the Common Application?

9. How much is tuition (cost of classes) for a year?

10. How much is room and board?

11. How much financial aid did the average freshmen receive in recent years?

12. What is the average range of scores on the SAT /ACT for students there?

13. Find a fun fact about the college:

Applying to college may seem like a confusing process, but follow this "map" and you will successfully apply to the college(s) of your choice.

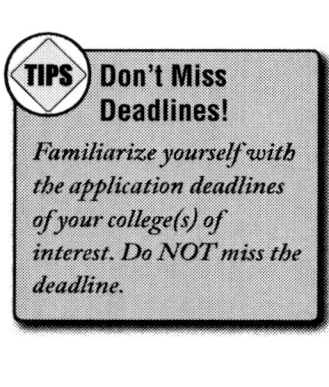

TIPS ⬦ Don't Miss Deadlines!

Familiarize yourself with the application deadlines of your college(s) of interest. Do NOT miss the deadline.

GO! Practice Application

When you're done reading everything in this section, there's a full practice application later in this unit for you to work on based on the actual Common Application.

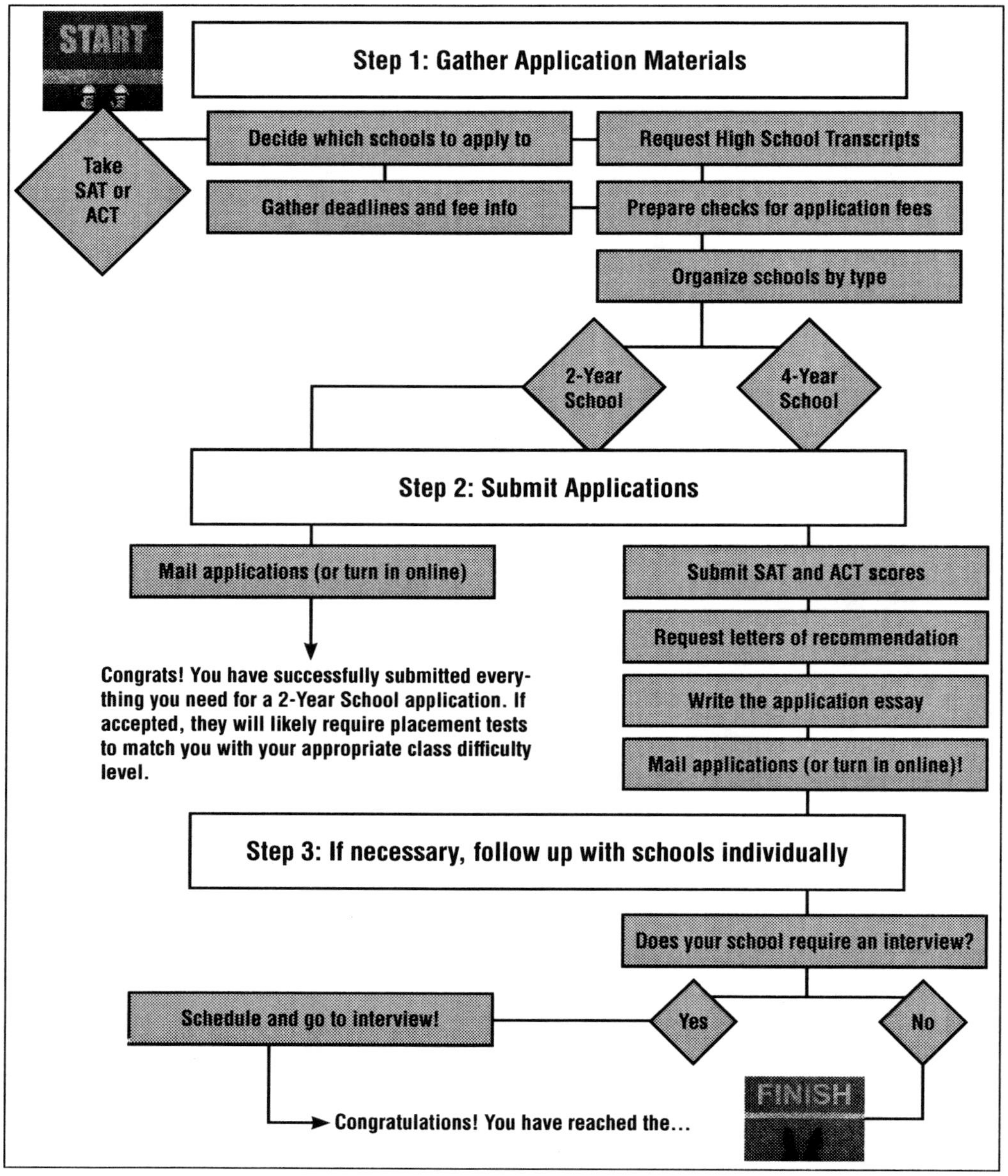

START

Take SAT or ACT

Step 1: Gather Application Materials

Decide which schools to apply to

Gather deadlines and fee info

Request High School Transcripts

Prepare checks for application fees

Organize schools by type

2-Year School

4-Year School

Step 2: Submit Applications

Mail applications (or turn in online)

Submit SAT and ACT scores

Request letters of recommendation

Write the application essay

Mail applications (or turn in online)!

Congrats! You have successfully submitted everything you need for a 2-Year School application. If accepted, they will likely require placement tests to match you with your appropriate class difficulty level.

Step 3: If necessary, follow up with schools individually

Does your school require an interview?

Schedule and go to interview!

Yes

No

FINISH

Congratulations! You have reached the...

Believe it or not, most college applications are relatively straightforward - so don't panic. Here's the basic breakdown:

Personal Information

Your name, address, phone number, e-mail address (if you don't have one, get one), what you might want to major in, your ethnicity and your social security number (if you have one).

Educational Information

This could include where you went to school, when you graduate, the name of your guidance counselor, and a list of the courses you are taking your senior year in order of difficulty. More importantly, you want to ensure that you sign up, in your high school's registrar office, to have your official transcript sent to each college you are applying to. The **transcript** will give the college admissions office your class rank, your cumulative high school GPA, and the official report of the classes that you have taken throughout high school, as well as any Pre-AP, AP, or honor courses that you have taken.

Test Scores

Your scores on standardized tests including AP exams, the ACT, the SAT or both. You must check with your school counselor or registrar to find out if you are required to send the SAT or ACT scores online.

Family Information

Basically, the same information you provided in the personal information section, but for your parents. Put whomever you live with for the majority of the year if you don't live with your parents.

Extracurricular Activities

List the activities you were involved in, how many years you have been involved in them, and how many hours a week you spend or have spent on them. It is hard to remember all of these after four years of high school, which is why you want to consistently update your résumé throughout school. Be relatively accurate here – colleges won't believe that you spent 60 hours a week playing golf.

Academic Honors

Did you win any awards in high school? Were you valedictorian? Win the school history prize? Honor roll? Nominated for band secretary? Most improved in Spanish? Co-captain of the soccer team? This is where you list all of those prizes and awards you have won. Show what a great leader you are!

Work Experience

Did you have an after school job? Have an internship or job over the summer? This is where you record all of the work experience you have.

Short Answer

If the application has a short answer section, the instructions will limit you to either just enough words to capture the facts or will challenge you to reveal something about yourself in a concise manner. If there are essays of one to three paragraphs, work on supplying specific details and a vivid picture of yourself in the short space.

Personal Essay

You will learn more specific information about the college application essay later in this chapter. Make sure you spend more time than you think is necessary on this part - it is a major component of your application.

Almost all four-year colleges and universities require one or more long essays – about a page to two pages typed. The college will supply specific questions giving you an opportunity to explore aspects of your mind and life experiences. The admissions committee will closely read any long essays for intelligent responses, excellent grammar, and essay form. Expect to write several drafts, and try to find a teacher or an adult who has experience with writing to give you feedback on your drafts.

TIPS **Transcripts**
Get your official transcripts from your school's registrar office.

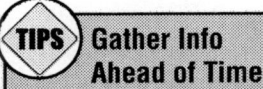

TIPS **Gather Info Ahead of Time**
Don't forget to gather all of your test scores and financial aid information well before the deadline! You definitely don't want to be in a race to finish your applications at the end.

Unit 6: Apply to College

About the SAT and the ACT

Most colleges consider your SAT and/or ACT score as part of the admission process. These tests are given to students on specific days over the school year and must be signed up for online, through the mail, or through the school counseling service. It is strongly recommended that all students take one or both tests during their junior year.

Why are These Tests Important for You?

Not only do colleges look at your test scores from the ACT or SAT for admission, but many offer scholarships based on your scores. They may also use your test results for course placement and course credit. This means if you can show that you are academically ready to succeed in college-level courses, you may test out of some foundational classes. Since the tests assess information you are learning in your high school classes, it is important to work hard all four years. The harder you work in school, the more prepared you will be to do well on the tests.

What is the SAT?

The **SAT** is a widely used test in college admissions. It assesses lifelong learning and subject matter learned in high school. The recently redesigned SAT, which took effect in Spring 2016, focuses on evidence-based reading and writing, math, and an optional essay. It includes three kinds of questions: multiple-choice, student-produced responses (in mathematics only), and an essay. The test is scored from 200 to 800 for Evidence-Based Reading and Writing, 200 to 800 for Math, and 2 to 8 on each of three traits for the essay. The highest possible score for the first two tests on the SAT is 1600; the essay score is reported separately.

A Few Key Facts about the SAT

- Most students take the SAT once or twice. College Board, the organization that administers the test, does not recommend taking it more than twice. There is no evidence that taking the SAT multiple times significantly changes your score.

- **Collegeboard.org**, the website for SAT, has free practice questions, practice tests, and study guides. Take advantage of the free access!

- When you register for the SAT, you can choose up to four schools to send your scores to for free. You may change this up to nine days after the test date. Take advantage of these score reports, as additional reports are subject to a fee.

- **SAT Subject Tests:** Some highly competitive colleges require you to take an SAT Subject Test to demonstrate high competence in individual subjects. Check the official website or with the admissions department of your prospective college to see if they require or prefer certain SAT Subject Tests. Subject areas with these tests include Literature, American History, World History, Mathematics, Biology, Chemistry, Physics, and several foreign languages.

My Turn! Rate My Confidence for the SAT

DIRECTIONS: In the SAT Summary chart below, read the description for each section and, in the third column, rate yourself between 1 and 10 on how well you think you would do on that particular section. For example, a 1 would mean you do not think you have historically scored well and a 10 would mean that you usually do very, very well on that topic.

SAT Summary

Section of Test	Description	Rating
Evidence Based Reading and Writing	**Reading Test:** Measures understanding of passages from U.S. and World Literature, History/Social Studies, and Sciences. **Writing and Language Test:** Measures "Expression of Ideas" and "Standard English Conventions" through passages relating to Careers, History/Social Studies, Humanities and Sciences.	
Mathematics	Measures ability to solve and analyze real world problems; emphasis on algebra and some advanced math.	
Essay	Measures reading, analysis, and writing skills; students must analyze a source document and explain how the author builds an argument. OPTIONAL; however, many colleges may require students to complete the essay.	

Test Details: The SAT Test includes 5 sections and takes 3 hours to complete (plus 50 minutes for the Essay [optional])

*Scoring: Range from 200-800 on the other two sections of the test. Highest possible score is 1600. The Essay is optional and the score ranges from 2 to 8 on each of three measured traits. *Note: You are NOT penalized for guessing on the SAT.*

> **GO!** *For additional test taking tips* visit `http://info.methodtestprep.com/blog/bid/58010/SAT-Quick-Facts`

> **TIPS Save Time** *Don't worry about memorizing a bunch of formulas; those that are commonly used are provided for you.*

SAT Specific Test Taking Tips

- **Take the PSAT seriously!** The PSAT is usually offered in school during your 8th or 9th grade year and provides practice for the SAT. Students who score high on the PSAT may have a chance to enter scholarship programs.

- **Don't spend too much time cramming vocabulary words.** Vocabulary is still valuable on various sections of the test, but comprehension is more important than memorization of vocabulary.

- **Brush up on your math.** A good knowledge of Algebra I is just as important as Algebra II.

What is the ACT?

The **ACT**, or "American College Test," is the other standardized test used in the college admission process and colleges and universities nationwide accept it. The ACT is a curriculum based achievement test that is meant to measure information you have learned during high school.

TIPS **Not Just Tests**
Keep in mind, testing scores are not the only part of your application used to determine admission.

A Few Key Facts About the ACT

- You can take it up to 12 times, so do not be afraid to retake it.

- There are several different mobile phone apps that you can download and use for preparations however, two of these apps have been created by ACT.

- By answering questions about your interests and courses, ACT develops a profile for you including your work in high school and your career choices. It also shows your strengths and weaknesses in the subject areas tested. This information is informative both for you and for colleges.

- Take advantage of the fact that you can send your scores to four colleges for free. If you send more than one score to a school, their database will automatically drop your lowest score.

- ACT changed to a new scoring system in 2015. While the new scoring system will not change the types of questions or the format of the test, it will provide sub-scores allowing you to identify your strengths and areas for improvement. For example, there will be A STEM (Science, Technology, Engineering, and Mathematics) score based on your scores on the math and science sections. If you score well in these areas, then you may want to consider a college major in a STEM discipline or a career in a related field.

My Turn! Rate My Confidence for the ACT

DIRECTIONS: In the same way you completed the last exercise, please rate yourself on your confidence level in the third column of the ACT Test Summary chart below. Also, on the next page, please answer the two questions at the bottom.

ACT Summary

Section of Test	Description	Rating
English	Measures knowledge about the use of standard written English; no vocabulary or analogies, five reading comprehension passages.	
Mathematics	Math reasoning skills; mostly Geometry and Algebra, but also has four questions on Trigonometry/Pre-Calculus.	
Reading	Measures reading comprehension and reasoning skills, which will compare or draw information from four passages.	
Science	Measures ability to interpret, analyze, and evaluate information related to the natural sciences. It is focused more on scientific process and not as much on specifics for science courses such as chemistry and physics.	
Essay	Measures writing skills emphasized in high school English classes. OPTIONAL; however, some colleges may require this section for scores to be considered.	

Test Details: Includes four test sections and takes three hours and 25 minutes (including a 30 minute optional writing test).

Scoring: Your score is averaged across the four sections of the test. e highest possible score on each section is 36. Note: You are NOT penalized for guessing on the ACT either.

ACT Specific Test Taking Tips

- **Answer the questions you find easiest first.** Come back to the others last.
- **Don't waste time.** You shouldn't spend more than a minute or two on any question.
- **Answer every question.** There is no penalty for guessing and the easy questions are worth just as much as the hard one, when answered correctly.
- **Mark only one answer** choice per question. Be careful!

Comparing the SAT and ACT

SAT		ACT
50 minutes, optional	Essay	30 minutes, optional
7 times a year	Administrations	6 times a year
Evidence-Based Reading and Writing, Math, Essay (optional)	Components	English, Math, Reading, Science, and Writing (optional)
Algebra, Problem Solving and Data Analysis, and Passport to Advance Math (skills that must be mastered in order to take advanced Math classes in college)	Math Content	Algebra I, Algebra II, Geometry, and some Trigonometry
No	Is there a penalty for wrong answers?	No
• 200 to 800 for Evidence-Based Reading and Writing; • 200 to 800 for Math; • 2 to 8 on each of three traits for Essay. • The highest possible score for the rst two tests on the SAT is 1600; the essay score is reported separately	How is it scored?	• 1-36 for each subject. A 36 is the highest score, made from averaging each subject's score. • The new scoring system offers students additional sub-scores in English, Math and Reading that range from 1 to 18. • On the optional writing test, you will receive your overall score and separate additional scores in the following areas: ideas and analysis, development and support, organization, and language use.
Yes, all of your scores are sent to the colleges you choose. The good news is that schools are only concerned about the highest scores.	If you take the test more than once, are all of your scores automatically sent to schools?	No, students can choose which scores the schools will see. If you take the test more than once, ACT will send scores only for the date you select.
Yes, but you can send your scores to up to 4 colleges or universities for free. Take advantage of this.	Are there fees for sending your scores to colleges?	Yes, but you can send your scores to up to 4 colleges or universities for free. Take advantage of this.
Yes, but there are fee waivers that you may qualify for, so ask your guidance counselor.	Do you have to pay to take the exam?	Yes, but there are fee waivers that you may qualify for, so ask your guidance counselor.

1. Which test do you feel you will score the highest on? _____

2. Where can you find the most up to date information on college admission tests? _____
   _____
   _____

3. Explain three ways in which the SAT or ACT are different than a typical classroom test or final: _____
   _____
   _____

Test Taking Tips

General Test Taking Tips

- **Dress comfortably,** as there is no dress code and you're going to be testing for several hours.

- **Get plenty of sleep** the night before. You won't perform nearly as well if you're tired.

- **Eat a big breakfast** with a good amount of protein before the test. Studies have shown this leads to a significant increase in performance on tests.

- **Wear a reliable watch** so that you can keep track of time as you work on each section of the test.

- **Remember to bring photo identification** with you to the testing center on test day. You will need it to register.

- **Write neatly** so that others can read your handwriting with no confusion.

- **On multiple-choice questions, consider all answer choices before you choose one.** Use the process of elimination to narrow your choices. You will not be penalized for wrong answers that you give, so it's still worth your while to guess.

- **Make your essay structured:** a clear introduction, supporting paragraphs and a conclusion. Graders will take only 60 to 90 seconds to grade each essay, and they'll look for clear, evidence-based arguments more than stylish, graceful writing.

My Turn! Envision My Test Success

DIRECTIONS: Draw a picture of yourself showing up on test day. Be sure to include all of the tips on the list above.

Unit 6: Apply to College

Understanding your SAT and ACT scores

GO! *Remember to go talk to your guidance counselor to gather more information.*

Since the SAT and ACT are scored on different scales, it is important to understand what your score means when you get it back. You need to know if you have scored high enough to start the application process or if you need to register for the next upcoming test. As a general rule of thumb, the higher your scores are, the better. Your chances of acceptance increase at a given school based on how much higher your scores are than the average scores of students who already attend that school.

For example, the average score for the ACT is around a 21 (remember this is out of a 36). If your scores are below a 15 on the ACT, those are considered low and will be more challenging to get accepted to a 4-year college. In this case, hit the books hard and study again to retake them. Also you can increase your chance of getting in even if you have low test scores as long as you keep up your grades in high school, have a high class rank, and submit a quality application.

During your junior year, talk to your guidance counselor or look online to find out when the registration deadlines and test dates are for the upcoming SAT and ACT. Once you decide which test you are going to take, take the necessary steps to register. Remember, you will be able to send your scores to up to four colleges for free when you register, so make sure you have decided where you want to have them sent. Also, for the ACT, you will need to submit a photo in order to complete your registration. This does not need to be fancy. A picture taken of only you by yourself with your cell phone is perfectly acceptable - no "selfies" though!

In the table below, list the upcoming registration dates and test dates:

	Registration Date	Test Date
SAT		
ACT		

Final Words of Advice:

Since the ACT and SAT are structured and graded differently, some students may score significantly higher on one test over the other. For this reason, it makes a lot of sense, and it is recommended, to take both tests. Also, you can take each test more than once, so don't be discouraged if you do not score as high as you would like to on your first attempt. Instead, try again and don't forget to study in advance before each test. You will find that local bookstores carry a wide variety of study books to help you do well on these tests, and buying one is definitely worth the money. The websites for both the ACT and SAT also offer practice tests.

NOTE: *It is important to note that the SAT and ACT design, timing, reported scores, and scoring rubrics can change. Check college board.org for the latest information on the redesign.*

The College Application Essay

What is the College Application Essay?

The college application essay is your chance to tell the college(s) you are applying to about yourself in a compelling and personal manner; this is where you make yourself stand out from the other applicants. It is written by you as part of your application and in response to a set of essay questions chosen by the college. Having a well-written application essay can help students with lower SAT or ACT scores get into the schools of their dreams. On the other hand, a poorly written essay can keep even a top student from being accepted. This is the part of the application that gives the admissions officer a glimpse into who you are, what makes you ready for college, and why you would be a great fit at their school.

Key Point
An admissions committee is a group of people who review submitted college applications and make decisions on acceptance or denial.

Know Your Audience

An **admissions committee** at the university reads most application essays and they read through thousands of them every year. In light of this, it's important to let them know why you are unique. The best application essays tell a student's story in a compelling way that makes the person reading it feel positively about the writer. Don't ask, "What does the admission committee want to read?" Instead, ask yourself, "What is it about me that I want to be sure colleges learn?" When admission officers read application essays, they'll be looking for students who have been true to themselves and pursued their passions, even if they haven't always succeeded.

TIPS **The Importance of the Essay**
The college application essay can make or break your acceptance. Every moment you spend writing and making it the best it can possibly be is completely worth your time.

Getting started is often the hardest part to writing any application essay. Follow the steps below to help you take that first step and to keep focused on what to include in your essay.

1. **Find a place to write.**

   Get all the tools you'll need in one place and find a quiet place where you can focus on the essay for at least an hour or two. Pick a comfortable place, turn off your electronics (your cell phone, the TV, etc.), and get to work.

2. **Start brainstorming about yourself.**

   Use a graphic organizer and start to list out the things you are especially good at, the things you struggle with, the things you are interested in, and your strengths and weaknesses.

3. **Create your personal brand statement.**

   Choose one part of yourself you want to make sure that the college you're applying to will know after reading your essay. This will be the most important part of your application essay.

4. **Begin outlining your story.**

   Choose a hook that will grab your audience from the first sentence by using a quote, action, or by describing a scene. Outline important points by organizing your paragraphs in a logical way. Don't worry about grammar, spelling, or how it looks right now. The point of this is to just get your ideas on paper.

Key Point
Application essays provide the opportunity for you to tell colleges about who you are, what makes you ready for college, and why you would be a great fit for their school.

Key Point
To write a strong application essay, you should show your story instead of telling it, avoid lists, revise and edit, and be "you."

Unit 6: Apply to College

My Turn! Tips for Writing an Application Essay

DIRECTIONS: Read each tip below and brainstorm ideas or ways to utilize the tip in your application essay.

TIPS **Get Help!**

Even William Shakespeare needed help writing and rewriting his work, averaging over 12 drafts per play. You should ask for help, too. Your teachers, parents, and anyone else whom you think is a good writer could give you great feedback and improve your essay.

1. **Show, don't tell.**

   When writing, always remember that actions speak louder than words. Don't tell your reader that you care about animals; write about how you once rescued an injured cat.

   _____

   _____

   _____

   _____

   _____

2. **Avoid listing everything.**

   Many times, applicants try to fit everything they have ever done in their application essay. This kind of essay reads like a long, boring list. There are other parts of your application to mention all the things you've done, so save the listing for there. A detailed story of a challenge you overcame tells the reader a lot more about you than a list of all the awards you've won.

   _____

   _____

   _____

   _____

   _____

helpful tips

3. **Pull your reader into your story.**

   Set the scene with just enough detail so the reader feels like he or she is there. Hook your reader by grabbing the reader's attention from the start. Describe the moment you approached the podium to give a big speech, instead of starting with a lot of background information about joining the debate team and how you prepared for the speech.

   _____

   _____

   _____

   _____

   _____

   _____

4. Simplify.

Cut any paragraph, sentence, or word that doesn't move the story ahead or give compelling new information. Start your story as early as possible and get it out fast.

_____

_____

_____

_____

_____

_____

5. Grammar matters.

Capitalization, usage, punctuation and spelling errors can hurt your chances of being accepted. These often distract your reader and make your essay difficult to understand. Errors tell the admissions officers that you don't care enough to edit your work. Once you've got all the ideas on paper, find someone, maybe even a former teacher, to help you edit your essay.

_____

_____

_____

_____

_____

_____

6. Be yourself.

Don't write what you think others want to hear. Tell a story that only you can tell. Don't feel that you have to go for extreme drama. Give details of your normal life supporting the image of you as a mature, hard-working person who reacts positively to school.

_____

_____

_____

_____

_____

_____

My Turn! Practice

DIRECTIONS: Practice using the tips on the previous pages in both correct and incorrect ways by writing a sample paragraph.

Correct Usage	**Incorrect Usage**

Notes

The Personal Statement

Some high schools, colleges, and graduate school programs will require a personal statement as part of your overall application. **Personal statements** are an opportunity for you to showcase either your personal background or your opinion on a particular topic. This gives the schools a feel of who you are as an individual while also showcasing your ability to persuade an audience through writing. Because of this, the personal statement is often known as the heart of the application. The purpose of the personal statement is to:

1. Produce a picture of you as a person and your future academic potential.

2. Provide an indication of your judgment and priorities – what you say and how you phrase it is crucial!

3. Grab the readers' interest and make them want to pursue you further as a potential student!

4. Address any unusual circumstances or hardships you have faced and how you have overcome them.

5. Highlight your achievements.

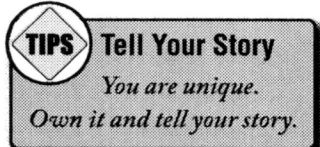

TIPS Tell Your Story
You are unique.
Own it and tell your story.

Tips for Getting Started

1. **Start Early.**

   Because a personal statement reflects your unique style of writing, you typically have total creative license when structuring your statement. Therefore, you are required to think outside the box. Starting early allows time for thought, reflection, and revision.

2. **Choose a topic (or topics) for your statement that addresses any lingering questions an admissions director may have.**

   Try to come up with a topic that may not be addressed or clear within other parts of your application. The personal statement may be the only or final opportunity you have to answer these questions before the admissions committee makes their decision.

3. **Be persuasive.**

   While you have complete creative license, you want to make sure your statement has a logical structure. Explain your points clearly and provide specific, concrete examples for each. Remember, simply listing your accomplishments is *not* persuasive!

4. **Pay special attention to your opening paragraph.**

   The opening paragraph of any statement or essay is generally the most important. It is also the point where you either grab or lose the readers' attention, so make sure to provide a unique angle or hook to keep them invested in your topic.

5. **Avoid clichés.**

   While your personal statement is the place to address who you are and how it relates to the school of your choosing, sticking to reasons unique to you is crucial. Phrases such as "I want to go into medicine to help other people" are overused and do not distinguish you from other applicants. These so-called understood statements should be avoided.

6. **Compose your personal statement in a word processing program.**

   Avoid typing your personal statement directly into an application. By creating it in a Word document, you are able to revise and edit more thoroughly before pasting the final draft into your application. Make sure to save the document as a PDF so it is compatible with the computers in the admissions office if you are submitting your application online.

7. **Proofread and revise (multiple times).**

   Make sure to check for grammatical errors, spelling, and the overall flow of your statement. Have parents, teachers, or trusted adults review your work and provide feedback. Be sure to not plagiarize from other sources – your personal statement should reflect *your* writing style.

8. **Copy and Paste the final draft into your application, and relax.**

   Remember: while your personal statement is a critical component to your application, it is one part of many pieces. Try to not stress and be confident in your statement!

My Turn! Brainstorm

DIRECTIONS: Brainstorm information to include in YOUR personal statement. Write or draw your ideas in the box below.

Unit 6: Apply to College

Sample Essay Questions

Although colleges change their application essay prompts every few years, the following types of prompts tend to show up pretty frequently.

Topic A

"Write an essay to discuss the impact of one person in your life. How has this person changed your life? Explain why this person is important."

Topic B

"Choose an issue that is important to you - the issue could be personal, related to school, political, local, or international in scope. Explain the immediate significance of that issue on your life. Examples include yourself, your family, your community and environment, or your generation."

Topic C

"Please write a one-page personal statement."

Topic D

"What single adjective do you think would be most frequently used to describe you by those who know you best? Briefly explain."

Topic E

"Tell us about a conversation you've had that changed your perspective or was otherwise meaningful to you."

Topic F

"Evaluate a significant experience or achievement that has special meaning to you."

Topic G

"Name one book you have read in the past year; describe your reason for considering this book significant and what you gained from reading it."

Topic H

"There may be personal information that you want considered as part of your admissions application. Write an essay describing that information. You might include exceptional hardships, challenges, or opportunities that have shaped or impacted your abilities or academic credentials, personal responsibilities, exceptional achievements or talents, educational goals, or ways in which you might contribute to an institution committed to creating a diverse learning environment."

Key Point

College admissions departments select the essay topics for your application.

TIPS **Personal Statement**

A personal statement is often an extra requirement in addition to an application essay. Not all schools require one, and it is a more common requirement for graduate programs than undergraduate schools.

TIPS **Check Your Sources**

Use a reliable source (a book or trusted website) to read exemplar student essays.

Sample College Application Essay

By Christian Duarte
Dallas, Texas

When Fried Chicken *isn't* Comfort Food
University of Texas at Austin

I arrived home, exhausted from working at Church's Fried Chicken after my 6-hour shift. Walking through the door to my home, I was greeted by a wave of intense heat. Baffled, I asked my mother who was sitting on the couch drenched with sweat, "Why is it so hot in here?" She replied that the air conditioner had broken again. "Then call someone to fix it," I said, as I began to strip off my grease-stained work uniform. "I would, but we don't have the money to pay for it," she responded. I knew exactly where this was heading. I smacked my lips, gave out a huge sigh, and asked her how much she needed. Before she could answer, I had already started to head to my room to get the $400 that I had been setting aside for new parts for our car.

My family asks for help on a regular basis. Since my mother's divorce, we have struggled financially. She works two full-time jobs as a shift leader at two different restaurants for 70-80 hours a week. I have an older brother who just finished high school this past year and a younger sister who lives with my grandmother because we cannot support her financially. Since I turned 15, my responsibilities at home grew significantly. I became a full-time employee, brother, son, and high school student. Starting the summer before my junior year, I joined my mother at Church's Chicken to help pay some of the bills that were accumulating at home. Every week I work 40 hours at Church's getting paid $7.25 an hour. Although I'm exhausted and can barely keep my eyes open, I always push for more hours because I know that my hard work helps alleviate my family's financial struggles.

Almost every day I leave school for my job at 4p.m. and come home after 11p.m. to start my homework. I know that my responsibilities do not end when I come home from work. I know that if I don't continue to push myself to complete my homework assignments to the best of my ability, I will never move past this job or my grease-stained uniform. I continue to perform as a top student, always taking the most rigorous classes available at my school. No matter what, I refuse to let my academics suffer because of my financial responsibilities at home.

This summer I received a unique opportunity to be one of three students in my senior class selected to intern at The Millennium Foundation. Through the foundation I helped support my school's college access program. For the first time I worked in an environment where I was able to apply what I learn at school to projects that truly challenged me, and my perspective. I worked for the Director of College Admissions for my school district and saw how my summer research projects directly impacted the training of the college counselors at my high school. I saw the path of my long-term goals become clear by rooting myself in the importance of my continued education.

I know that Church's Chicken is a high school job, temporarily patching the financial problems in my family. My goal is to gain a higher education that will push me toward a successful career path. I know that college is the only solution for me. I will break barriers by going to college as the first person in my family to attend and take this leap. I will show my younger sister, older brother, and mother how education will pay off as I am able to support them better when I return. I am proud of my mother and brother for working hard every day at Church's to support the family, but I know that my time there is coming to an end. I look forward to the next stage of my life and am ready to trade my grease-stained uniform for a degree, facing the challenges ahead and pushing limits to turn my dreams into a reality.

 Pull Your Reader into Your Story
In the first paragraph Christian captured the readers attention by telling a story that is unique to HIM.

 Show, Don't Tell
In the fourth paragraph he is letting the reader know how he stands out from all of his other classmates.

TIPS **Be Yourself**
In the final paragraph, Christian let the admissions team know why continuing his education to college is important to him.

Unit 6: Apply to College

My Turn! Application Essay Free Write

DIRECTIONS: Select one of the "Sample Essay Questions" from the previous page. Use the lines below to write out at least a 5 paragraph essay answering the prompt. Try to include as many personal details as possible and be thorough and personal in your writing.

My Turn! Application Essay Final Draft

DIRECTIONS: Using your free write page, now use this space to formulate your thoughts into a formal essay. Refer back to the essay writing tips as needed.

TIPS **Type It Out!**
A real final draft of a college application essay needs to be typed.

College Application Tracker

My Turn! Track My Applications

DIRECTIONS: Use this college application tracker, or create a soft copy version to save on your computer, to organize each of your applications and stay on top of all the necessary deadlines and details.

Application Number	Name of the College (No Initials)	Application ID Number	Date the App was submitted	Have you sent your SAT/ACT scores to this campus?	Date transcript / fee waiver was mailed	Is there anything left to do for this application?
1						
2						
3						
4						
5						
6						
7						
8						
9						
10						
11						

Practice College Common Application

The Common Application

If the college application process seems a bit overwhelming, just remember that it is worth it! Also, available to you is a college application called **The Common App**. This is an application for undergraduate admission that can be completed online or in print. Once you have completed it, it can be sent to any number of participating colleges along with your recommendation letters and your transcripts or school report forms. The goal of The Common App is to allow you to spend less time on admission paperwork and more time on college research and visits, your essays, and your high school work. It is important to note that NOT ALL colleges accept this form of application. Do your research first. If your college does not accept it, do not be discouraged but instead apply according to the specific criteria that each school requests.

Below you will find a practice college Common Application. While this is not an exact copy of the Common Application that you will find from their website, the questions and information below are modeled after it as closely as possible.
NOTE: Also please be aware, specific schools that don't use the Common Application will likely require a separate application which may ask for similar information, but look different.

First Choice School and Major: _____

Second Choice School and Major: _____

BIOGRAPHICAL INFORMATION

1. **Enter your US Social Security Number:** ████████████████

2. **When were you born?** ____ / ____ / ____ *(mm/dd/year)*

3. **Full, legal name:**
   Last/Family Name: _____
   First Name: _____
   Middle: _____ Suffix: *(Example: Jr., III, etc.)* _____

4. **Other names or aliases:**
   If you attended school using a different name or took a standardized test (ACT/SAT) using a different name, please list them below:
   Last/Family Name: _____
   First Name: _____
   Middle: _____ Suffix: *(Example: Jr., III, etc.)* _____

5. **Your gender:** *(circle one)*   **Male   Female**

6. **Place of Birth:**
   City: _____
   State/Possession: _____
   Country: _____

7. **Ethnicity or Race of which you most closely identify:** _____

TIPS **Not All Schools Accept the Common App**

While many schools do accept the Common App, some schools require their own application and many request supplemental (additional) documents as well.

GO! *Research your schools of choice to see if they accept The Common App. It is used by hundreds of universities in the U.S. and around the world!*

TIPS **Why Is There a Black Box?**

Never, ever write your Social Security Number (SSN) anywhere that is not an official document from a trusted/secure source.

Unit 6: Apply to College

8. **Are you a US citizen?** *(circle one)*   **YES   NO**

Non-US Citizens Complete the Following:

a.   If no, of what country are you a citizen? _____

b.   Do you hold Permanent Residence status (valid I-1551) for the US?
(If yes, please submit a copy of the front and back of card in your application.)

YES   NO

c.   If you are not a U.S. citizen or permanent resident, do you have an application for permanent residence (form I-485) pending with the U.S. Citizenship and Immigration Services (USCIS)?
(If yes, please submit a copy of Notice of Action from the USCIS, form I-797C.)

YES   NO

d.   If you are not a citizen or permanent resident or have no application pending with the USCIS, did you live or will you have lived in your home state for 36 consecutive months leading up to high school graduation or completion of the GED?
(If yes, please submit a completed Affidavit of Intent to Become a Permanent Resident.)

YES   NO

e.   If you are not a U.S. citizen or U.S. permanent resident, are you a foreign national here with a visa that makes you eligible to domicile for your home state residency purposes (see list of eligible visas) or are you a Refugee, Asylee, Parolee or here under Temporary Protective Status?

YES   NO

Type: ☐ Refugee
☐ Asylee
☐ Parolee
☐ Temporary Protective Status
☐ Qualifying Visa Type: _____
☐ None of the above

9. **Status as a current U.S. military service member, veteran, or dependent:**
A U.S. military service member is a person who is serving in any branch of the U.S. Armed Forces, including the National Guard or Reserves. Please select any of the following that apply to you. I am a:

☐ Veteran (former U.S. military service member)
☐ Current U.S. military service member
☐ Spouse or dependent of a veteran or a current U.S. military service member
☐ Spouse or dependent of, or a veteran or current U.S. military service member with an injury or illness resulting from military service (service-connected injury/illness)
☐ Spouse or dependent of a deceased U.S. service member

10. **Your Permanent Address:**

_____
_____
_____

11. **Your Phone Number:** _____
Type: ☐ Cell   ☐ Work   ☐ Home

12. **Emergency Contact:**

Name: _____
Relationship to You: _____
Phone Number: _____
Address: _____
E-mail: _____

13. **Your personal e-mail address:** _____

14. **Family's Educational Background:**
Please indicate the highest level of your parents' or legal guardians' educational background:

> **Father:**
> - ☐ No High School
> - ☐ Some High School
> - ☐ High School Diploma or GED
> - ☐ Some College
> - ☐ Associate's Degree
> - ☐ Bachelor's Degree
> - ☐ Graduate/Professional Degree
> - ☐ Unknown

> **Mother:**
> - ☐ No High School
> - ☐ Some High School
> - ☐ High School Diploma or GED
> - ☐ Some College
> - ☐ Associate's Degree
> - ☐ Bachelor's Degree
> - ☐ Graduate/Professional Degree
> - ☐ Unknown

15. **Other than English, what language(s) do you speak fluently?**

> Language _____ Years Spoken: _____
> Language _____ Years Spoken: _____

16. **Please indicate the amount of your family's gross (total) income based on the previous years taxes.**
> - ☐ Less than $20,000
> - ☐ $20,000 to $49,999
> - ☐ $50,000 to $79,999
> - ☐ $80,000+

17. **How many people, including yourself, live in your household?** _____

18. **Do you have family obligations that prevent you from participating in extracurricular activities?**   **YES   NO**

If yes, do you....

a.	Have to work to supplement family income?	**YES**	**NO**
	Describe: _____		
b.	Provide primary care for a family member?	**YES**	**NO**
	Describe: _____		
c.	Have other family obligations that prevent you from participating?	**YES**	**NO**
	Describe: _____		

EDUCATIONAL BACKGROUND

1. **High School Name:** _____

2. **High School City or County:** _____

3. **High School State:** _____

4. Expected Graduation date: ____ / ____ *(month/year)*

5. Number of college credits gained by high school graduation? _____

6. Are you Home Schooled?   YES   NO

7. Do you plan to graduate with an IB (International Baccalaureate) diploma?
                                    YES   NO

8. If you did not graduate from high school, do you have a GED?
                                    YES   NO

9. Please list all previous colleges you have attended, including dual credit courses in high school.

    Name of Institution: _____

    Location *(city, state)*: _____

    Dates of Attendance *(month/year)*: ____ / ____ to ____ / ____

    Major: _____

    Degree Date: ____ / ____ / ____

    Type of Degree: _____ *(Associates, Bachelor's, etc.)*

10. Are you currently on academic suspension from a previous college or university?   YES   NO

EDUCATION INFORMATION

1. Semester and year you expect to enter: _____ of _____ *(year)*

2. If you plan to pursue a pre-professional program, please indicate which one:
    ☐ Pre-Law
    ☐ Nursing
    ☐ Medicine
    ☐ Veterinary
    ☐ Physical Therapy
    ☐ Other: _____

3. Will you seek a teacher certification? YES   NO

4. List all of the courses you will complete your senior year:
    Please place an X in each box that is applicable after writing each course name.

Course Name	AP/IB Credit	Dual Credit	Taken Sem 1	Taken Sem 2
Ex: Physics				

5. Indicate those that you have taken or plan to take.
    Please have official test scores sent directly from the testing agency to your top choice schools of which you apply.

    ☐ **ACT** Date taken or plan to take: ____ / ____ *(month/year)*
    ☐ **SAT** Date taken or plan to take: ____ / ____ *(month/year)*

EXTRACURRICULAR AND VOLUNTEER ACTIVITIES

Do you plan to submit a paper resume and cover letter?   **YES   NO**

Note: A paper resume is not an alternative to filling out the information below. You must also complete the information below and the FAFSA to be considered for scholarships.

Organization/Activity:					check one	Activity Level
Participation						Local
						City
Year (circle all that apply)	Positions Held	Elected?	Hours per Week	Weeks per Year		District
Freshman		YES / NO				State
Sophomore		YES / NO				Regional
Junior		YES / NO				National
Senior		YES / NO				International

Organization/Activity:					check one	Activity Level
Participation						Local
						City
Year (circle all that apply)	Positions Held	Elected?	Hours per Week	Weeks per Year		District
Freshman		YES / NO				State
Sophomore		YES / NO				Regional
Junior		YES / NO				National
Senior		YES / NO				International

Organization/Activity:					check one	Activity Level
Participation						Local
						City
Year (circle all that apply)	Positions Held	Elected?	Hours per Week	Weeks per Year		District
Freshman		YES / NO				State
Sophomore		YES / NO				Regional
Junior		YES / NO				National
Senior		YES / NO				International

COMMUNITY OR VOLUNTEER SERVICE

1. Place of Service: _____
   Description: _____
   Total Hours: _____ from _____ / _____ (month/year) to _____ / _____ (month/year)

2. Place of Service: _____
   Description: _____
   Total Hours: _____ from _____ / _____ (month/year) to _____ / _____ (month/year)

3. Place of Service: _____
   Description: _____
   Total Hours: _____ from _____ / _____ (month/year) to _____ / _____ (month/year)

TALENTS, AWARDS, & HONORS

1. Award, Honor, or Distinction: _____
   Description, Basis, Sponsor: _____
   _____ Date(s) of Award _____

2. Award, Honor, or Distinction: _____
   Description, Basis, Sponsor: _____
   _____ Date(s) of Award _____

3. Award, Honor, or Distinction: _____
   Description, Basis, Sponsor: _____
   _____ Date(s) of Award _____

4. Award, Honor, or Distinction: _____
   Description, Basis, Sponsor: _____
   _____ Date(s) of Award _____

5. Award, Honor, or Distinction: _____
   Description, Basis, Sponsor: _____
   _____ Date(s) of Award _____

EMPLOYMENT, INTERNSHIPS, & SUMMER ACTIVITIES

Your specific Job Role/title	Employer	Hours per Week	Employed from: (month/year) to (month/year)

Whew, that was a long one! You likely won't have the time or energy to fill out this entire application in one sitting. You also may need to ask for some help from parents or other adults to answer some of the questions. That is perfectly okay, and this is a great opportunity to learn that starting early, giving yourself multiple times to work on the application, and asking for help, are all great ways to apply to college successfully.

College – An institution of higher education that gives out degrees and certificates. The term is also used to refer to the different parts of large universities such as the College of Education or the College of Engineering.

Common Application (informally known as the Common App) – An undergraduate college admission application that students may use to apply to any of hundreds of member colleges and universities both in the United States and Internationally.

Community College – A two-year institution of higher education. Course offerings are usually divided into two categories. There is a "transfer curriculum," which contains courses designed to be transferable toward a bachelor's degree at a four-year college, and an "occupational" or "technical" curriculum with courses of study designed to prepare students for employment in two years.

Community Service – May include any experiences you have giving back to your classmates, school, or community. Activities such as tutoring a classmate, walking your neighbor's dog, or reading to the kids at your sibling's daycare may all be considered community service.

Compound Interest (Banking Setting) – Earned interest on both the money you've saved and the earned interest.

Course Fee – The tuition a student pays per credit hour for the college courses, or classes, they attend each semester. The course fee will vary depending on the overall cost of the institution.

Cover Letter – A one page summary of how your skills, past experience, and goals align with the organization you are applying to.

Credit hour – Credit given for attending one lecture hour of class each week for 15 weeks or equivalent. Most college classes are three credit hours, meaning their total meeting time for a week is three hours. Note that this does not include homework and other work done outside class.

CSS (College Scholarship Service) PROFILE – A financial aid application provided by the College Board in the U.S. It allows a number of private institutions that provide scholarships to get a closer look into a student's family finances. Along with the FAFSA, it is the most common financial application students fill out, although unlike the FAFSA the CSS PROFILE is much more comprehensive and requires a small fee.

Cumulative GPA – Calculates your grade point average (GPA) from the very beginning of your freshman year.

DACA Students (Deferred Action for Childhood Arrivals) – Undocumented youth granted DACA are protected from deportation for two years, subject to renewal, and provided with a work permit. In almost every state, DACAmented students can apply for a driver's license. For more information on eligibility and resources to apply for DACA, search United We Dream and DREAM Educational Empowerment Program.

Deferred Admission – Permission from a college where you have been accepted to postpone enrolling in the college. The postponement is usually up to one year.

Degrees – Degrees are what students get for completing a program of study at a college or university. There are three basic types of degrees: Associate Degrees - obtainable at a two-year community or junior college, Baccalaureate or Bachelor's Degrees - offered by four-year colleges and universities, and Graduate Degrees - obtained after the bachelor's degree, i.e., Master's Degree or Doctoral Degree.

Dissertation – A dissertation is a requirement for a Doctoral Degree. The lengthy essay based upon scholarly research, and it must be an original contribution to the field.

Doctoral degree – A doctoral degree, also known as a PhD or doctorate, is the most advanced degree that can be earned. This is why people who have a PhD are often called doctors even if they don't work in a hospital or clinic.

Dorm – These are buildings on college campuses that students live in. Freshmen are normally required to live in a dorm, but sophomores, juniors and seniors are usually given the option of finding their own housing. That said, many students might live in a dorm for all four years of college.

Dual Credit – High school students may be "dually" enrolled in a high school course that also counts towards college credit hours. Dual enrollment is helpful because it gives high school students a head start on their college careers.

Early Action (EA) – An option to submit your college applications before the regular deadlines. When you apply EA, you get admission decisions from colleges earlier than usual. EA is not binding, so that means that you do not have to enroll in a college if you are accepted early action.

Early Admission – A college admission plan where students apply earlier in the year and then receive their acceptance notifications early. This is good for students who want to reduce their number of admissions at one time. Early admission deadlines are usually between October and November.

Early College – High schools designed so that students can receive both a high school diploma and an Associate's degree or up to two years towards a Bachelor's degree. Early Colleges are free, but students must usually go through an application process before being granted admission.

Early Decision (ED) – An option to submit an application to your first-choice college before the regular deadline. When you apply ED, you get an admission decision earlier than usual. Early decision plans are binding. This means that you agree to enroll in the college immediately if admitted and offered a financial aid package that meets your needs.

EFC (Expected Family Contribution) – An important part of the FAFSA where a student lists the expected amount of money that his or her family will be able to contribute towards their education. The EFC is subtracted from a college's COA (Cost of Attendance) before an institution decides how much financial aid a student will receive. The general rule is the lower a student's EFC, the higher the amount of financial aid offered.

Extracurricular Activities – These are non-classroom activities that students can get involved in at school. They can include such activities as athletics, clubs, student government, recreational and social organizations and events.

FAFSA (Free Application for Federal Student Aid) – The FAFSA is an almost universal application for financial aid, including loans, grants, college work-study and other federal and state programs. It is often required before a student can be considered for many scholarships.

Financial Aid – Aid is made available from grants, scholarships, loans, and part-time employment from federal, state, institutional, and private sources. Awards from these programs may be combined in an "award package" to meet the cost of education. The types and amounts of aid awarded are determined by financial need, available funds, student classification, academic performance, and sometimes the timeliness of a student's application.

Freshman – A student in their first year of high school/college.

Full-Time Enrollment/Part-Time Enrollment – A full-time student is enrolled in 12 or more credit hours in a semester (full-time status for a Summer term is usually 6 credit hours). A part-time student is enrolled in less than 12 credit hours in a semester (less than 6 in a Summer term).

GPA (Grade Point Average) – GPA is the average of your class grades, generally based on a 4.0 scale.

Graduate Student/School – Colleges and universities around the country offer graduate programs for students who want to study a subject area in further depth beyond their undergraduate (traditional four year school setting). A student who is enrolled in this type of program is described as a graduate student.

Grants – Financial assistance that does not require repayment.

Informational Interview – An interview conducted to collect information about a job, career field, industry or company. An informational interview is not a job interview. Rather, it's an interview with an individual working in a career you would like to learn more about.

In-State Tuition – A reduced tuition rate that students pay if they attend a college in their home state.

Interest (Banking Setting) – A payment that banks pay you to deposit (store) your money with them.

IB (International Baccalaureate) – IB is an impressive twelve-year curriculum that offers an international perspective on education. Only select schools are IB schools. The high school program is called the Diploma Program (DP) and is completed during the final 2 years of high school.

Internship – A temporary job that students take over the summer during high school or (usually) college, usually in the same area they are studying. A student majoring in science, for example, might get an internship with a laboratory. Internships are required in some academic programs. Note that internships may include pay and college credit, or in other cases may not.

Interview – A formal meeting in which one or more persons question, consult, or evaluate another person for a potential job or acceptance to a school.

Junior – A student in their third year of high school/college.

Junior College – See Community College.

Loans – Financial assistance that must be repaid, usually with interest added.

Major – A student's concentrated field of study.

Master's degree – A graduate degree that usually requires two or more years of study after completing a bachelor's degree. A thesis is required of a master's student.

Minor – A student's secondary field of study. It may be aligned with a student's major or completely different. For example, a student whose major is Public Health could minor in Hospital Administration (to further career opportunities) or English Literature (to show diverse personal interests and abilities) or Spanish (to increase job opportunities in Spanish-speaking areas). A minor usually consists of 5-8 courses, which is less than half of the courses required for a major.

Networking – Meeting, interacting, and following up with people who could use your help or who could help you.

Nonresident ("Out-of-state tuition") – Any student who lives out of state or does not meet specific state residency requirements. This is especially relevant for students applying to state universities; it is much harder to get in if you are not a resident of the state and tuition is much higher. For example, a Texan will find it much easier than a Californian to be admitted to the University of Texas and will pay less to go there.

Online courses – Classes held on the Internet instead of in a traditional classroom.

Out-of-State Tuition – Tuition rate that students have to pay if they choose to go to attend a college that is not in their home state. This tuition rate can cost just as much as the most expensive schools in the country.

Percentile – Percentiles are a way of comparing scores or GPAs across a population of students. For example, a percentile rank of 50% means that the student scored or had a GPA the same or better than 50% of the students in his or her population of students. It does not mean the student scored a 50 on the test.

Personal Statement – An essay about yourself that is included in your application essay that will make you stand out from the rest of the applicants.

Postgraduate (Graduate Student) – A student who continues to study for an advanced degree, such as a lawyer or doctor, after earning a bachelor's degree or other first degree.

Priority Date or Deadline – The date by which your application — whether it's for college admission, student housing or financial aid — must be received by a college to be given the strongest consideration.

Private College/University – A non-state assisted college or university that relies on private funding, tuition and fees. For example, Southern Methodist University (SMU) in Dallas is a private university.

Professionalism – Professionalism refers to the appropriate behavior expected of a person in a business setting, both in person and online.

Public College/University – A state-assisted college or university. For example, the University of Texas at Austin is a public university.

Recommendation Letter – A recommendation letter is a written document you request from a professional where they assess your skills and qualifications. The purpose of the letter is for the organization or school to learn about you as a candidate. A letter of recommendation is typically confidential.

Reference – Someone who can comment on your personal character, work ethic, or past work experiences. References should be given to employers on request, which means you should usually wait for the employer to ask for your references before giving them a reference list.

Registrar – The registrar of an institution is responsible for the maintenance of all academic records. This may include duties such as: keeping track of class enrollments, certification of athletic eligibility and student eligibility for honor rolls, administering academic probation and verification of the completion of degree requirements for graduation.

Regular Admission – This is the type of admission that most schools offer. There is a set deadline by which an applicant has to submit their application.

Resident ("In-state tuition") – A student who meets state residency requirements.

Résumé – A document that highlights one's contact information, education background, professional experience, honors, extracurricular activities and coursework. A résumé is almost always required when applying for any sort of professional job or internship and is usually what determines whether an applicant will receive an interview.

Rolling admission – A policy in which a school sends out acceptance letters to students as they are accepted.

Room and Board – The amount of money it costs for housing in dorms and meals in the dining halls, or cafeterias, per semester. This is usually a requirement for freshmen year of college, but is an option the following years.

SAP (Satisfactory Academic Progress) – Students receiving financial aid under federally supported programs must follow certain standards to continue receiving aid. These standards include holding a certain GPA and completing a minimum number of credit hours per semester.

SAR (Student Aid Report) – A summary of responses filed on one's FAFSA. It is sent to the student and colleges/universities the student listed on his or her FAFSA.

SAT (Scholastic Aptitude Test) and ACT (American College Test) – Both tests are designed to measure a student's level of knowledge in basic areas such as Math, Science, English, and Social Studies. Most colleges require the results of either the SAT or ACT before granting admission.

Scholarships – Financial assistance based on merit; does not require repayment.

Semester – A half-year term in a school or college, typically lasting fifteen to eighteen weeks. For example, at colleges that use the semester system, the school year is divided into two semesters.

Semester GPA – Calculates your grade point average (GPA) for a single semester.

Senior – A student in their fourth year of high school/college.

Senioritis (The Senior Slump) – A noticeable decline in motivation or performance of students during their senior year of high school or college.

Soft Skills – Abilities that characterize your relationships with other people such as communication, leadership, and managing others.

Sophomore – A student in their second year of high school/college.

Student activity fees – A required fee that is separate from your tuition each semester/year. This fee helps fund student organizations, activities, and other services provided on campus.

Study Group – A group of people (usually 4 to 6 students) who meet as often as necessary to help each other with schoolwork, prepare for tests, share information, and discuss knowledge gained in class.

Subsidized Loans – Stafford subsidized loans do not build interest for at least the first half of one's college education. They are called subsidized loans because the government "subsidizes" (or pays back) any interest that builds for at least the first half of college.

Syllabus – An outline of the important information about a course. Written by the professor or instructor, it usually includes important dates, assignments, expectations and policies specific to that course. Some are quite lengthy.

Thesis – A thesis, in the context it is used in this book, is an extensive research paper undertaken and written by college students on a specific topic. They are usually presented to a committee as part of the latin honors award process.

Trade School – Trade schools, also called vocational or technical schools, are where you go to learn a set of specific skills and knowledge related to a particular job or career field.

Transcript – The transcript is a permanent academic record of a student at college. It may show courses taken, grades received, academic status and honors received. You may be asked for an official transcript for an internship application, scholarship application, or graduate school application. The official transcript is printed on formal paper with your school's seal and Registrar's signature. If you receive an official transcript, make sure not to break the seal open. If you do it will be considered unofficial.

Transcripts (Official) – An official transcript is a complete record of your collegiate academic history printed on formal paper with your school's seal and Registrar's signature. Colleges will usually mail them directly to where you want them to go, though they will charge a fee for doing this. If you receive an official transcript make sure not to break the seal or open it; if you do, it will be considered unofficial. You might need an official transcript for an internship application, scholarship application, or graduate school application. In order to request an official transcript, contact your school's registrar.

Transcripts (Unofficial) – An unofficial transcript is a complete academic history at your college, but is not sealed. Unofficial transcripts are often cheaper or even free, as it is just a print out of all of your classes and credits. At many colleges, you can even find your unofficial transcript online. In order to request an unofficial transcript, contact your school's registrar.

Tuition – Tuition is the amount paid for each credit hour of enrollment. Tuition does not include the cost of books, fees, or housing. Tuition charges vary from college to college and are dependent on such factors as resident or out-of- state status, level of classes enrolled in (lower, upper or graduate division), and whether the institution is publicly or privately funded.

Undergraduate – An undergraduate is a student who is pursuing either a two- or four-year degree.

University – A university is composed of undergraduate, graduate, and professional colleges (for example, law schools) and offers degrees in each.

Undocumented Students – Students who lack lawful status in the country. They are not U.S. citizens, U.S. Nationals or "eligible non-citizens."

Unsubsidized Loans – A Stafford unsubsidized Loan is federally funded and is not based on financial need. Interest builds as soon as one begins college and is not paid back by the government.

Waiting List – Students who apply to a college and may be admitted if space becomes available. Colleges wait to hear if all the students they accepted decide to attend. If students do not enroll and there are empty spots, a college may fill them with students who are on the waiting list.

Work-Study – This program provides college students with part-time jobs to help pay for school. There are two different kinds of work-study: Federal Work-Study (run by the government) and non-Federal Work-Study (usually run by the college a student attends).

Academic Probation – All colleges require students to maintain a minimum GPA (Grade Point Average) to remain in school. Students who fail to do this will be placed on probation for a semester. If this happens, you need to work with you Academic Advisor to improve.

Advanced Standing Credit – These are credit hours that a college accepts toward a degree from courses that a student completed somewhere else. You can get credit for work done at another college or by "testing out" (think high school AP courses).

Alma mater – A phrase used to describe the school from which one graduated.

Alumni – People who have graduated from a school.

Audit – A student who does not want to receive credit in a course may, with approval of the instructor, sit in on the class. This is called an "audit." A student who audits a course usually cannot ask the college at a later date to obtain college credit for the audited course.

Catalog – College catalogs provide all types of information parents and students need to know about a school. It lists, for example: the university's history and philosophy, policies and procedures, what courses are available, degrees and certificates offered, physical facilities, admission and enrollment procedures, financial aid, student life information, etc.

Class Schedule – Colleges publish and distribute a Class Schedule before the beginning of each semester. With the help of academic advisors and/or faculty members, students use this book to create their own individual class schedules for each semester they are enrolled. Courses are designated in the Class Schedule by course department, course number, time and days the course meets, the room number and building name, and the instructor's name.

CLEP (College Level Examination Program) – The CLEP can be administered to students who want to receive college credit by taking proficiency tests in selected courses. If the student scores high enough on the test, college credit can be awarded. There is a charge for each test taken. Information concerning an individual institution's policy about CLEP Tests can be found in the institution's catalog.

Co-Ed – A school, facility, or program that includes both men and women. This term is usually used when referring to a university or dorm.

Commuter – A commuter is a student who lives off-campus and drives to class, or commutes.

Concurrent Enrollment – In some cases a student can enroll in (attend) two educational institutions at the same time. For example: In Oklahoma, a high school senior can concurrently enroll in high school and in college provided he/she meets certain requirements. Another form of concurrent enrollment is when a college student attends two colleges at the same time. Permission for concurrent enrollments is generally made in advance.

Course numbers – Numbers assigned to specific classes.

Degree Requirements – The requirements listed by colleges for completion of a program of study are generally known as degree requirements. Degree requirements may include a minimum number of credit hours, a required GPA, prerequisites and elective courses within the specified major, and/or minor areas of study.

Department – Departments are the pieces that most colleges are divided into, and are responsible for the academic functions in a field of study. For example: the chemistry department, the English department, etc.

Drop and Add – Students are generally allowed to drop courses from their class schedules and/or add other courses. Different colleges give students varying amounts of time to do this at the beginning of each semester or quarter. The college catalog or class schedule should note the correct procedures. Students usually need written approval from designated college officials to initiate dropping or adding a class. A small fee is often required.

Enrollment – This is the procedure by which students choose classes each semester. It also includes the collection of fees. Pre-enrollment is a form of enrollment in which students select courses well in advance of the official enrollment date of the next term.

Fees – Charges students must pay to take courses at college.

Finals – Stands for "Final Exams." Most courses will have final exams (those who do not will usually have some type of cumulative paper or project). Most colleges have a certain amount of time that final exams are given in – anywhere from 3 to 7 days. During these days regular classes do not meet so students have time to study. Check the syllabus for specific information about exams, and your college's website for final exam dates. Many schools have policies to keep you from having too many exams on one day, so be sure to check your school's website on that procedure.

Fraternities/Sororities (also called the Greek System) – Fraternities (for men) and sororities (for women) are social organizations that are active in various activities in colleges. Through a process called Rush or Recruitment (which takes place during a specified period of time), students may be offered the opportunity to "pledge" (join) a certain fraternity or sorority. Not all colleges have these organizations.

GA – Stands for "Graduate Assistant." See TA.

Gen Ed – Stands for a "General Education" course, which are courses all students must take, regardless of major. Colleges typically have different Gen Ed requirements – talk to your advisor about specific requirements.

Humanities Courses – Humanities courses are classes covering subjects such as literature, philosophy, and the fine arts. Most undergraduate degrees require a certain number of humanities credit hours.

Laboratory – Most science lecture courses have a lab course attached to them. It is recommended that you take the lab course during the same semester as the lecture course (for example, Chem 101 L = Introduction to Chemistry Lecture, 3 credits and Chem 101LL = Chemistry Lab, 1 credit). Laboratory courses are usually longer than lectures, lasting from 3 to 5 hours, and are offered one time per week. During lab course you will be conducting experiments and doing the hands-on portion of your class. Outside of class you are usually responsible for lab write-ups, group work, pre-lab work, and studying topics related to the course. Grades in lab courses are usually based on lab procedures, experimental accuracy, lab reports, and often on additional exams. Grades and credit can be separate or attached to the lecture depending on the course.

Lecture – Class session where professor talks and students take notes with little or no interaction between students and professor during this time. These classes usually have between 50-300 students in them.

Lower Division Courses – These courses, usually referred to as 100 or 200 level, are the first classes you take in college (usually as a freshman or sophomore). Most are general courses providing an introduction to a certain area (for example, Introduction to American Government), and in many cases are prerequisites for more advanced courses.

Mid-Term Exams (Midterms) – During the middle of each term, instructors may give mid-term exams that test students on the material covered during the first half of the term. Some classes have only two tests, a midterm and a final.

Non-Credit Courses – These are classes or courses that do not count towards a degree at a given college. Non-credit courses may serve one of several purposes: to explore new fields of study, increase knowledge in a particular area, develop useful skills or enrich life experiences.

Pass/Fail Courses – Pass/fail courses do not earn letter grades or grade points for students. If a student passes a pass/fail course, he/she receives a "P" (pass) or "S" (satisfactory) on the transcript and the credit hours. If the student does not pass the course, they will receive an "F" (fail) or a "U" (unsatisfactory) on the transcript and no credit hours. The evaluation for the pass/fail course is not figured into the student's GPA.

Petition – A petition is the name for both the process and the form a student fills out to request consideration of special circumstances. For example, if a student is denied admission to the college of their choice, they may petition for admission based on exceptional circumstances such as a death in the family.

Prerequisite – A course that must be taken prior to enrollment in another course. For example, a student must take Calculus I before they can take Calculus II.

RA (Resident Advisor) – An upper-class student (junior or senior) living in a freshman dorm as a peer counselor and hall supervisor.

Reading Days – Also known as "dead day(s)" or "dead week". This is a scheduled time after regular classes and right before final exams. On these days, professors do not have classes so that students may study for finals.

Summer session – A summer term of approximately six weeks.

TA (Teaching Assistant) – A graduate or undergraduate student who works with a professor and sometimes leads a discussion class.

Transfer of Credits – Some students attend more than one institution during their college career. When they move or transfer from one college to another, they also transfer accumulated credit hours from the old college to the new one. The new institution determines which courses will apply toward graduation requirements.

Trimester – At colleges that use the trimester system the school year is divided into three trimesters. These usually correspond to the seasons; a fall trimester, a winter trimester and a spring trimester.

Upper Division Courses – Classes (300+) that usually have prerequisite courses, and are taken later in college (usually junior or senior years). They are typically specific to your major and provide more in-depth understanding about the material (for example, The Current American Presidency).

Withdrawal – Students may withdraw from (or stop taking) courses during a semester, but there are established procedures for doing so. The college catalog and/or Class Schedule generally specifies the procedures and deadlines for withdrawing from a course. Written approval from a university official must be secured, and in some cases fees must be paid.

Citations

The following sources were referenced in the creation of this manual.

Bureau of Labor Statistics. "Employment Projections."*Bureau of Labor Statistics*. Bureau of Labor Statistics, 15 March 2016. Web. 14 June 2016. <http://www.bls.gov/emp/ep_chart_001.htm>.

Bureau of Labor Statistics. "Top Ten Industries Employing 16-19 Year Olds." *U.S. Bureau of Labor Statistics*. U.S. Bureau of Labor Statistics, 1 Jun 2006. Web. 14 Aug 2013. <http://www.bls.gov/opub/ooq/2006/summer/oochart.pdf>.

Center for Disease Control. "Nutrition Facts." *Center for Disease Control*. Center for Disease Control, n.d. Web. 30 September 2012. <http://www.cdc.gov/healthyyouth/nutrition/facts.htm>.

Clark, Kim. "Tuition at public colleges rises 4.8%." *CNN Money*. CNN Money, 24 Oct 2012. Web. 14 Aug 2013. <http://money.cnn.com/2012/10/24/pf/college/public-college-tuition/index.html>.

Texas Education Agency. "Chapter 24: Curriculum Requirements, Subchapter F: Graduation Requirements." *Texas Education Agency*. Education Opens Doors, 28 Apr 2012. Web. 28 April 2013. <http://ritter.tea.state.tx.us/rules/tac/chapter074/ch074f.html>.

U.S. Census Bureau. "Average Earnings of Full-Time, Year-Round Workers as a Proportion of the Average Earnings of High School Graduates by Educational Attainment: 1975 - 2011." *U.S. Census Bureau*. U.S. Census Bureau, 01 Mar 2012. Web. 14 Aug 2013. <http://www.census.gov/hhes/socdemo/education/data/cps/historical/fig10.jpg>.

Wardlaw, G.M., and R.A. Disilvestro. *Perspectives in Nutrition*. Boston: McGraw Hill, 2004. Print.

Salary Sources:

Teacher: http://www.payscale.com/research/US/All_K-12_Teachers/Salary
> What am I worth? (n.d.). Retrieved June 22, 2016, from http://www.payscale.com/research/US/All_K-12_Teachers/Salary

Superintendent: http://www1.salary.com/School-Superintendent-Salaries.html
> School Superintendent Salaries. (n.d.). Retrieved June 22, 2016, from http://www1.salary.com/School-Superintendent-Salaries.html

Non-Profit Analyst: http://www.simplyhired.com/salaries-k-non-profit-analyst-jobs.html
> Non Profit Analyst Salaries. (n.d.). Retrieved June 22, 2016, from http://www.simplyhired.com/salaries-k-non-profit-analyst-jobs.html

Counseling Psychologist: http://www.bls.gov/ooh/Life-Physical-and-Social-Science/Psychologists.htm#tab-5
> Summary. (n.d.). Retrieved June 22, 2016, from http://www.bls.gov/ooh/Life-Physical-and-Social-Science/Psychologists.htm#tab-5

Librarian: http://learn.org/articles/School_Librarian_Salary_and_Career_FAQs.html
> School Librarian: Career and Salary Facts. (n.d.). Retrieved June 22, 2016, from http://learn.org/articles/School_Librarian_Salary_and_Career_FAQs.html

Principal: http://www.bls.gov/ooh/management/mobile/elementary-middle-and-high-school-principals.htm
> Elementary, Middle, and High School Principals : Occupational Outlook Handbook : U.S. Bureau of Labor Statistics. (n.d.). Retrieved June 22, 2016, from http://www.bls.gov/ooh/management/mobile/elementary-middle-and-high-school-principals.htm

IT Coordinator: https://www.glassdoor.com/Salaries/it-coordinator-salary-SRCH_KO0,14.htm

Salary: IT Coordinator. (n.d.). Retrieved June 22, 2016, from https://www.glassdoor.com/Salaries/it-coordinator-salary-SRCH_KO0,14.htm

SAT:

"Compare SAT Specifications." SAT Suite of Assessments. N.p., 2015. Web. 22 June 2016.